Cultivating Cooperation

Cultivating Cooperation

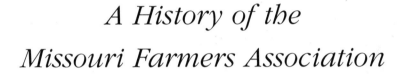

A History of the
Missouri Farmers Association

Raymond A. Young

University of Missouri Press
Columbia and London

Library of Congress Cataloging-in-Publication Data

Young, Raymond A., 1912–1993.

   Cultivating cooperation : a history of the Missouri Farmers
Association / Raymond A. Young.

      p.   cm.

   Includes index.

   ISBN 0-8262-0999-8 (cl. : acid-free paper). — ISBN
0-8262-1000-7 (acid-free paper)

   1. Missouri Farmers Association—History. 2. Agriculture,
Cooperative—Missouri—History. 3. Farmers—Missouri—Political
activity—History.   I. Title.
HD1485.M58   1995
334'.683'09778—dc20   95-7298
                                                             CIP

⊗™ This paper meets the requirements of the
American National Standard for Permanence of Paper
for Printed Library Materials, Z39.48, 1984.

Designer: Stephanie Foley
Typesetter: Connell-Zeko Type & Graphics
Printer and binder: Thomson-Shore, Inc.
Typeface: Garamond

History is to a country as memory is to an individual.

—Arthur Schlesinger

Contents

Foreword by Bud Frew   ix

Preface: *What Is MFA?*   xi

Acknowledgments   xv

Introduction by Michael L. Cook   1

Prologue: *The Post-Civil War Era in Missouri, 1885-1910*   13

I. The Hirth Era, 1914–1940

One.   William Hirth and the Farm Club Movement   19

Two.   The Creation of a Statewide Organization   32

Three.   Continued Growth: *The Early 1920s*   49

Four.   Politics and Conflict   69

Five.   MFA in the 1930s   87

Six.   The End of an Era   102

II. The Heinkel Era, 1940–1979

Seven.   Expanding Business Ventures: *The 1940s*   133

Eight.   MFA in the 1950s   154

Nine.   Reorganization: *The 1960s*   165

Ten.   MFA, a Good Neighbor   180

Eleven.   MFA in the 1970s   183

Twelve.   Heinkel Defeated by Thompson, 1979   200

Epilogue 208

Appendix One. MFA Oil Company: *A Brief History* 211

Appendix Two. MFA Livestock Association:
  A Brief History 216

Appendix Three. Members of the Board of
  Directors, Missouri Farmers Association,
  1917–1994 219

Notes 227

Index 231

Foreword

Bud Frew

President, Missouri Farmers Association

Raymond A. Young was without question the logical person to record the history of the Missouri Farmers Association. His long and dedicated service with and support of the organization—his first job with MFA was in 1933, and at the time of his death in 1993 he was president emeritus of MFA Oil Company—gave him a unique understanding of its growth and development. He was a leader and guided MFA as its executive vice president for many years.

Among Ray's greatest attributes was his astuteness as a businessman—a businessman who was totally honest and fair in all his dealings. During the trying years of the 1970s, it was his efforts that held MFA together. At that time MFA had lost direction and was pursuing a purely political agenda. Ray brought back the good business principles to the organization that he had always applied so successfully to the operation of MFA Oil Company. Moreover, he had a deep concern for farmers and wanted to see them prosper.

Ray had the gift of friendship. Practically everyone who ever knew him considered him a friend, and his colleagues, including the managers and the membership of the organization, held him in the highest esteem. Through his capacity to care and his genuine interest in the problems, achievements, and happiness of individuals, he made them feel as though they were important. Ray Young was a student of human behavior. His understanding of people and events helped him lead the Missouri Farmers Association through good times and bad.

Ray was an important part of the transition as the organization moved from behind the mule to modern times. In his fifty years of MFA service, he reported briefly to William Hirth, the founder of the organization, and eventually worked with the first president of the so-called new MFA, Eric Thompson. Ray rightfully should have taken over the reins, for his business acumen and his focus were the steadying force behind MFA for many years. But he was never one to boast about his achievements. His reward was the success of the business and what it meant to the farmers. He enjoyed watching people he brought into the organization become loyal and productive employees and friends.

And so it was not only Ray's dedication to MFA and his keen intellect that made him the best possible person to write the association's history; indeed, he was part of most of that history.

Preface

What Is MFA?

From the meeting on March 10, 1914, that saw the creation of the first farm club, a giant, sprawling organization named Missouri Farmers Association (MFA) has grown and prospered. In spite of the association's size and visibility, few people have a clear-cut idea of what MFA is. The leaders of the three thousand farm clubs that held meetings in rural schoolhouses throughout most of Missouri first organized the Missouri Farmers Association to serve as the central body around which farmer-owned businesses could revolve. MFA in turn provided leadership in starting farmers exchanges, livestock marketing associations, feed mills, creameries, produce plants, and numerous other businesses. William Hirth, the powerful farm leader, and his magazine, *The Missouri Farmer,* provided the glue that held the farm clubs and businesses together. Each MFA agency elected its own board of directors, which, in turn, chose the agency's manager. Each MFA member received a free subscription to *The Missouri Farmer,* which was the association's official organ, and participated in the election of delegates to the annual MFA conventions.

Even though MFA was a loosely knit organization with little legal clout to keep all its disparate units together, the common goal of improving their economic lot assured the farmers' loyalty to MFA. Hundreds of volunteers carried word of the organization's objectives to their neighbors. Small wonder that outsiders have occasionally compared MFA to a religion.

For some time, I have told myself that the story of the Missouri Farmers Association needed to be written in order to preserve the early history of the organization. As time passes, the trail grows dim. Les Stegh, Deere and Company archivist, said, "Corporations tend to be notoriously bad about saving material. . . . People tend to save memorabilia such as watch fobs and throw away the correspondence, which is often much more important."[1]

Frank Stork, general manager of the Association of Missouri Electric Cooperatives, explains the need for workers to remember accomplishments of their predecessors. Not only do "those who are passing from the leadership scene, and their accomplishments, deserve to be remembered," but the new leaders can "look ahead with anticipation to achieving even better things" because they have "a solid foundation on which to build." And they "will need to know what has gone on before them if they are to be constructive builders."[2]

Unfortunately, the history of MFA has not received significant attention, perhaps because of its uniqueness. Joseph G. Knapp, the best-known historian of cooperatives in the United States, devotes only half a page to MFA in his *Rise of American Cooperative Enterprise, 1620-1920,* even though MFA's volume of business, number of members, and political influence were much greater than those of cooperatives that receive a much fuller treatment. As James Rhodes, University of Missouri professor of agricultural economics, has commented, "Few people outside of Missouri, even those in cooperatives, have understood the unique organization of MFA."[3]

In 1953, MFA was the subject of a doctoral dissertation done at the University of Missouri by Ray Derr. MFA bought the rights to the study and published it as *Missouri Farmers in Action: A Public Relations Study.* Although Derr's emphasis was on the public relations of the organization, his study is the only history of Missouri Farmers Association from its origin through 1953.

Besides Derr's dissertation, other sources of MFA history, which I have used herein, include issues of *The Missouri Farmer,* beginning in 1909; minutes of MFA board meetings, beginning in 1917; MFA audit reports; papers of the Western Historical Manuscript Collection, which include holdings of the State Historical Society of Missouri, in Ellis Library, University of Missouri in Columbia; numerous publications of cooperatives; interviews with MFA leaders; and my personal memories from my association with MFA, dating back to my grade-school days in the 1920s at Walnut Grove, a rural school in Stone County, where my parents were active members of a farm club.

The focus of the history of any organization is on individuals, and for the first sixty-five years, from 1914 to 1979, the story of MFA is largely that of two powerful leaders, William Hirth and Fred Heinkel. Hirth, the founder, led MFA from 1914 until his death in 1940, and Heinkel headed it from 1940 until his defeat as president in 1979.

I was fortunate to have worked for both Hirth and Heinkel. My first job was as bookkeeper and clerk, from 1933 to 1935, at MFA-affiliated Producers Produce Company, a poultry and egg processing plant in Springfield; and from 1935 to 1938 I was a traveling auditor for MFA. In 1938 I became an employee of MFA Oil Company, serving for one year as assistant manager and for forty-two years as general manager and president. I was also executive vice president and CEO of MFA from 1968 until 1981. When I retired in 1981, I became senior vice president and consultant for both MFA Oil Company and MFA for two and a half years. Thus my career offered a wealth of involvement in MFA agencies and the opportunity to know key personnel and business operations during fifty years of MFA history.

Derr commented, "It would seem that some historian might find a fertile field in the development of the cooperative movement in Missouri." This book will not attempt to be that, but it will introduce the people and the events that have gone into the evolution of this organization through 1979. I will not attempt to relate happenings following the end of Heinkel's tenure as president except in brief outline. As I recall former senator Tom Eagleton saying, in commenting on his impression of the Reagan years, "A decent judgment requires a decent interval, the benefit of distance and perspective, and freedom from the bias of proximity."

At present, 46 locally owned retail cooperatives (farmers exchanges) and 116 MFA Agri-Service centers are affiliated with MFA (a prerequisite for membership in a local cooperative is membership in MFA). Some large major agencies that were sponsored and organized by the Missouri Farmers Association have separated from the organization but are still in business. These include Shelter Insurance Companies (formerly MFA Insurance Companies), Mid-Am Dairymen (Producers Creamery Company of Springfield became a part of the formation of this company), and Farmers Livestock Marketing Association of Illinois (originally Farmers Livestock Commission Company). In addition, two major cooperatives formerly affiliated with MFA continue in operation with the MFA name, though they no longer have common membership or overlapping directors. Those are MFA Oil Company and MFA Livestock Association. Both cooperatives are licensed to use the MFA name and emblem, and they maintain a close working relationship with Missouri Farmers Association. Histories of both these affiliates are provided as appendixes herein.

Acknowledgments

First, my thanks and deep appreciation go to my secretary, Mary Lee Sebastian, who helped not only in typing the manuscript but also in providing many suggestions, corrections, and additions to the text. My thanks go also to Bud Frew, president of Missouri Farmers Association, who offered encouragement and made documents and records available without restrictions. Mary Gonnerman, secretary of MFA, helped locate documents and offered suggestions. Ormal Creach nudged me along and contributed valuable information. Dale Creach, president of MFA Oil Company, graciously provided an office and permitted me to steal part-time help from his employees.

Finally, my grateful thanks go to my wife, Virginia, whose constant encouragement and support were a great incentive to "keep at it."

To all those who kept asking "When are you going to finish the book?," here it is. I have used great care in getting my facts right, but I realize there may be some mistakes. If I have left out something that should have been included, I apologize; it was difficult to condense more than sixty-five years of history in a few hundred pages.

Cultivating Cooperation

Introduction

Michael L. Cook

*Robert D. Partridge Chair in Cooperative
Leadership, Department of Agricultural Economics,
University of Missouri–Columbia*

My first substantive exposure to the MFA organization came
in 1984 when I attended a Farmers Export Company board
of directors meeting. Across the table sat two no-nonsense
cooperative businessmen, Bud Frew and David Jobe. Their spirited
questioning, their unflinching courage in confronting intimidating
tactics of so-called grain professionals, and their pro-farmer feistiness
left an indelible impression on me. What organizational roots, what
corporate culture, would create an environment that fostered the evolution of this type of unabashed and indomitable cooperative leader?
In this volume, *Cultivating Cooperation,* Raymond Young helps an-
swer these ponderings. With directness and discretion, Young brings
alive the economic hardships, social challenges, and organizational
dilemmas faced by leaders during the evolution of agricultural producer groups in the United States. His story—that of the birth and
development of an organization sculpted by an audacious group of
economically driven, philosophically sensitive Missouri ruralists—is
truly inspiring. This is the story of what a geographically dispersed
group of human beings faced with economic hardship did to gain
control over their own destiny. It is a story that complements, and in
many cases surpasses, the documented experiences of many other
cooperative-oriented groups during the past 140 years. Before delving

1

into the MFA story according to Raymond Young, it might be useful to summarize briefly the historical evolution of the United States agricultural cooperative movement. It becomes apparent in this introduction, and is confirmed by Young's observations, that MFA plays a prominent role in the twentieth-century development of agrarian collective action in the United States.

Following the Civil War, the imbalance of power between farmers and business gave rise to farmers' efforts to organize. To a large extent, cooperatives were a response by farmers to the risk and uncertainty generated by volatile price swings and by "hold up strategies" executed by major input suppliers, transportation monopolies, and food processing trusts. The formation of cooperatives became a primary means of providing power to farmers without their having to give up social and economic independence. The Grange in the 1870s, followed by the Farmers Alliance in the 1880s, were attempts to form state and regional cooperative federations. The organizations were active both in marketing farm products and in processing farm supplies. A primary contribution of these groups was the establishment of an English Rochdale type of cooperative system in the United States. Major tenets of this cooperative form were that goods were handled at prevailing prices and that net savings were distributed to user members on the basis of patronage. For the most part, the efforts of the Grange and Farmers Alliance failed. Investor-owned firms possessed sufficient market power to adjust prices and access to markets in order to lure farmers away from cooperatives.

In an attempt to control the monopoly power and predatory trade practices of business, the Sherman Antitrust Act was passed in 1890. This act was sponsored primarily by farmers in the hope of restoring the benefits of competition to them. However, the act was ineffective for two reasons. First, the courts placed more emphasis on prohibiting practices that restrained trade than on decreasing the monopoly power of noncooperatives. Thus, farmers and cooperatives remained at a disadvantage in competing with investor-owned firms. Second, farmers were not granted exemption from antitrust under the act and were subsequently limited in their ability to form cooperatives. While the Clayton Antitrust Act of 1914 was an attempt to remedy some of the weaknesses of the Sherman act, it did not go far enough in meeting the needs of the cooperative movement.

It was in this period of considerable uncertainty and blatant market failures that Aaron Bachtel and six other Chariton County farmers met and formed the first (officially recognized) Missouri farm club. The date of their meeting—May 10, 1914—is considered to be the founding date of today's MFA cooperative system.

During the next several years, while World War I raged, shortages plagued farmers but increased demand for farm products, temporarily diminishing the need of farmers for strong cooperatives to offset the power of large investor-driven firms. However, with the end of the war came the farm depression of the 1920s. By 1921 farm prices had fallen to one-half of their 1919 level, demand for farm products had significantly decreased, and the price of farm inputs had risen significantly. In an attempt to improve the plight of agriculture, national legislation was passed to further the progress of cooperative marketing associations. The Capper-Volstead Act of 1922 granted farmers the right to organize in associations. This act, in effect, gave the go-ahead for developing strong, well-organized, and well-financed cooperative associations.

In the 1920s the federal government took other steps, along with the Capper-Volstead Act, to offset the farm depression and to improve the legal standing of cooperatives. Building on the German-influenced foundations of the 1916 Federal Land Bank System, the Federal Intermediate Credit Banks were established to set up a short-term credit system to aid the depressed state of agriculture. The Cooperative Marketing Act of 1926 set up a government function to provide research and service activities to cooperatives. Further, the Agricultural Marketing Act of 1929 created the Federal Farm Board to help stabilize the farm sector. The Federal Farm Board encouraged the organization of cooperatives, advised them on crop prices and production situations, and set up a stabilization corporation to control surpluses. These steps by government represented a major change in the role of the states with regard to cooperatives and agriculture. The federal government became proactive in its relationship to agriculture and cooperatives and was firmly committed to nurturing the cooperative movement.

At the same time that government was trying to take a more active role in supporting cooperatives during the 1920s, cooperative leaders were seeking to develop the most advantageous philosophy of cooperative growth. Two competing views emerged during this period: Aaron Sapiro's centralized "top down" philosophy and Edwin Nourse's federated "ground up" philosophy. Sapiro urged cooperatives to organize along commodity lines in order to control a large enough proportion of a crop to be the dominant factor in the market. He advocated the organization and management of areawide cooperatives.

Sapiro based his philosophy on the belief that local cooperatives acting alone could not solve the numerous problems facing agriculture. These problems included production stabilization, product inspection and distribution, financing, bargaining, research, and the utilization of by-products. He felt only large-scale, producer-contracted, centralized cooperatives with monopsony control over supply could be formed soon enough to end the crisis in farming and farm prices brought on by the 1920s depression. Interestingly, the problems facing cooperatives were the same as those facing noncooperatives during this time. The response of noncooperatives to these problems was to increase in size and scale and to form monopolies. Noncooperatives from 1890 through the 1920s pursued a strategy of merger and vertical integration in order to develop a stable production process and to control prices. Their primary goal was to manufacture a product without interference from competitors. Thus, what Sapiro advocated for cooperatives was to emulate noncooperatives' behavior in the form of a manufacturing, vertically integrated strategy and to use tactics similar to those of the noncooperatives in competing with them. He urged cooperatives to pursue a strategy of monopoly production and supply in order that state or regional single-commodity cooperatives would control enough of a particular crop to be a decisive factor in determining prices.

The commodity-marketing movement espoused by Sapiro gained strength during the early 1920s and reached its peak in 1924, the year MFA introduced a producers contract. However, at this point, the mainline philosophy of Edwin Nourse began to gain strength. Nourse favored a local-federated approach through which larger cooperatives were formed from associations of locals along natural commodity lines. These federations were responsible for central selling and other overhead services. In the end, it was Nourse's philosophy of cooperative development that prevailed. By the mid-1930s, few strong, centralized commodity-marketing organizations based on the Sapiro model existed. As Young explains, after ten years of frustrating experiences, MFA also, in the mid-1930s, decided to eliminate most Sapiro ideas, including the producers contract approach. The federation of locals acting as a competitive yardstick became the dominant cooperative form.

The 1930s were characterized by increased momentum in the cooperative movement. The support and guidance of government agencies were key factors in fostering cooperative growth and in lessening the impact of the depression on cooperatives. The Agricultural Adjustment Administration relieved cooperatives of the responsibility of controlling production and allowed cooperatives to center their attention on ways to increase business efficiency and marketing proficiency.

Also during this period, the effects of the Farm Credit Administration could be seen in many areas of cooperative development. Funds from cooperative banks were used to reorganize thousands of creameries and cheese factories to make them viable economic entities. The Bank for Cooperatives helped establish regional grain associations to provide a centralized marketing arm for grain cooperatives. Purchasing cooperatives experienced phenomenal growth during the 1930s, partly due to the financial support and inflow of capital from the Bank for Cooperatives.

One effect of government support for agriculture and cooperatives during the New Deal era was to put cooperatives in a position to respond positively to changes in business institutions and procedures. As marketing strategies became more universally accepted, cooperatives found themselves competing with investor-owned firms characterized by large, integrated national marketing organizations. As a result, farmers found that they needed larger and stronger organizations to compete with noncooperatives.

One way they responded was by increasing the rate at which local cooperatives became members of regional marketing federations. This was especially prevalent in the dairy sector. Further, cooperatives increased the number and kind of marketing services they performed during the 1930s. Transportation departments were established to move products to the consumer. Dairy as well as fruit and vegetable cooperatives increased their reliance on advertising and brand-name identification to sell their products. Dairy cooperatives were in the forefront in implementing many of the shifts to a more consumer-oriented, marketing-based organization. MFA's efforts in this area were nationally recognized.

The 1930s saw cooperatives increase their involvement in processing operations. Dairy cooperatives began processing and distributing milk; fruit and vegetable cooperatives moved into canning, freezing, dehydrating, and packaging; and rice cooperatives acquired milling and drying facilities. Also during the thirties, cooperative wineries were begun in California. After 1936, cottonseed oil and soybean oil mills were started. By 1940 MFA had become the first poultry cooperative to process and market broilers.

Agriculture experienced a boom from 1941 to 1945 as farmers were called upon to increase production to meet increased wartime demand. Cooperatives responded to this increased production by revamping plants to produce better products and to further diversify the types of products being manufactured. New plants were built and storage and operating facilities were expanded. As in the 1930s, government support and cooperative support institutions provided the key to cooperative growth. Price supports for farmers bolstered farm prices. The Bank for Cooperatives supplied credit to cooperatives to expand their facilities and operations, and Production Credit Associations provided farmers with credit necessary to expand production. During this period national cooperative organizations improved their policy positions as representatives of farmers and their cooperatives. Significant among those that were established were the National Council of Farmer Cooperatives, the Milk Producers Federation, and the National Federation of Grain Cooperatives. A primary result of these organizations' efforts was a strengthening of the political position of cooperatives at the national level.

Investor-owned firms emerged from World War II greatly strengthened compared to their status during the depression years, and were poised for growth. They faced a growing United States economy, increased demand by consumers, and an expanded international market. They pursued horizontal mergers to increase their market share within an industry and vertical integration to control the manufacturing, processing, and distribution of a product. By the mid-1950s, investor-oriented firms had become large, powerful organizations and represented formidable competitors for cooperatives.

World War II had a similarly positive influence on cooperatives. They had grown during the war years and had become strong, viable business entities. After the war, cooperatives saw noncooperatives growing through mergers and acquisitions, and responded by trying to emulate this behavior in order to meet their increasing power.

In the period before 1940, cooperatives engaged in 500 to 600 mergers. Most of these were horizontal in nature and consisted of local cooperatives becoming part of federations or centralized organizations. By 1945 most local cooperatives were part of a larger regional structure, so further integration of this nature was limited. Therefore, much of the integration in the post–World War II period took place in order to expand the cooperatives' range of services and diversify their operations. From 1940 to 1955, only 485 mergers took place among farm cooperatives. Most of these were among dairy and farm supply entities. This merger activity increased the average size of cooperatives by 7 percent and accounted for 13 percent of total cooperative growth from 1940 to 1964. Thus, even though cooperatives tried to emulate investor-oriented firms' merger behavior after World War II, their success was limited. Their primary vehicle for growth during this period was internal.

The period from 1955 to 1975 was a time of significant change and growth for cooperatives. Net sales volume for cooperatives increased by 600 percent. The number of marketing and purchasing cooperatives decreased from over 10,000 to 7,700, yet, at the same time, farmer investment in cooperatives rose from $4 billion in 1955 to $8 billion in 1975 and their marketing and supply market shares continued to increase.

One significant development in cooperatives during this period was the increased merger and consolidation activity. The emphasis was primarily on vertical integration. Some of this integration took the form of contractual arrangements that linked production, financing, processing, and marketing together with the management function. Consolidation allowed supply cooperatives to capture economies of scale in the production of farm inputs. By increasing their scale of operations, supply cooperatives in the 1960s and 1970s were able to move aggressively into manufacturing by building fertilizer and pesticide plants, by building and operating oil refineries, and by integrating backward into raw materials. The net result of this activity was that by the mid-1970s supply cooperatives had significantly increased their market share of farm supplies purchased in almost all categories. In some of these categories, cooperatives dominated productive activities. Examples of this were in fertilizer production, where two cooperatives (CF Industries and Farmland, Inc.) were the largest producers, and in oil refining, where cooperatives produced 30 percent of the farm petroleum demanded. In the supply sector, the success of cooperatives in capturing market share was, in part, due to the formation by regional cooperatives of interregional cooperatives. By banding together to perform a particular manufacturing or service function, they were able to achieve maximum economies of scale.

The merger and consolidation trend was most pronounced in the dairy cooperative sector. Technological change, which widened the area over which milk produced moved and which prompted a shift to large-scale plants, was a prime motivator for consolidation in the dairy sector. These changes necessitated a new organizational structure to increase the bargaining strength of dairy cooperatives and to coordinate their marketing activities. The initial response of dairy cooperatives in the early 1960s was to establish marketing or bargaining federations. These set the stage for the development of more completely integrated regional centralized associations of dairy cooperatives. By the mid-1970s, the market position and structure of dairy cooperatives was greatly expanded and strengthened by mergers and consolidations. Further, dairy cooperatives had purchased fluid milk plants, had expanded their capacity to process surplus milk into butter, dry milk, and cheese, and controlled one-third of milk processing in the United States.

Grain, fruit, and vegetable cooperatives increased their merger activity during the same period in order to capture the advantages of larger volume, modern equipment, and more capable management. Some of the merger activity in these areas took the form of joint ventures between cooperatives and noncooperatives.

The 1970s constituted the most recent golden age of agriculture and represented a time of relative prosperity in farming. Many changes took place during this time. Farms grew smaller in number, larger in size, and increasingly more specialized. As a result, farmers produced a smaller proportion of their inputs. The increased demand for previously on-farm-produced inputs led to growth in the agribusiness sector. This, in turn, provided growth opportunities for cooperatives. Cooperatives captured a proportionately larger share of the increased agribusiness market than did noncooperatives in the 1960s and 1970s. A similar trend was observed concerning cooperative growth in marketing farm products. As farmers faced greater inability to affect prices on the input side, they sought to maintain greater control over market outlets and prices on the demand side. This led to increased involvement by farmers in cooperatives and the push for cooperatives to escalate their marketing and processing activities.

To finance these activities, cooperatives increased their use of debt. Between 1963 and 1970, cooperative debt increased by 132 percent as cooperatives pursued a strategy of financing fixed assets with long-term debt. To further increase equity, marketing cooperatives stepped up their use of advertising and branded products in order to bolster prices and margins. The net effect of the financing strategy of cooperatives in the 1970s was that they experienced a significant increase in their debt-to-equity ratios and a higher burden of debt.

During the early 1980s, cooperatives faced additional challenges. First, the agriculture recession of the 1980s placed severe constraints on growth potential for farmers and their cooperatives. The reduced level of growth resulted in problems related to member loyalty, market access, financial stress, and the burden of debt servicing. Second, cooperatives found themselves located in industries where they exercised little market power. This resulted from the fact that coopera-

tives were a vertical extension of their farmer-members' asset base
and were, as such, very user oriented and product driven. And third,
even at the first handler level, where cooperatives were a more dominant force in the market, they had been losing ground. Since 1952,
their share in this market had been increasing at a lesser rate.

Yet the crises of the 1980s brought renewed conviction by producer leaders and their management teams that collective action was
in their social and economic interest. By the 1990s marketing and
supply cooperatives, including MFA, had reversed their market-share
decreases and were regaining some of their former ability to be leaders
in meeting members' needs.

In this volume, Raymond Young graphically captures the important
role of MFA in this evolution of collective action by Missouri farmers
and their chosen leaders. His text has two subtle but powerful con-
ceptual underpinnings. He argues that the MFA founders relied on
economic and *philosophical* arguments to convince their fellow farmers to join in the historical development of a leading Missouri agricultural institution. According to Young, the two most frequent economic
justifications for forming cooperatives were: (1) individual producers
needed an institutional mechanism by which they could bring economic balance under their control and because of excess-supply-induced
prices, and (2) individual farmers needed countervailing power when
confronted with monopsonistic and monopolistic market structures.

Young succinctly describes the *economic* conditions and macro
responses in the form of the McNary-Haugen movement, the Federal
Farm Board, and the Agricultural Adjustment Act. He eloquently describes the dream of a grandiose role for cooperatives along the Sapiro
line of thinking, which would incorporate price controls and supply
management. But as the evolution of agricultural cooperatives pro-
gressed, the Nourse rational competitive yardstick arguments began
to supersede the more idealistic and cooperatively ambitious dreams
of the less economically inclined. Young pragmatically describes this
period.

The author's second *economic* argument in explaining why collective action in Missouri evolved was his belief that market failures
existed. He explains from a personal point of view that many product

and input markets were less than optimally competitive. Firms operating in these imperfectly competitive markets behaved in a manner that reduced the farmers' producer surplus. The fifty-year evolution of major cooperative legislation from 1890 to 1940 produced over eighty-five state cooperative incorporation laws, the Sherman Antitrust Act, the Clayton Antitrust Act, and the Capper-Volstead Act, each of which in some way attempted to address these real and perceived market failures.

Young intertwines his economic reasons for MFA's development with philosophical points. It is clear that the *philosophical* foundation of cooperatives evolved from the principles and practices developed by the Rochdale Society members during the mid-1800s in England. By the 1920s these rules had been consolidated into the three hard-core principles of democratic control, service at cost, and limited return on equity. Young implicitly concludes that cooperatives are user-owned, user-controlled, user-benefited agricultural producer organizations. More explicitly, (a) MFA farm member owners are the major users of the cooperative, (b) the benefits received by the farm members are tied to the concept of use of the cooperative in the form of patronage, and (c) the control of the cooperative by the farm member users is structured democratically in the use of voting power. Young implies that by staying close to these basic cooperative principles, producer-driven organizations have a higher probability of success. The bottom line of Young's story is that for a cooperative business organization to be successful it needs strong and visionary leadership, well-defined economic objectives, close employee-patron relationships, and a progressive, well-formed, cooperatively oriented membership.

This volume documents, from one visionary leader's point of view, how Missouri farmers constructed and molded an organization to meet their economic needs. Young approached his task in the only manner that he knew—with enthusiasm, compassion, professionalism, and humility.

The Post–Civil War Era in Missouri, 1885–1910

The end of the Civil War in 1865 marked the beginning of expanded farm production in the United States as well as several decades of farm depression. With rapid expansion into the western prairies and Great Plains in the years between 1860 and 1910, farm acreage more than doubled. Wheat output had a fourfold increase, cotton production doubled, and there were nearly two and a half times as many cattle on farms in 1910 as there had been at the end of the war. Between 1870 and the end of the century, the wheat price dropped from $1.50 to $.50 a bushel, and cotton from $.19 to $.05 a pound. Other farm commodities suffered price declines equally severe.

At the turn of the century, Missouri had 285,000 farms. Corn was the leading crop, with an average yield of thirty bushels per acre. Missouri had more registered Hereford cattle than any other state and more than twelve million acres planted in bluegrass. Dairy production was important, with fifty creameries, twenty-nine cheese factories, and twenty skimming stations. Approximately two thousand carloads of strawberries were produced annually. By the end of the second decade of the new century, Missouri was first in the nation in poultry production, first in hay marketing, first in bluegrass acreage, second in wheat acreage, fourth in value of livestock, and fifth in corn acreage. Farms were small, and farming was diversified, with most farmers growing corn, wheat, oats, and hay, and raising dairy and beef cattle, sheep, horses, mules, and chickens.

Since farmers could not control production as well as industrial producers could, they were at a disadvantage economically. As long as farmers tried to compete individually, they had no control over the prices they received for their commodities, the prices they paid for machinery and supplies, or the interest rates they paid. Many farmers strove for some kind of federal assistance, and others sought help through cooperatives. It is not surprising, therefore, that farm organizations made their start during this era.

One of the reasons for the success of the Missouri Farmers Association in its early years was that its leaders had the opportunity to learn from the mistakes of farm organizations that flourished and failed in the period from the Civil War to the early 1900s. The first such group was the Patrons of Husbandry, known as the Grange. Founded in 1867, it made its appearance in Missouri in 1870 and by 1874 consisted of fourteen hundred local units, or "sub-unions." In 1875, Missouri had the largest membership of any state.

Although the Grange was primarily social and political in nature, members pooled carload orders of farm supplies, thus reducing costs for each individual. Some of the state's Granges organized local stores, but these enterprises were not too successful. The stores had poor managers, sold goods at unprofitable prices, and extended credit too loosely. Loyalty was also a problem, since members would not patronize their cooperatives if they could save a few pennies by shopping elsewhere. Consequently, the Grange died out rather quickly, though its efforts provided valuable experience.

Another group, the Farmers Alliance, had its start in Texas in 1874 and reached Missouri in 1887. By the next year the 615 chapters in the state had a total of 13,000 members. Shortly before, in 1886, the Agricultural Wheel had also entered Missouri, and in 1887 it formed a state organization. By 1889, the Wheel claimed to have 120,000 members in Missouri with many stores and mills, and the Alliance had a membership of 20,000 and organizations in thirty-eight counties. The two groups met together in Springfield that year and consolidated under the new name Farmers and Laborers' Union. The group's emphasis thereafter was largely political, and it made demands rather than requests of candidates for office. Like the Grange, it was ultimately unsuccessful in its aims.

In 1902 the Farmers Union was organized in Texas. Missouri had its first local unit by 1905 and a state organization by 1907. Missouri membership reached its peak of 3,400 in 1910, and in 1913 the Farmers Union had 125 cooperative stores in the state. By 1919, however, state membership had dropped to 1,100.

Although the early farm organizations did not survive as viable statewide units, some local farmer-owned businesses in Missouri did endure as the result of the efforts of early farm leaders. For example, cooperative creameries begun in 1892, 1899, 1900, and 1908 were still operating thirty or forty years later. Of greater importance, however, was the valuable experience that the early MFA leaders gained from the mistakes of their predecessors. William Hirth, of Audrain County, was one of those leaders.

I.

The Hirth Era, 1914-1940

Chapter One

William Hirth and the Farm Club Movement

Winlliam Hirth was born on March 23, 1875, in Tarrytown, New York. His parents had migrated from Germany several years earlier. His father, Henry, worked at various times as a driver of a horse-drawn cab and as a factory worker. When William was three years old, the family moved to a farm on Lead Creek in Pike County, Missouri. Shortly thereafter, they moved to a 120-acre farm near Rush Hill in Audrain County.

Young Bill attended a rural one-room school where his schoolmates gave him the nickname "Baker's Choice"—the brand name on the flour sacks from which his mother made his undershirts. He was well acquainted with the hard work that accompanied farm life and deeply resented the backbreaking work required of his mother. In an article entitled "The Old Farm Home," which appeared on the front page of the February 1, 1916, issue of *The Missouri Farmer,* Hirth vividly described his early life on the farm.

> It is a great privilege to have been born on a farm. Some months ago I chanced to attend a conference of big business men in a big city when the subject of agriculture came up— and one after another a half dozen of the speakers boasted of the fact that they had been born and raised on the farm and referred to it with a pride which was splendid to witness. And

some of these men dwell behind the great bronze doors of the mighty. Their salaries run into the thousands and at their beck and call an army of men move as they will. Broadly speaking, like all other men who think clearly, these men realize that Agriculture is the very corner stone of the Nation's well-being. Again, I have no doubt that down in the depths of their hearts they realize that their success in life has largely come from the stern lessons they learned in the old farm home of the long ago—that it was there they acquired the brawn and courage which enabled them to win while the weaker ones fell by the wayside.

As I write these lines, memory carries me back once more to the days of my boyhood on the old farm up in Audrain County. Once more I set my old box traps where the rabbit tracks were thickest between the brush piles in the old briar patch and once more I make the rounds with beating heart early the next morning—and then when Saturday finally came I once more see myself trudging to town with a half dozen frozen cotton tails flung across my back. And think of it! For each one of those cotton tail I used to get a nickel. As the old timers would say, "money was easy in them days." Once more I proudly "break a path" through the drifted snow across the "big pasture" to the little school house—for in those times the boy who "broke the path" for the girls and smaller kids was considered something of a hero. Once more I defy the parental mandate and "go in swimmin'" and then sit bare-headed out in the sun for my hair to dry lest the dripping locks tell tales. Once more I hear the symphony of sweet throated birds as I sit and watch my cork in breathless expectancy on the old creek bank, and once more I show my utter recklessness by joining "the gang" for a midnight visit to the "haunted house"—an experience without which no farmer boy's life is complete. Once more I try to pick a hedge thorn out of my calloused heel with an eight-penny nail. Once more I swear by all the gods on high that nature committed a horrible and senseless blunder in its construction of the cow—and once again as the kindly shadows of the night are falling I make the rounds with the old basket filled with golden corn, climb up into the loft and throw down a goodly allowance of sweet-scented hay and then, when every horse and pig and cow and sheep has been tenderly looked after I turn my weary but gladsome steps toward the beacon light which shines forth from the old kitchen window.

It may be that I don't know how to tie my necktie as deftly as do these hot-house fellows who were raised on the boulevards. Perhaps I would look like an old draft horse if I tried to dance the tango or the fox trot. Very likely I would get mixed up on the idiotic array of forks and spoons which lie beside their dinner plates—but just the same I wouldn't trade my humble knowledge and view of life for all their graces, though I received a king's ransom in the bargain. For back there on the old farm I learned the things which enable men to take punishment—to come again if perchance they stumble—to meet life's battles fearlessly—to be thankful for God's favors, and patient in the hour of trial and disappointment. It is your duty and mine, my friend, to see to it that the old farm house is spared from the avarice and greed of our time—that in the future, as in the past, it may continue to be the source of the Nation's finest manhood and womanhood.

Early farm organizations in Missouri influenced Hirth in his strong desire to do something for the welfare of the farmer. When he was fifteen, he joined the Farmers Alliance at Rush Hill and soon afterward became its secretary and the lecturer for the county organization. His fame as a speaker spread, and before his twenty-first birthday, he stumped Missouri for the Democratic Party in support of William Jennings Bryan for president. Hirth's father, Henry, was a stalwart Republican.

Hirth attended McGee College in Macon, Missouri, for one year and then Central College in Fayette for two years until his money ran out, in 1897. Francis Pike, a longtime employee of the *Columbia Daily Tribune,* relates that his grandfather, John F. Pike, gave Hirth financial help to attend college during those three years. Henry Hirth was adamant that his son stay on the farm and refused to give him money for school. Years later Francis Pike applied for a job in William Hirth's publishing plant in Columbia. Remembering the help he had received from Pike's grandfather, Hirth promptly gave the young man a job.

After he left college, Hirth became a salesman for New York Life Insurance Company, moved to Oklahoma, and enjoyed much success. In his first year he became a member of the $100,000 Club, and in his second year the $200,000 Club—an achievement that was comparatively greater than being a member of a $1 Million Club today.

In 1900 Hirth married Lillian Vincent of Kansas, the daughter of a former U.S. congressman. That same year, they moved to Columbia, where Hirth resided and farmed until his death forty years later.

According to Hirth, he had decided early in life to be a lawyer. Consequently, he read law at a law firm in Columbia, was admitted to the bar, and was offered positions with several firms. Hirth explained that the real reason he finally decided not to practice law was that when he was a member of the Farmers Alliance, he became so deeply interested in the unfair economic conditions faced by the farmers during that period that he decided to try to do something about it. It would become a full-time job.

In 1906 Hirth and A. C. Talley, the former state secretary of the Populist Party, bought a weekly newspaper, the *Columbia Statesman*. Through the newspaper, Hirth sponsored a variety of campaigns, including formation of the Commercial Club in Columbia, a forerunner of the Chamber of Commerce. He joined in a proposal to build a new Boone County courthouse through a bond issue. The issue had been defeated three times previously, but with Hirth's help it passed by a margin of three to one. Hirth was also instrumental in encouraging the Hamilton-Brown Shoe Factory to locate in Columbia. Ray Derr, in *Missouri Farmers in Action,* points out that farm-related subjects were addressed in the *Columbia Statesman* far more extensively than in the other Columbia papers. Hirth was also a strong supporter of the College of Agriculture at the University of Missouri, though he disagreed with the approaches taken by some of the college's staff members.

In 1908 Hirth was on the verge of running for Congress, but instead he embarked on a new venture, the publishing of a farm magazine. His newspaper's printing plant was adequate for the task, and on October 15, 1908, the first issue of *The Missouri Farmer and Breeder* appeared. It started as a monthly publication, in 1912 the name changed to *The Missouri Farmer,* and the following year it became a semimonthly publication. Hirth, listed on the masthead as publisher, wrote several articles in each issue, including "After Thoughts," which appeared on the front cover. George B. Ellis was the original managing editor, and his editorials and articles were reminiscent of those by Hirth in both style and philosophy.

Some have contended that Hirth had two objectives in starting *The Missouri Farmer*—to provide helpful advice for farmers and to provide a voice for a farm organization. He attained the first objective by printing numerous articles by experts in the field of agriculture, primarily staff members of the University of Missouri College of Agriculture. There is some question, however, that Hirth originally intended the founding of a large cooperative farm organization as a primary purpose for his magazine.

During its first two years, *The Missouri Farmer* contained little advertising and concentrated on articles that would benefit farmers in producing crops and raising livestock. In 1910 an editorial lamented the low returns farmers were receiving; another editorial plugged for better rural roads. In 1911 a four-day convention of farmers held at the College of Agriculture of the University of Missouri received considerable publicity, and in May 1911 a message from University of Missouri president Albert Ross Hill, stressing the need for farmers to continue to learn and cooperate in all efforts, ran on the front cover. The first article on cooperatives, "Benefits Derived from Cooperative Societies among Farmers," appeared in November 1911.

In its early days, *The Missouri Farmer* made references to the grass-roots farm clubs founded through the Grange, the Farmers Union, and similar organizations. Throughout the early teens, articles such as "Benefits of Cooperation among Farmers," written in 1913 by Henry J. Waters, the former dean of the College of Agriculture, regularly appeared, extolling the advantages of group buying and selling by farmers. They cited examples from other states, including cooperative creameries in Minnesota and Wisconsin. During these years, Hirth dedicated himself to the farm club concept. He "single-handedly and without funds started to work and for several years hammered away through *The Missouri Farmer* at 'the kind of organization I had in mind. . . . I delivered hundreds of public addresses [on the subject] whenever a handful of farmers would listen.'"

By 1914 *The Missouri Farmer* had been designated the official organ for several groups, including the Missouri Farm Management Association, Missouri Cattle Feeders Association, Missouri Corn Growers Association, Missouri Dairy Association, and others. The February 1, 1914, issue of *The Missouri Farmer* reprinted an article from a Minnesota bulletin, "Advantages of a Farmers' Club," stating that "a farmer who can use two dozen self-binders can purchase them more cheaply than the man who uses only one. The farmer who can sell many carloads of farm products of one class can get a better price for his products than can the one who has only a wagonload or less to market." An editorial in the same issue stressed the need for farmers to raise their voices.

> When conditions are such that out of every dollar paid by the consumer only 45¢, less than half, goes to the producer, the farmer, then evidently something is wrong in the division of the dollar. We believe, however, this is largely the farmer's fault. Farmers are at a disadvantage because of their independent action, the lack of organization, and [the lack of] cooperation. The individual farmer may raise his voice against an injustice of railroad rates, stockyards charges, or the exorbitant prices of the Standard Oil Trust, but what does it amount to? Let a million or ten million protests go up against these great interests through a united organization, and something will be done.

Hirth prepared and distributed material to be used in organizing farm clubs, including suggested bylaws and speeches. It is difficult to determine when the first farm club was organized, but the beginning date of the Missouri Farmers Association has traditionally been designated as May 10, 1914, when a group of seven farmers gathered at the Newcomer School House north of Brunswick in Chariton County and elected Aaron Bachtel as its first president.

Bachtel, a reader of *The Missouri Farmer* and a prominent farmer in Chariton County, described the meeting in a speech at the MFA annual convention in August 1933 that was reprinted in the October 1 issue of *The Missouri Farmer.*

> I have been a reader of *The Missouri Farmer* for a long time. In the February, 1914, issue there was a short article wherein it stated that farmers should organize into school district Farm Clubs and how they could be benefitted by such organizations. After reading the article, it looked so simple and at the same time so far reaching, that it appealed to me very forcibly. So I wrote to Mr. Hirth and asked him to send me a bundle of the papers containing that article which he did by return mail. I distributed these among my neighbors, asking them to read the article and to meet at the Newcomer School House the following Tuesday night. And how well I remember that cold and blustery winter night on the third of March and the discussion that took place as to the needs of the farmer, but they hesitated to organize.

> Although it looked good, they were afraid the farmers would not stick. I was very anxious for an organization and told them to think the matter over until the next week when we met again with a good attendance. I told them I thought this plan to organize the farmers was sound and would like very much for them to try it. This was March 10th. After talking the matter over at some length the following seven men agreed to band themselves together in a Farm Club: Aaron Bachtel, T. E. Penick, W. J. Heisel, George Heisel, Earl Smutz, John Kohl, W. L. Armstrong. At our next meeting we added ten more members.

> As spring work began we didn't do much, only had our regular meetings and added a few members. As time rolled on harvest came and we made up an order for 1,150 pounds of penitentiary binder twine, which we received through Mr. Hirth. This was the first Club order that was ever given. That fall Mr. Hirth made a contract with the West Virginia Coal Company for coal—I think the contract was to last until the following March. The price of coal went up, and I shipped in several carloads. One car I got in I told all the farmers, regardless of whether they were members or not, to come in and get coal just the same, with one provision, that when they

got their coal, if they thought the Farm Club was really worth
while they were to pay their dues and become members,
which they did, all but one man. And I've never liked him
since.

Virgil Bachtel, the son of Aaron Bachtel, remembered going to the
meeting on March 3, a week before the organizational meeting on
March 10. "It was a rainy and muddy night when dad and I rode
horseback to the school. There weren't many there, and they were
skeptical of the idea. Many of them weren't readers of 'The Missouri
Farmer,' and they feared it was a get-rich quick scheme of Hirth's.
Others didn't believe farmers could stick together."

Aaron Bachtel remained active in the Missouri Farmers Association, serving as a board member from 1923 to 1944, and is sometimes
referred to as the father of MFA. The Newcomer School House was
purchased by MFA in 1950, and at one time MFA Insurance Companies
(now Shelter Insurance Companies) contemplated moving the building to its grounds in Columbia, but a replica was built instead.

As farm clubs were organized, news items concerning their meetings appeared in *The Missouri Farmer* and, in Hirth's words, "set the
woods on fire." In every issue of the magazine, editorials urged
farmers to join together in rural schoolhouses and form farm clubs.
Following are excerpts from editorials in the November and December 1915 issues:

> Heretofore, the farm organizations scattered here and there
> have devoted themselves chiefly to social matters and a dis-
> cussion of farming methods—and while such subjects are
> very necessary and splendid, yet in the present crisis, we must
> have an organization much farther reaching and more serious
> in its aspirations than this; we must, in short, boldly and
> fearlessly take in hand the marketing of the things which the
> farmer produces—and this must be a battle cry to which
> farmers may rally in every nook and cranny of the land. The
> first essential step is to organize a "Farm Club" in your school
> district.
>
> So light up the little school house and send the word out into
> the highways and byways for the clans to assemble—and as

they come trooping in from the cornfields and barnyards, tell them they are about to engage in a solemn struggle in which every farmer must do his whole duty. Tell him that we propose to shake off the strangle hold of a gang of conscienceless conspirators who waxed fat upon our toils, who are setting at naught the victories of better farming methods, who have taken the joy and enthusiasm out of our fields and feed lots, who levy their unholy tribute upon every morsel of meat and bread which the toiling millions must eat to hold body and soul together, whose black shadow rests across the threshold of every farm home in the land and whose remorseless greed in driving thousands of our brightest boys and girls away from the old "home nest" to the overcrowded cities with their pitfalls of vice and crime. In the light of a cause so just, is there in this great commonwealth a farmer with soul so craven as to whisper "What's the use?"

Evidence that farm clubs started simultaneously throughout Missouri appeared in the April 1, 1914, issue of *The Missouri Farmer.* The Glendale Farm Group in Barton County, with about thirty farmers present, adopted the sample bylaws and constitution secured from the secretary of the Missouri State Board of Agriculture. They ordered four cars of corn, two cars of feeding oats, two cars of Texas seed oats, and a hundred bushels of seed potatoes. "We have saved 9¢ a bushel on our first car of seed oats. This broke the local price 4¢, so it helped everyone some." In Cooper County, the Willow Grove Farm Club was organized in the fall of 1914, according to Albert Widel, who became a veteran MFA leader and manager at the Blackwater Farmers Exchange.

In a 1934 pamphlet entitled *The Romance of the Missouri Farmers Association,* Hirth recalled that in the beginning the farm club movement "spread like a prairie fire into different parts of the state, and thus soon the school houses were lit up in every direction, and the Fords rattled far into the night; meanwhile I made three or four speeches per day . . . and thus before I knew it we had better than 10,000 members, and the organization of new Farm Clubs went on with ever increasing speed."

Hirth persuaded many local banks to buy blocks of yearly subscriptions to *The Missouri Farmer* to be used in persuading farmers to join up. Meanwhile the magazine continued to send its message to farmers in powerful language.

> Too long, we farmers have been content to plan, plant, and reap and leave the buying of what we use and what we raise to others. Why not arouse ourselves to the great need of the hour and use the power of cooperation and organization to give us the fruits of our labor?
>
> The organization of farmers should begin right at home in the school district where farmers know each other and where leaders and representatives can be chosen who can be trusted. Let the organization start work on something that will bring immediate results. Enough can be saved on buying a carload of fertilizer, lime, tankage, coal, or other like products to make it worthwhile.
>
> After a half-dozen districts are organized and have found something to do, a County Club should be formed. And where a half-dozen counties are organized, a state federation should be perfected, and the final aim should be a national union, which, under wise direction, can become the great controlling force in the economic life of the farmers in every state in the Union. Such an organization can also be made a great social and educational movement.

In addition to urging formation of farm clubs through the columns of *The Missouri Farmer*, Hirth addressed many mass meetings in rural areas of the state. It was not uncommon for him to make several addresses per day. He paid all the expenses himself, including renting the hall and taking out newspaper notices. Through his intimate knowledge of early farm organizations such as the Wheel and the Farmers Alliance, he knew what a farm organization needed to survive, as he explained to the women in the Farmers Alliance in Audrain County. "We have got the cart before the horse . . . . No farmer organization can live on politics alone. It must enter the marketing field and save its members some money, and having done this, its leader should then make it wholesome and powerful politically. But no farm organization can become permanent by merely raising political cain."

Originally, the individual farm clubs placed their orders for commodities through *The Missouri Farmer*. Hirth contracted for the commodities, with some difficulty at first, but ultimately thousands of carloads were shipped. The local merchants' profit margins were high, so the average savings to farm club members on a carload of flour and feed was about four hundred dollars. The bulk purchases of binder twine from the state penitentiary in Jefferson City saved farmers many times more than their annual club dues.

In an editorial in *The Missouri Farmer* on August 15, 1916, the advantages of pooling purchases through farm clubs were explained.

> On account of the drought, considerable feed will have to be bought this year, and if farmers can make a saving of $2 or $3 a ton on alfalfa or on mill feed or of 5¢ or 10¢ a bushel on corn, is not that worthwhile? . . . Aside from the business reasons for organizing Farm Clubs, there are many social and educational advantages to be gained. Better schools, better churches, good roads, and a better environment all around for the enjoyment of living will come with a complete organization of farmers.

Another report in *The Missouri Farmer*, in April 1916, told the story of a farm club in Boone County that made arrangements with a flour mill to buy the amount the club needed at a savings of forty cents per hundred pounds. The members also pooled their order for twelve hundred rods of woven-wire fence at a savings of two cents a rod and purchased seed potatoes at a discount of ten cents a bushel. In addition, "a Club arrangement was made with the local papers, and $1.45 was saved for each member on his reading material."

The November 15, 1916, issue of *The Missouri Farmer* reported:

> At Centralia more than a dozen new Farm Clubs have been organized during the last thirty days. . . . Up around Richmond, in Ray County, a dozen new Clubs have been formed during the last three weeks. . . . Down in Vernon County more than 20 Clubs have been formed. . . . Even down at Branson, in the heart of the Ozarks, Mr. Renshaw and a few courageous souls are trying to start the ball rolling among the crags where

Harold Bell Wright found the characters and setting for a beautiful story, *Shepherd of the Hills.*

At Hirth's urging, the first county association was founded in War-ren County in December 1915. Hirth and Sam Jordan, a staff member of the State Board of Agriculture and the first county agent in Mis-souri, addressed the meeting, the largest ever held in the county courtroom, with farmers literally hanging out the windows. The county association was "composed of three district units—the school district, the township, and the county . . . [and was] later to become part of a Missouri Farmers Association." Gust C. Polsten of Warrenton was elected president; Garrett Bockhorst of Hickory Grove, vice pres-ident; and E. H. Winter of Warrenton, secretary. Assuming one of the tasks of the individual farm clubs, the county association became the agency that placed orders for farm supplies, thus allowing larger or-ders to be placed with suppliers.

Hirth was concerned that the process of pooling orders for mer-chandise might become tedious at meetings and that interest would wane. So he urged that farm clubs get an old-time fiddler or a local orchestra to perform at their meetings. He further suggested "a lec-turer from the College of Agriculture, or a local minister, teacher, law-yer, doctor or dentist." However, he warned, "none of these should take the place of practical farm topics or of the better methods of buy-ing and selling."

Some farm clubs came forth with unique activities. For example, several clubs in the Union area bought a fine jack for breeding pur-poses. Members of the Harrison Farm Club, of Centralia, held an an-nual rabbit hunt each December 31 and one year captured sixty-two rabbits. According to *The Missouri Farmer:*

> H. E. Klinefelter, of Labadie, reported:
> One of the best Farm Clubs in Franklin County is North Bend, a small one with fifteen members paid up. This group of men have met regularly once a month for years. And why do they meet? Because the meetings alone are worth the dol-lar MFA dues. He says it is worth a dollar to get together and discuss the affairs, local, county, state, and national. If the

local telephone line needs repairing, the North Bend Farm Club looks after it. If a road needs repairing, the Club lets the county court know about it. If a neighbor is sick and needs his wood sawed and his corn shucked, the Farm Club saws the wood and shucks the corn.

A report in the January 1, 1916, issue of *The Missouri Farmer* entitled "Farm Clubs Forming Everywhere" summarized the status of the movement at that time.

> Every mail brings letters to "The Missouri Farmer" telling about Farm Clubs which have been formed or which are in the process of formation, and we believe we are safe in saying that not less than one thousand such organizations will be perfected in different parts of the state before the end of January. In the meantime, more than a dozen big county farmers' mass meetings have been planned in as many different counties for the purpose of organizing a County Farmers' Association.
>
> Perhaps Warren County has more Farm Clubs at this time than any other county in the state—but the interest is very keen in Livingston, Macon, Lafayette, Bates, Audrain, Henry, Sullivan, Atchison, and a number of others. This is also true of Boone in which perhaps a dozen clubs have been formed within the last two weeks—the latest one being in the Wade district, which starts in with 25 members.
>
> Thus this great new movement is thoroughly launched and before long Missouri should be "on fire" from end to end.

Chapter Two

The Creation of a
Statewide Organization

irth's first effort to found a statewide organization occurred in January 1916. In the December 15, 1915, issue of *The Missouri Farmer,* he stated, "We believe the time is ripe to hold a great state meeting of farmers to consider the marketing of farm products and to lend an added impetus to the organizing of County Farmers Associations, with the idea of later joining them together in a powerful statewide organization." Hirth suggested that the annual Farmers Week, sponsored by the College of Agriculture of the University of Missouri and held from January 3 to January 7 in Columbia, would be an opportune event for such a gathering.

In the January 15, 1916, issue of *The Missouri Farmer,* a report by George Ellis entitled "Missouri Farmers Take First Step for Better Marketing" gave these details:

> At the suggestion of "The Missouri Farmer," the secretary of the State Board of Agriculture, Hon. Jewell Mayes, issued a call for a state convention on marketing and market conditions to meet in Columbia Wednesday, January 5, 1916 during Farmers Week.
>
> About 100 met at the Boone County Court House and heard David Lubin, a worldwide authority on organization and marketing for farmers. The conference adjourned until the next

day when 500 or 600 farmers met and completed the temporary organization of a state marketing association. On the same day, the Missouri Association of County Farm Bureau Boards met in Columbia in connection with Farmers Week. The Farm Bureau organization was headed by President E. H. Bullock, of Edina, and he was made temporary chairman of the group called by Mayes. J. Kelly Wright, of the State Board of Agriculture, was made temporary secretary. The chairman was authorized to name a committee of fifteen and call a meeting to perfect a permanent organization.

Little information is available on action taken by that first group of leaders during 1916. A "Farmers Marketing Committee," possibly the executive committee of the board, was quoted in the August 15, 1916, issue of *The Missouri Farmer* as calling for a two-day mass meeting in every county to form county associations.

> The undersigned committee will actively assist in the organization of a strong County Farmers Association through which the foundation of a Farm Club [can be achieved] in as nearly as possible every school district in your county. . . . The College of Agriculture and the State Board of Agriculture will doubtless cooperate as far as possible. . . . As soon as 25 or 30 counties have been organized in this manner, a powerful Missouri Farmers Association will be formed.

The committee members signing this call were Anderson Craig, the chairman, of Maryville; W. H. Thompson, the secretary, of Columbia; W. A. Ferguson of Houstonia; T. B. Ingwersen of Bowling Green; Floyd Trigsle of Gallatin; E. H. Bullock of Edina; and H. H. Weaver of Rush Tower. Ingwersen would be elected the first president of Missouri Farmers Association in August 1917.

During 1916 the farm club movement continued unabated. In August a two-day farm club meeting was held in Chariton County. Two representatives from the State Board of Agriculture spoke on the first day, and Hirth spoke on the second. The crowd was estimated to be from fifteen hundred to two thousand. In September, at a two-day meeting in Higginsville, the Lafayette County Association was organized. The association expected to organize one hundred farm clubs in 129 school districts for a total of two thousand members in the county and to take over the job of purchasing for all the individual farm clubs in the county. It also expected to sell apples by the carload.

The year 1917 dawned with the farm club movement in high gear. In the January issue of *The Missouri Farmer,* Hirth commented on the growth of farm clubs in the counties of Ray, Chariton, Laclede, Scotland, Boone, Vernon, Audrain, Cass, and Ste. Genevieve. He was confident that one thousand farm clubs would be in existence before the end of the winter. Because no real progress had been made toward the statewide organization of farm clubs at the January 1916 meeting, Hirth again called for a farm club convention to be held in connection with Farmers Week, January 2–5, 1917. Approximately five hundred farm club members attended, with Lafayette and Saline Counties having the largest delegations. On Wednesday afternoon, after two half-days of discussion, the group created a temporary organization with S. R. Schmutz of Mayview as temporary president, and B. P. Smoot of Centralia as temporary secretary. The group also provided for a board of directors of twenty-five, to be named later, and agreed that the temporary association would continue until summer, when the permanent organization would be completed. Hirth commented that "nothing attracted greater attention during [the 1917] Farmers Week than the convention of Farm Clubs."

Hirth instructed the temporary board of directors to get busy at once contacting legislators about implementing the resolutions adopted by the delegates before the present session of the state legislature adjourned. The resolutions, written by Hirth and passed by the delegates, dealt with the weighing of livestock and recommended that a searching inquiry be made into other matters at stockyards; that a stringent dog law be passed to protect sheep; and that a close eye be kept on the road laws. The temporary board also asked farm club members to contribute fifty cents each to defray the costs of the organization and recommended that *The Missouri Farmer* become the official organ.

In the meantime, reports in *The Missouri Farmer* told of the continued surge of farm club activity. "Something has broken loose in

Franklin County. The first Farm Club was organized near Union about two weeks ago . . . and since that time several other big Clubs have been put on the map." On April 11, Hirth wrote, he had "helped to perfect a Saline County Association at Marshall." He declared: "It was one of the greatest farmer meetings I have ever attended in the state. Although work was exceedingly pressing in the fields, between 700 and 800 farmers took part in the meeting. . . . up to the present time over 80 Farm Clubs out of a total of 114 rural school districts have been organized."

No substantial development occurred between January and August 1917, but the executive committee of the board did issue a call for a "State convention of the Missouri Farmers Association" to be held in Sedalia on August 28 and 29, following the state fair. Farm clubs were entitled to name one delegate for each ten members or fraction thereof. In an announcement of the meeting, Hirth urged farmers who had automobiles to come to the first annual MFA convention and suggested they plan to travel in groups so they could help each other in case of a tire blowout. He also asked farmers to bring their wives. "[The] women's building will be open both days. There will be comfortable chairs, couches, wash and toilet rooms and plenty of good drinking water."

Arrangements for the meeting were made through the Sedalia Chamber of Commerce. Evidently, chamber officials became dubious when, on the day before the convention was to open, nothing had been prepared; and the publicity man for the state fair asked if there was really going to be anyone there. The next day, when he saw the two thousand people in attendance, he reportedly said, "Well, I'll be damned!"

Those in attendance were described as "big cattle feeders by the score . . . many old gray and grizzly veterans who helped to make history years ago for the Grange, the Farmers Alliance, and the old Wheel." Speakers included Frank Myers, secretary of the Iowa Farmers Cooperative Elevator Association; Sam Jordan, county agent from Chariton County; and Cornelius Roach, chairman of the State Tax Commission.

When the call went out for nominations for president of the new association, J. S. Littrell of Chariton County led off by nominating T. B. Ingwersen of Pike County, a pioneer in the farm club movement. W. W. Walker of Lafayette County made the second nomination, of Samuel J. Kleinschmidt, also from Lafayette County. A ballot was taken and Ingwersen was elected. Immediately, Kleinschmidt asked for the floor and proposed that the assembly make the election of Ingwersen unanimous. Following the call for nomination of a vice president, several jumped up to nominate Kleinschmidt, and the assembled group elected him. The next action was election of a treasurer; the group selected another Lafayette County leader, E. W. Schowengerdt of Mayview, for that position.

A constitution was also adopted. It gave power and authority to six directors-at-large and to a board of thirty-two directors, including two from each congressional district except the tenth, eleventh, and twelfth, which were all within St. Louis. The first board consisted of twenty-six members: T. B. Ingwersen, president, Bowling Green; Samuel J. Kleinschmidt, vice president, Higginsville; E. W. Schowengerdt, treasurer, Mayview; Ned J. Ball, Montgomery City; Walter Barrett, Elwood; C. C. Brown, Elsberry; Welton Buford, Gorin; A. J. Crawford, Atlanta; T. H. DeWitt, Green City; Clarence Fitzpatrick, Higginsville; William Hirth, Columbia; J. A. Hudson, Columbia; W. A. Kearns, Granger; George M. Kelley, Tipton; B. F. Kline, Knobnoster; J. S. Littrell, Keytesville; W. E. McClure, Irwin; C. O. Niebrugge, Washington; R. T. Pence, Marshall; Frank Pierce, Nashville; Earl Rea, Marshall; A. C. Rosier, Butler; Sherman Rybolt, Grant City; B. C. Smutz, Brunswick; C. A. Wiggenstein, Fredericktown; and Estes Youtsey, Gallatin. Of these members, Rea, Crawford, Littrell, Hudson, Ball, DeWitt, and Hirth were chosen to serve as the executive committee. Interestingly, of the twenty-six members of the board of directors, all but five resided north of Highway 50, which runs from Kansas City through Warrensburg, Sedalia, Jefferson City, and on to St. Louis. Those south of Highway 50 were two board members from Barton County and one each from Bates, Greene, and Madison Counties. The heaviest concentration was three from Lafayette County and two each from Saline, Chariton, and Boone Counties. Within a few years, however, the geographic distribution changed as membership increased in southwest Missouri.

The organization's Articles of Purpose, written by Hirth and adopted at this first convention, were described as a "battle cry of production cost, together with a reasonable profit for the fruits of the farmers' sweat and toil." The more formal constitution and bylaws adopted at the convention began with the Object of the Association, which grew out of Hirth's Articles of Purpose.

> It shall be the duty of this Association to assist the various Farm Clubs and county Farmers Associations which are in good standing in the purchase of such commodities as may be considered proper items of Farm Club activity; to render every possible aid in the building up of a system of marketing by which our members may receive production cost, together with a reasonable profit for the fruits of their sweat and toil and to otherwise assure to the agricultural interests of Missouri the reward and recognition to which their fundamental importance entitles them in the life of our great commonwealth.

The remainder of the bylaws included a listing of officers, duties, and other details.

The resolutions that were adopted included naming *The Missouri Farmer* as the official publication; urging the building of grain elevators and the creation of livestock shipping associations; and warning against the establishment of general merchandise stores in competition with country merchants. Memories of the experience of previous farm organizations such as the Grange, the Farmers Alliance, and the Wheel, which had opened farmers' stores, were still fresh. Hirth pointed out that the management of general merchandise stores was a business unfamiliar to farmers. He also pointed out that the goodwill of bankers, who did not look kindly on competition with hometown merchants, was important to farmers. Additional resolutions called on the federal government to set farm prices during wartime with the same profit margin allowed for other industries; to conduct the war on a pay-as-you-go basis; and to allow farm boys to stay home and produce food. Finally, the group resolved to amalgamate all state farm organizations into one.

The contracting for and purchasing of farm supplies to be handled by farm clubs and county associations became the concern of the Missouri Farmers Association instead of Hirth, who had been handling those details personally, along with help from Joseph Goeke, business manager of *The Missouri Farmer,* and his staff.

Minutes of the first two board meetings do not show their dates or locations, but the board got down to serious business quite soon after the first convention. Hirth pointed out the opportunities and possibilities of the organization. He said that it should gain enough members so that it could have its own flour mill and a seed house at the earliest opportunity. The executive committee was given power to search for and procure a site for a cement plant; a motion was made to have stationery printed for use by the directors; and *The Missouri Farmer* was confirmed as the official organ for the farm clubs.

At its second meeting, the board made plans to raise money for a flour and feed mill in Kansas City at a cost of three hundred thousand dollars. The chairman appointed an auditing committee consisting of T. H. DeWitt of Green City, R. T. Pence of Marshall (who would later serve as president and vice president of MFA, respectively), and J. A. Hudson of Columbia. The auditing committee was given authority to hire one or two men to do organizational work.

Hudson, a native of Montgomery County and one of Hirth's closest friends, had been born in 1853 on a small farm and had later become one of Missouri's noted country editors. After the turn of the century, he had moved to Columbia, where he owned extensive property, including a large farm where he fed out some five hundred steers annually.

Hudson proposed the following resolution endorsing Hirth and *The Missouri Farmer,* which was adopted:

> 1) "The Missouri Farmer" planned and inaugurated the Farm Club movement; 2) "The Missouri Farmer" carries many important messages; 3) Hirth has made hundreds of speeches at his own cost; 4) Hirth made arrangements to contract flour, feed, twine, coal, salt, etc., and paid his own postage, phone, etc.; 5) Hirth's fight against special interests has resulted in his losing advertising revenue for "The Missouri Farmer"; 6) Will

be impossible to develop Farm Clubs which will live without keeping in touch with activities through "The Missouri Farmer."

Members of farm clubs were admonished to pay their dues before they could enjoy the benefits of doing business with the Missouri Farmers Association. These membership dues were originally $2.50, divided as follows: $.50 to the local farm club, $.50 to the county association, $.50 to the state association, and $1.00 to *The Missouri Farmer* for a two-year subscription.

The second annual MFA convention was held in Sedalia on September 9 and 10, 1918, with sixty-two counties represented. Samuel J. Kleinschmidt was elected president and W. E. May of St. Clair, vice president. Numerous resolutions were passed, including one calling for unity and loyalty.

> We hereby re-affirm our faith and loyalty to the principles of our splendid organization, to the Articles of Faith adopted in last year's convention and to the principles and policies enunciated in the regular constitution and bylaws of the local Farm Clubs. Manifestly, we cannot hope to build up a truly powerful organization unless the local club and leaders bear willing allegiance to the plans and policies of our state organization, and there must be no straying away or lax regard of the wishes of the central organization which is bending every energy to the winning of the great fight we have undertaken. Ours is the first farmers organization in the history of American agriculture which deliberately started out to put the farmers in position to demand "production cost, together with a reasonable profit for the fruits of the farmers' sweat and toil."

A few months later, the MFA board of directors authorized hiring a secretary and some fieldmen to assist the farm clubs. Some of the first fieldmen included F. L. Cuno of Franklin County; George M. Kelley of Tipton; and George McCarthy of Passaic, who was hired for "elevator and general MFA work." McCarthy, affectionately known as "Mac," had been born in Nebraska and moved at an early age to a farm near Passaic. He had converted his literary club in Passaic to a farm club, was manager of the local MFA livestock shipping association, and became manager of the Passaic Elevator Company. Later, as chief auditor, he would design an accounting system for MFA agencies and play an important leadership role in MFA.

Not only were the "Fords rattling far into the night," their drivers rounding up new MFA members, but according to a report in the December 15, 1918, issue of *The Missouri Farmer,* two New Haven members, Fred Schventer and Albert Allersmeyer, rowed across the Missouri River in a skiff and walked to twenty-five or thirty farmhouses in Warren County soliciting memberships. They could not hold a meeting because of the flu epidemic.

Early Conflicts

The farm clubs were not the only organizations established during this period in an effort to alleviate farmers' problems; Hirth faced substantial competition. Strained relations between Hirth and the Extension Division of the University of Missouri surfaced early in the history of the Missouri Farmers Association. In the November 1, 1917, issue of *The Missouri Farmer,* Hirth noted: "It is a personal matter, which need not disturb or concern my friends. My only plea is that He who rules on high will continue to bless me with vigorous health . . . for granted this priceless boon, their petty schemes will cause me no alarm, for, to tell the truth, I rather enjoy a fight, once I know there is no way out of it. So 'lay on McDuff and damned be he who first cries, hold, enough.'"

To understand Hirth's displeasure, a brief background is helpful. In 1910 the university had founded the Extension Division to oversee the offering of off-campus education.[1] As part of the extension effort, the College of Agriculture in 1912 began a program to place farm advisers in counties throughout the state. These advisers were to be hired by the college but sponsored by county farm bureaus made up of local interests. On May 8, 1914, Congress established the national Agricultural Extension Service by passing the Smith-Lever Act, providing further financial support for county extension agents (farm advisers). By that time, ten county farm advisers were already at work in Missouri. Included were Sam Jordan, F. W. Faurot of Buchanan County (the father of Don Faurot, the legendary University of Missouri football coach), and C. M. McWilliams of Cape Girardeau County.

As reported by Vera Schuttler in *A History of the Missouri Farm Bureau Federation,* Jordan began work in Pettis County on March 15, 1912, as county farm adviser and manager of the Pettis County Bureau of Agriculture; he was employed with funds raised by the Sedalia Boosters' Club. In Cape Girardeau County, the county court appropriated fifteen hundred dollars annually for three years, and on August 1, 1912, McWilliams became county farm adviser. He was the first county agent employed under the program being developed by the College of Agriculture, in an agreement involving the college, the county court, and the U.S. Department of Agriculture. In Pettis County the same plan went into effect on January 1, 1913. In keeping with the College of Agriculture's scheme for sponsorship by county farm bureaus, Cape Girardeau set up a bureau on April 26, 1913. As Schuttler noted, "It should be remembered that at this time County Farm Bureaus had no other function than to promote and help Extension activities within the county. County agents assisted in the organization of Farm Bureaus as part of their regular duties and largely directed the activities of the Bureau after they were set up."[2]

Thirteen counties had organized farm bureaus by early 1915. Their officers and farm advisers were called to a meeting in Slater on March 24 and 25, 1915, to consider forming a statewide organization. Over two hundred were in attendance, and they elected E. H. Bullock as president of the group, to be called the Missouri Farm Bureau Federation (MFBF). Hirth, who had been invited to the meeting, sent the following wire: "Sorry I can't attend meeting, but am there in spirit. Upon the fight that you and others like you are waging depends the future of agriculture. In it is involved not merely the happiness and prosperity of the farmer, but of the entire nation. Despite the knockers we must push on."

The close ties between the national Agricultural Extension Service and the farm bureaus continued, as Schuttler emphasized.

The Department of Agriculture sent out suggestions for organizing Farm Bureaus; the Missouri Extension Service made the services of a number of men available to help counties organize Farm Bureaus—including six in the state office and five county agents in different parts of the state; a school of instruction in Farm Bureau organization was arranged and full strength of the Extension Service was put behind the movement.[3]

Hirth's response to the activity was expressed in the May 1, 1917, issue of *The Missouri Farmer.*

> It is with astonishment that I have just read the plan of "farm organization" which is being promulgated by the College of Agriculture. . . . [T]he Extension Department is proposing an entirely new plan of farm organization for the entire state and . . . some 40 men have already been put into the field to carry it into immediate effect. . . . [T]his new organization shall be composed "of local groups such as farmers clubs, Granges, farmers unions or others." There are at this time something like 700 Farm Clubs in the state, with, I would judge, 18,000 to 20,000 members. . . . It is also said that one of the objects of this new conception is to put farming on a "more systematic business basis." Well, what constitutes a "systematic business basis"—and who is to be the judge—the farmers or the Extension Dept.? "In all communities there is a certain amount of buying and selling which can be done in a cooperative way"— The Farm Clubs have already saved tens of thousands of dollars in the buying of mill feed, flour, corn, hay, oats, cotton seed meal and cake, linseed oil meal, coal, potatoes, fertilizers, etc.—When a member of the army of splendid young men who are now attacking the state in "mass formation" heave[s] in sight, [you should] stop the corn planter long enough to pump them dry on seed bed preparation, methods of cultivation, soybeans, cowpeas, rape, silos, etc.—But when they ask you to be "assimilated" on a "systematic basis," say "Giddap."

A report in the March 1, 1918, issue of *The Missouri Farmer* stated that R. T. Pence of the MFA board of directors wanted to meet with the College of Agriculture Extension Division officials to see if their help could be obtained in working with farm clubs. J. A. Hudson, Hirth, and Pence met with Professor A. J. Meyer, head of the Extension Division. Meyer's response was, "The more I consider the matter and the more I discuss it with different people, the farther I get from being able to offer a clean-cut plan of cooperation between the Farm Bureau organization and your organization." Meyer went on to say that the farm bureaus served exactly the same purpose as the farm clubs, but Hirth pointed out to Meyer the huge savings the farm clubs had made on binder twine and asked if the College of Agriculture had taken care of its farm bureau members in a similar manner.

At the second MFA annual convention in September 1918, one of the resolutions adopted was as follows:

> We heartily commend and offer our fullest cooperation to the [University of] Missouri College of Agriculture in its efforts to increase production, but we submit that in all communities where the Farm Clubs have obtained a powerful foothold, the College should manifest a cheerful willingness to work through those agencies rather than to seek to bring into being an organization of its own and then compel the farmers of such communities to maintain two separate institutions— an effort which entails double cost and which invariably results in confusion, friction, and misunderstanding.
>
> As an institution maintained by the state, the College of Agriculture is not permitted to assist farmers in the buying of commodities at wholesale price or to engage in other activities which may incur the displeasure of individuals or business enterprises and therefore when a farmer joins an organization for which the college stands sponsor, he is shut off from all vital benefits and activities such as has been and are being promoted through the Missouri Farmers Association, which is in a position to act upon all matters and in all circumstances upon its own responsibility and initiative.

Another irritating action of the Extension Division was the hiring of MFA president Samuel J. Kleinschmidt by the College of Agriculture as assistant county agent leader for the state. Kleinschmidt had just been elected as president of the Missouri Farmers Association at the annual convention in September 1918, after having served one year as vice president.

The Missouri Farm Bureau Federation and the Missouri Farmers Association continued to try to find some basis for merger or cooperation, however. In January 1921 A. J. Meyer, who had taken a year's leave of absence from the Extension Division to help guide the development of the farm bureau program, wrote a letter to Hirth suggesting closer cooperation and outlining a possible basis for doing so. The reply from MFA was a proposed agreement that became known as the Peace Treaty. It was signed by Ned J. Ball, then president of MFA, and J. A. Hudson, chairman of the executive committee. Schuttler, in *A History of the Missouri Farm Bureau Federation,* wrote, "The Peace Treaty provided, in effect, that the MFBF refrain from cooperative marketing and purchasing activities—confining its efforts to education programs." The following resolution was adopted at the 1921 MFA convention:

> We desire to heartily endorse and reiterate the recent communication of the directors of the Association to the leaders of the Missouri Farm Bureau Federation, and we here and now request that the endeavors of the latter to force the farmers of this state to finance two sets of cold storage plants and two sets of grain and livestock commission firms at the central markets is not only an undertaking of blind folly, but one which is fraught with the gravest menace to the entire cooperative movement in Missouri.

Not everyone within the Missouri Farmers Association agreed with this policy. On July 11, 1920, Clarence Fitzpatrick, a member of the board of directors, wrote to Hirth that he did not agree with a letter that had been sent to the MFBF, which he felt was "nothing more or less than a dictation of what the Federation should do." He said he was out of sympathy with certain MFA policies, and that he was sending his letter of resignation to the secretary. Hirth, in a letter of reply dated August 1, 1920, spoke of the great work that Fitzpatrick had done, and concluded:

> There are today two Clarence Fitzpatricks. The first one was every inch a fighting Farm Club man—proud to stand at the head of the most constructive farmers' organization the Corn

Belt has ever known. The other is an entirely new Fitzpatrick who sips pink tea and splits hairs over matters of imaginary ethics in the shade on the front porch, while 60,000 Farm Club members are in the backyard in overalls, engaged in the greatest hand-to-hand battle with selfish private interests in the history of American Agriculture—and I have such a genuine admiration and affection for the first Fitzpatrick that I shall endeavor to forget all about the latter.[4]

The organizations made further attempts to work together throughout the 1920s, but they could not reach any agreement. MFA insisted on its members signing a contract agreeing to sell their produce only through MFA, and the MFBF insisted that the new organization that would be formed by joining the two should become a member of the American Farm Bureau Federation. As late as 1945, MFA appointed a committee to meet with an MFBF committee, but nothing came of the committees' efforts. Even in 1961 MFA negotiated with officials of the MFBF relative to MFA purchasing facilities of the State Bureau Service Company, but the asking price was more than MFA officials felt the facilities were worth.

Early Legislative Activities

Following the first MFA convention in August 1917, the freshly elected board members quickly began to fight for fair prices for farm products, which were effectively under control of the United States Food Administration during World War I. After an exchange of correspondence between J. A. Hudson and the Food Administration, in which an effort was made to set up a meeting in Kansas City between livestock producers and Food Administrator Herbert Hoover, a letter was sent from the board of directors of the Missouri Farmers Association to Congressman Champ Clark of Missouri, Speaker of the House of Representatives. The letter pointed out that the government had guaranteed profits from 9 to 15 percent for the packinghouses, whereas livestock producers were suffering losses. In addition, the letter stated:

We are coming to Congress because there remains no other place for us to go—and all we ask is that through your great body of final authority you compel the Food Administration to forthwith establish such prices for cattle, hogs, and sheep as will at least assure the feeder of production cost . . . we leave the operation of a profit beyond production cost entirely in your hands.

To grant us less would not only be grievously unfair to the producers of food, who are laboring under handicaps little short of pitiful, but any other course would make a mockery of the cry that "Food will win the war."

Early in 1918, within the first year after MFA's organization, a group of MFA leaders made a trip to Washington, D.C. This group included William Hirth, J. A. Hudson, A. C. Rosier (who had served as treasurer of the Missouri Farm Bureau Federation), C. S. Gilpin, A. J. Crawford, Earl Rea, and J. S. Littrell. They appeared before the Senate Agriculture Committee in opposition to the Food Administration's desire to keep down the cost of meat to the armed services "regardless of the cost of production, saying nothing about a legitimate profit which is cheerfully vouchsafed to all other vital industries." In his account of the Washington, D.C., trip, Hirth reported that in Congress Hoover made a suggestion to a prominent member of the Missouri delegation that the margin on hogs and cattle be increased by reducing the price of corn. "That was when the parting of the ways hove in sight so far as the leaders of the Missouri Farmers Association were concerned."[5]

In February 1919 MFA hosted both houses of the state legislature at a dinner at the Madison Hotel in Jefferson City, an occasion that *The Missouri Farmer* reported on March 1 "was heralded by every legislative speaker as a most commendable innovation." Among the requests from MFA to the legislators was a state statute under which MFA agencies could incorporate and do business as a cooperative. Other requested legislation included a pure seed law, aid for rural schools, and help in getting farm boys home from the armed services to help out on the farm.

Rapid Growth

The years 1919 and 1920 saw an explosion of activity in the organization of additional farm clubs, with their number growing to an estimated twenty-five hundred to three thousand. In addition, these years saw the establishment of livestock shipping associations, farmers exchanges, and local elevators, as Hirth pursued his dream of controlling the marketing of farm products.

One of the biggest cash crops for Missouri farmers in the early days of MFA was livestock. In many cases farmers drove the livestock to town, placed it in holding pens, and sold it to local dealers who, in turn, shipped the livestock via rail to terminal markets. The need for correct weights and measures during this process was one of the problems addressed by the first board of directors of MFA. To address this need, the organization sponsored the formation of livestock shipping associations at local shipping points. The University of Missouri's Extension Division, in a 1921 report, stated that there were such associations in all counties in the state except those close to terminal markets. By the end of the decade, the number of MFA-sponsored shipping associations totaled approximately 375, but these disappeared rapidly as the trucking of livestock took the place of rail shipments.

On May 25, 1921, the MFA executive committee met with thirty-one MFA livestock shipping association managers, and the group decided to start a new commission company in National Stockyards, Illinois, rather than buy an established company. Over ten thousand dollars in stock was pledged, and the go-ahead was given to start the new company. In October 1921 the executive committee hired Frank B. Young as manager of the Farmers Livestock Commission Company, and within a year the new company was the largest of its kind in the country. Stockholders included MFA shipping associations as well as some Farmers Union shipping associations in Illinois.

The meteoric growth of the company was one of the most astounding early accomplishments of MFA. The farmers received higher returns through the establishment of better prices, grades, and weights. Frank Young, who had been assistant cashier of the National Stockyards National Bank, became an important cog in the MFA wheel in short order, and his help and advice extended beyond the stockyards.

On another front, in an article in the October 15, 1919, issue of *The Missouri Farmer,* Howard A. Cowden, secretary of the Polk County Farmers Association, recommended establishing a farm club exchange in any territory in which 75 percent of the farmers were MFA members. He suggested that the farmers rent a suitable building for storage of salt, flour, shorts, bran, barley, tankage, seeds, and other commodities. He also suggested that they acquire a cream-testing outfit, egg cases, and other equipment. Capital of only six hundred to one thousand dollars would be needed to get such an exchange started, and the chief expense would be the manager's salary of sixty-five to eighty dollars per month. The December 15, 1919, issue of *The Missouri Farmer* carried stories about exchanges being organized at Martinsburg, Centralia, Memphis, Montgomery City, Stockton, Browning, Buffalo, Wyaconda, McKittrick, Callao, and Albany.

During 1919 *The Missouri Farmer* told of other activities in Greene, Scotland, Knox, Shelby, Monroe, Montgomery, Callaway, Maries, and Phelps Counties. A thirty-five-thousand-bushel elevator in Slater was purchased from the Glasgow Milling Company and became Cooperative Association No. 1, the first cooperative to be chartered under the new 1919 statute that MFA had sponsored in the legislature. Farm clubs at Elsberry organized a farmers cooperative elevator and raised the money to fund it in forty-eight hours. The elevator manager also managed the local MFA livestock shipping association. B. D. Simon, a Columbia contractor, finished building an elevator at Washington, Missouri. And Wyaconda Farmers Exchange opened up with an initial capital of twenty-five hundred dollars and forced up the price of eggs by ten cents per dozen on the morning it opened its doors.

The MFA emblem, which originated in the early days of the organization, was symbolic of the unity among these and all the other various agencies that made up the association. The unconfirmed story of the emblem's origin is that Hirth observed the Union Pacific emblem on railcars as he traveled back and forth to Washington, and used it as a pattern for the MFA emblem. The similarity between the two emblems lends credence to the story.

Chapter Three

Continued Growth

The Early 1920s

The third MFA convention was held in Sedalia on September 2–4, 1919, with two thousand in attendance. Threshing was in full swing, resulting in a smaller crowd than expected. Delegates numbered 414, with the highest number, 64, coming from Saline County. Polk County was next with 41; Franklin had 26; Cooper, 24; and Greene, 23. Speeches were made by A. C. Rosier, Ned Ball, Fred Dunlap of Daviess County, and Henry J. Waters, the former dean of the College of Agriculture and the current editor of the *Weekly Kansas City Star.* W. J. Spillman of *Farm Journal* made an address and later reported in his national magazine that the Missouri Farmers Association was "the most successful farm organization in the United States."[1]

Throughout the state, the momentum of signing up new members continued. In Dallas County, Dan Gause and a fellow member named Seits were captains of two opposing sides in a contest to sign up the most new members. The captains devised numerous tricks to obtain new members, such as calling a meeting to sign new members in the opposing captain's territory. And when a flood occurred, one side built a raft of logs, went into the opponent's territory, and signed up a large number of farmers. The loser had to pay for fifteen hundred ice cream cones.

"The Farm Clubs of the Ozarks," an article in the January 15, 1920, issue of *The Missouri Farmer,* reported on the growth and enterprise of one group of clubs.

> The first Farm Club in Greene County was formed in February about three years ago six miles west of Springfield. Almost immediately it began to preach the gospel in adjoining districts, and after a little while eight Clubs were brought into being.
>
> Then a meeting of all of these Clubs was called at Nichols, Missouri. At the beginning of the second year we established a permanent County Association with ample headquarters in the big Convention Hall at Springfield.

Thus the Greene County Sales Association was incorporated, with an original capital of five thousand dollars. The association opened a salesroom next door to the office in the Convention Hall building and soon afterward added a commodities warehouse, with switching facilities on the Frisco Railroad, on the north side of Springfield. Other exchanges opened at Rogersville, Willard, Billings, Fordland, Strafford, Ash Grove, Seymour, and Walnut Grove.

Early in 1920 the farm club at Browning reported that it had shipped out four carloads of wheat and several carloads of livestock and received two carloads of flour and feed and one carload of tankage. And the Saline County Farmers Association reported that in the summer of 1918 it handled sixty thousand pounds of binder twine. On the following October 1, it opened an office and warehouse and put in a stock of feed; in the first year the volume of business there was $135,000.

A letter to *The Missouri Farmer* from W. S. Miller, the "Fighting Farm Club leader of St. James," reported:

> We now have 23 school districts organized that do business at St. James and about 15 Clubs that do business through Rolla. Our buying committee has handled 25 carloads of flour, bran, and shorts, 10 carloads of oats, six carloads of corn, two carloads of cotton seed meal, five carloads of mixed feeds, one carload of hay, two carloads of salt, four carloads of potatoes, one carload of molasses feed, ten carloads of fertilizer.
>
> We have put in our own scales and have it housed with a

Farm Club office adjoining. We have also rented a small warehouse, which will do for a few months until we can buy the old elevator or build a new one.

Before moving to St. James, Miller had been general manager of the St. Louis Car Works, with three thousand employees. He became interested in MFA while farming and joined the local farm club. Later in 1920 Miller would become manager of the St. James Farmers Exchange. He would serve in that capacity until 1952, as well as serving on the board of MFA from 1922 until 1948, most of the time as a member of the executive committee.

In March 1920 *The Missouri Farmer* noted that "the great Farm Club fight is coming with a roar from one end of Missouri to the other. Recently Howard Cowden, one of the fieldmen for MFA, set the woods on fire along the Frisco branch east of Springfield and now the school houses are being lit up all around Mountain View, Willow Springs, Cabool, and Houston." Howard Cowden was to play a major part in the development of the Missouri Farmers Association through the next decade. He was born and raised on a farm near Pleasant Hope and became interested in MFA from reading *The Missouri Farmer.* Cowden organized farm clubs in Polk County and became secretary of the Polk County Farmers Association in 1919. He soon caught the attention of Hirth. It was while acting as the association's secretary that Cowden helped organize and manage the farmers exchange in Bolivar. By 1920 he was regularly contributing articles to *The Missouri Farmer,* and early in that year he was hired by MFA as a fieldman.

The Missouri Farmer continued to print stories about farm clubs and farmers exchanges. In the August 1, 1920, issue, the following account of farm clubs appeared:

> Down at Aldrich in the Ozarks there is a Farm Club which is becoming known far and wide as the "Wild Cats." It is headed by C. M. Stiles, who they say is a regular Billy Sunday when it comes to preaching the Farm Club gospel—and as the mellow Ozark moon looks down on the hills these nights, jitneys of the "Wild Cats" are bringing some new school dis-

trict into line and preaching a loyalty that tells the private produce dealers with their market to go jump in the creek. Success to the "Wild Cats"—and may their tribe increase.

We have a letter from R. H. Van Houten, secretary of the Shale Farm Club at Clarence, in which he says that on the evening of July 3rd the Farm Clubs of Jefferson and Clay Townships in Shelby County met at the Shale School house and had a splendid time. The women folks and their daughters were in charge and ice cream and cake were served in abundance. The crowd numbered approximately 300 and [was] as good a bunch of Farm Club folks as can be found in the state. While it was chiefly a social occasion, the leading members talked about the financing of a Produce Exchange and also a cold storage plant which will soon be needed in that territory. At the conclusion of the meeting the crowd unanimously passed a resolution stating that the Farm Clubs of their community had been "tried and proven as if by fire," winding up with the statement that "the members proposed to hold out to the last for the principle of production cost and a square deal to everyone."

The fourth annual MFA convention, held in Sedalia on August 24–26, 1920, had approximately seven hundred delegates, with a total of about twenty-five hundred in attendance. Ned Ball was elected president, and Dan Gause was elected vice president.

Between conventions, farm club meetings provided opportunities for MFA members to interest other farmers in their cause and encourage them to join MFA. Hirth was continually urging farmers to overcome their shyness and deliver speeches in support of MFA. In one of his "Afterthoughts," he said: "And, my friends, what is true oratory? Is it polished phrases, faultless diction or harmony of gesture? Nay verily! On the contrary, it is a human soul on fire with a great cause—and such a soul, although garbed in the uncouth vestments of a cross-roads farmer has in it the power of the thunderbolt!"

The farm clubs of Barton County organized a county association in Lamar in May 1920. Hirth was the principal speaker at the meeting, and Chester Gray, president of the Missouri Farm Bureau Federation, also spoke. The *Lamar Democrat* reported:

Saturday was a great day in Lamar. Not many of the folks here in town, we fancy, grasped its full significance. To get to its real meaning, it was necessary to go over there to the Opera House, watch the farmers, and hear the speeches. The real mass feeling of the tillers of the soil built up to the surface and became plain. Hirth made a profound impression. Chester Gray, of Nevada, was present to try to organize a Farm Bureau in Hirth's teeth. He might as well have tried to sell the bonds of the alleged Irish Republic in King George's Royal household.

Among the many other speeches made by Hirth were those at meetings in Warsaw on the afternoon of January 11, 1921, in Cole Camp that night, and in Versailles the following morning. The crowd in Warsaw filled the circuit courtroom to capacity, but in Cole Camp the largest theater building in town could not accommodate the crowd. Dozens of farmers were unable to get in, and the same was true at Versailles, where a crowd filled the circuit courtroom an hour before the speaking began.

In March 1921 came this report from a Carthage newspaper: "A tremendous crowd of farmers came in today for the opening of the new Farmers Exchange on Central Avenue, which became so packed with automobiles that Marshal Hogan had to send for help to untangle the jam. The purchase of poultry, eggs, and cream is reported to be the largest ever made in Carthage in one day."

In the early days of the Missouri Farmers Association, it was customary for the leaders to travel by train as far as they could and then be driven to their destination by a local member. On one occasion, when Hirth was speaking in Wright County, a local farm leader from Loring by the name of Stanley picked him up and took him by car on a tour of the county. A few days later Stanley had a heart attack and died, leaving his wife, several small children, and a one-thousand-dollar mortgage on their farm. Hirth appealed for contributions to pay off the mortgage, and the money rolled in—mostly one-dollar bills. The mortgage was paid off.

Besides regular meetings, farm clubs also offered entertainment for farm families. H. B. Patterson of Lockwood published a book of farm club songs. And hundreds of clubs held debates every two weeks with topics such as: Is the present one-room school giving the country boy and girl a square deal? Will the tractor ever replace the horse? and Is it the farmer or his wife who has the hardest time on the farm? Old-time fiddlers' contests, pie suppers, and kangaroo courts added spice to many meetings. At a meeting of the Walnut Grove Farm Club, a farmer named Sam Spears accused my father of stealing guinea eggs from him. As I recall, the kangaroo trial lasted for two or three meetings for the entertainment of all.

In June 1921 A. C. Moore, the Grundy County Association secretary, reported that the farm club there had gone "on a fishing trip, and it required fourteen automobiles to carry the crowd of 80 people. The men caught fish while the ladies cooked them for dinner. After dinner more fish were caught and divided up to be taken home." In November 1921 *The Missouri Farmer* reported on a meeting of farm clubs at Lowry City, where it took seven barbecued beefs to feed the crowd. In addition, there was a big parade several miles long.

Hirth supplied a bit of humor in each issue of *The Missouri Farmer* through a seedy character named Jim Riley.

> Down at th' livery stable th' other night th' boys got t' talkin' about th' saddest thing in th' world, and various and sundry sad things was trotted out. But when old Si Thompson suggested an empty bottle of Old Crow, th' whole bunch voted unanimous that he had hit th' bull's eye.

> I see where th' Chamber of Commerce in Kansas City is goin' t' start a campaign for better bulls down in the Ozarks, and if th' hillbillies don't want t' be considered short sports, it seems t' me its up t' them t' start a campaign for better poodle dogs or angory cats in Kansas City.

In January 1921 Dan Gause, vice president of MFA, representing south Missouri, issued a challenge to Ned Ball, the president, who represented north Missouri, to see who could sign up the most new MFA members by March 1. If the south won, the next MFA convention would be held in Springfield. President Ball accepted the challenge. There were dire threats and predictions from both sides. The south won by a narrow margin, and so the 1921 annual convention was planned for August 30–31 in Springfield. In his typical style, Hirth described the upcoming convention in an August 15 article entitled "Gathering of the Clan."

> Another year has rolled around and once more the "Clan" is about to assemble in annual conclave—this time in the "Land of a Million Smiles" from whence the Farm Club tiger will send his challenging roar into the remote fastnesses of the Ozarks. And in all the Nation, there is not another roar like it, for back of it are the pent up longings and pulsing heart-beats of more than 70,000 determined farmers—farmers with grim set jaws whose big, gnarled hands tell a story of many a day's weary toil in the fields and feedlots and whose faces, seared and lined by the suns and snows of many moons are lit up by a strange new light which plainly says, "We have en-listed for the long fight, and there will be no turning back."
>
> And so from the borders of peaceful Iowa to where the lonesome pine lifts its stately head across the line in Arkan-sas and from the East where the Father of Waters sweeps on majestically to the sea to where the Kansas sunflowers kiss the gentle breezes, the faithful of the "Clan" will soon be "treking" [*sic*] to Springfield—and when once the mighty car-avan arrives and the bands begin to play, never since Daniel Boone, with coon-skin cap and long rifle, acted as the Path-finder of Civilization years ago, will our splendid old common-wealth have witnessed anything like it, for in point of size and in the scope of involved issues the great political conventions of the past will appear like child's play.
>
> An exaggeration, you say? Well, wait and see—for at this time the greatest anxiety of the leaders is whether the largest convention building in Southwest Missouri will accommodate the throng.

The September 15, 1921, issue of *The Missouri Farmer* described the meeting as "the greatest farm meeting in the history of the corn belt." The attendance was approximately seventy-five hundred. A huge parade through Springfield stretched for many blocks. The con-vention was held in the coliseum, just west of the square, and MFA had its headquarters in the Colonial Hotel just east of the square.

Dan Gause was elected president, and C. L. Moody of Macon was elected vice president. Gause delivered an address on loyalty, the principal theme of the convention, and Governor Arthur M. Hyde of Missouri and Governor Sam R. McKelvie of Nebraska also spoke. A telegram from President Warren G. Harding was read, offering this assurance: "Tell the Farm Club members of Missouri that we are doing all that is humanly possible for them." Everyone wore pins carrying the slogan "We'll Stick," which was also the title of a farm club song sung at the convention by its composer, H. B. Patterson.

The Women's Progressive Farmers Association

On the last day of the 1921 convention, a request that a women's state association be admitted to the MFA was read. Gause made a motion to grant the request, and the Women's Progressive Farmers Association (WPFA) became official.

As early as 1920 *The Missouri Farmer* had started a feature called "Our Women's Department." The section contained letters from various parts of the state describing women's auxiliaries of the Missouri Farmers Association. The following was typical: "Our women's club meets twice a month, and we talk about what women are or should be interested in, namely, the raising of children, good housekeeping, chicken raising, canning, making old clothes into new ones, short cuts in home work, and many similar things."

Years later an article in *The Missouri Farmer* described the formal beginning of the WPFA.

> In the summer of 1920 a group of women, long organized as a community club known as "The Pandora Club," decided to join the Farm Club movement. They declared themselves a WPFA Club and selected the name WPFA, but it was on November 20, 1920 that Mr. A. S. Humphrey, then secretary of Barton County MFA, was instrumental in helping organize the WPFA as a county organization. Thus the first WPFA County Meeting ever held was at Lamar on that day.
>
> The county constitution and bylaws were drafted by Mr. Humphrey. Officers elected were Mrs. C. B. McDermott,

president; Mrs. H. V. Eales, vice president; and Mrs. Charles LaForce, secretary.[2]

Following official recognition of WPFA by the MFA convention was the election of statewide officers: Mrs. G. O. Reid of Springfield, president; Mrs. C. B. McDermott, vice president; and Mrs. S. D. Allen of Buffalo, secretary-treasurer. An impressive ceremony, signifying the uniting of the two organizations, was performed when G. O. Reid, representing the MFA, married his wife, representing the WPFA, in a mock ceremony.

The primary objective of the WPFA was to help the Missouri Farmers Association. Its members served meals at MFA meetings, provided programs at farm club meetings, and organized subsidiary Junior Farmers Association (JFA) clubs. The WPFA held local and district meetings and statewide conventions in conjunction with those of the MFA. It published a cookbook and had an annual food canning contest. The MFA made an annual monetary contribution to WPFA, as did its later affiliates, such as MFA Milling Company, Producers Produce Company, and MFA Oil Company.

The JFA also held its annual meetings in conjunction with MFA's annual meetings. By the middle 1940s there were 101 JFA groups in thirty-four counties with two thousand members. One of the annual events sponsored by JFA was a three-day fair in Marshfield. In 1963, for example, the fair consisted of exhibits from twenty-nine counties, with eighty-nine entries in the dairy show and 1,712 handcraft exhibits. The JFA also had a four-day meeting at Camp Clover Leaf Point on Lake of the Ozarks. For many years Mrs. Ben Franklin of Greenfield was the director of JFA activities. At one time the largest JFA group was that from my hometown of Hurley, where my mother served as secretary of the Stone County WPFA.

The Political Presence Continues

The December 15, 1921, issue of *The Missouri Farmer* called for farm clubs to hold a Rally Day on January 15, 1922. At the Rally Day, farm clubs would collect the full $2.50 dues for 1922. And they would also "send out an 'Automobile Squad' to collect the dues of those who did not attend 'Rally Night'" and "enroll as members every worthwhile farmer who is not now in the fold." In the same issue, *The Missouri Farmer* discussed plans to organize the WPFA; described a resolution against any change in the laws that would turn over control of the state legislature to cities; asked every member to sign a referendum to prevent the issuance of bonds to build roads that would leave farmers in the mud; and described plans for a series of debates and entertainments to be held twice per month for the remainder of the winter.

In 1922 the Missouri Farmers Association continued to make its presence felt at the state legislature in Jefferson City, although a *Missouri Farmer* editorial on June 15 may have exaggerated slightly when it declared, "In matters of legislation, the MFA has, during the last two years, become the greatest power in the United States."

At an MFA executive meeting in June 1922, the most important agenda item was whether Dan Gause should resign as MFA president following his announcement that he was a candidate for the U.S. Congress. Hirth thought it best that he resign, and Gause agreed.

On August 29–31, 1922, the sixth annual MFA convention, in St. Joseph, had an estimated attendance of four thousand. Outside speakers included Milo Reno, president of Iowa Farmers Union, and H. J. Waters. Among the many MFA leaders who made speeches was George E. McCarthy, "head of the auditing department and one of the big guns of MFA, who understands its gospel as few men do and who numbers his friends by the thousands." C. L. Moody was elected president, and William L. Steiner of New Haven was elected vice president.

Business Operations

Evidence of the great growth in the business operations of MFA was reported in the January 1921 issue of *The Missouri Farmer.* "In the space of eighteen months we have put into operation more than 100 grain elevators, nearly 150 Livestock Shipping Associations, and approximately 250 Produce Exchanges, and we are today operating central produce plants at Springfield, St. Joseph, and Sedalia. We have something like $3,000,000 invested in these properties."

Unfortunately, MFA business units did not always practice good management in the early days. In June 1921 the board of directors passed a resolution stating that it was unwise for a man employed for pay by an exchange, elevator, or cold storage plant to be a director of such an institution. And at a board meeting in January 1922, Hirth suggested a resolution that MFA exchanges, elevators, and central plants be required to submit monthly financial statements to their boards and that the managers be given the right to hire and discharge any employee with the consent of their boards.

Until January 1, 1922, Hirth, together with Joe Goeke and his staff at the offices of *The Missouri Farmer,* handled all records and transactions of the statewide organization, and their operation bordered on the chaotic. With the tremendous amount of detail associated with the processing of MFA dues and the purchase of numerous commodities for farm clubs and farmers exchanges, someone was needed to step in and straighten things up. Thus, on January 1, Howard Cowden became the first full-time paid secretary of MFA. His offices were in rented space on the second floor of the Haden Building at the corner of Ninth and Broadway in downtown Columbia.

The close relationship between Howard Cowden and Hirth at this time was reflected in articles in *The Missouri Farmer* throughout 1922. In January, Cowden commented, "Very few realize what it cost Mr. Hirth in time and money to put out the tons and tons of literature which he has sent out." The next month Hirth described Cowden as "schooled to the last word in the lore of the Farm Clubs, modest in address and bearing but a young man of outstanding ability. He is one of the truly fine assets of the MFA." In his column in the September 15 issue, Cowden described the reception accorded Hirth at the 1922 convention and heaped high praise of his own.

> When Mr. Hirth was introduced to the Convention at St. Joseph, there burst forth a round of deafening applause, a moment later the audience was on its feet yelling until the Coliseum fairly shook. The great ovation given Mr. Hirth

shows how profoundly grateful the real dirt farmers of Missouri are for the great services rendered by him. It shows also that the old saying that farmers "won't stick" to their leaders is not true of Missouri farmers. The farmers of Missouri recognize that in order to accomplish their ends, they must follow a definite leadership.

Mr. Hirth's leadership of the MFA dates back to the first Club, and, while he holds no official position except membership on the board of directors, the farmers of Missouri are behind him in practically everything of importance. Perhaps he may make some mistakes now and then, but his work, considered as a whole, stands out conspicuously as the most constructive work of its kind in the history of American agriculture.

I have learned to know most of the farmer organization leaders of the country, and I consider him head and shoulders above all others—and I do the stalwart leaders of other states no injustice in making such a statement. It is true. His leadership has been questioned by some and cussed by others, but, again, I say, the great ovation given Mr. Hirth shows that the farmers of Missouri recognize leadership and are willing to support it.

At a December 1923 meeting of the executive committee, Hirth indicated his satisfaction with Cowden's work by making a motion to increase Cowden's salary to five thousand dollars per year. During the first year in which Cowden served as secretary, MFA made a contract with Hooven-Allison for 650,000 pounds of binder twine; the second year, it made a deal with the same company for 1 million pounds of twine with an option for an additional 250,000 pounds.

At that time and for several years thereafter, the only income for MFA came from the $.50 of the $2.50 yearly membership dues allotted to the statewide organization, plus brokerage fees on commodities purchased by MFA farmers exchanges and elevators. The earliest financial statement reported a net gain for MFA in 1921 of $373.18, with a notation that it was later changed to $64.78, and in that year membership totaled 33,424.

In the early days of the farm club movement, Hirth, with personal funds, helped finance a grain commission firm on the Merchants

Exchange in St. Louis in order to help sell grain from MFA elevators. At that time, the grain and livestock exchanges in St. Louis would not allow cooperative firms to operate on the terminal markets on the grounds that patronage refunds were illegal. MFA fought the case to the Missouri Supreme Court and won. When the Producers Grain Commission Company was organized by MFA in 1924, Hirth promptly liquidated the assets of his firm, and gave his five thousand dollars of profit to Producers Grain. The company soon became a successful operation, and by 1940, it was the largest receiver of grain on the St. Louis market, with 989 carloads of grain collected from fifty-five exchanges and elevators. Julius Schuermann was manager, and Roy Huettemann was secretary and number two man in the company.

The financial condition of MFA was such that early members of the board of directors endorsed notes in order to finance the association. For example, at a board meeting in Springfield on August 31, 1921, the following appeared in the minutes: "Motion that four notes of $2,500 each for ninety days be made to finance the Association and that the entire board sign them." Again, in October 1922, it was agreed that the executive committee should sign a joint note for $2,000 for the state association until the treasury was in better condition. And one year later, Hirth asked members of the board to sign another four $2,500 notes.

Board members signed a note again in July 1924 when the newly organized Producers Grain Commission Company of St. Louis received seventeen carloads of wheat and did not have sufficient funds to pay for them. Board members Crawford, Hirth, Pence, Chris Ohlendorf of Boonville, and George M. Kelley signed a $25,000 note.

Things were getting better when the executive committee in May 1926 reported: "The secretary presented to the President one of the $3,000 notes, which was signed by members of the executive committee in February. This note was burned; one for $2,000 having been burned at the meeting on April 17."

In the meantime, poultry and egg processing plants and Farmers Livestock Commission Companies were expanding rapidly. In June 1921 seven produce plants were in operation; one year later the number operating reached a high-water mark of nine, with locations in

Joseph, Springfield, Clinton, Sedalia, Chillicothe, Medill, Shelbina, St. James, and Kirksville. In 1921 the plants had two men in New York and one in Chicago working as salesmen for their products. In April 1922 A. B. Drescher of Hannibal was hired to assist the central plants in the sale of eggs and poultry.

Hirth pointed out in the September 1, 1923, issue of *The Missouri Farmer* that "the MFA with its 400 Elevators, Produce Exchanges, Cold Storage Plants and terminal grain and livestock commission companies and with its more than 300 Livestock Shipping Associations is the greatest 'farmer's machine' that can be found in any single commonwealth." In addition, that fall the big cooperative elevator at Sweet Springs voted to become affiliated with MFA.

In the early 1920s mixed feed had become an increasingly important supplement to grain and hay. Bran, shorts, and meat scraps were the early supplements, and a short time later cottonseed meal became important. To meet the need for mixed feed, MFA started a wholesale feed operation, the Farm Club Mill and Feed Company of Springfield, in the early 1920s. In January 1923 MFA loaned the mill three thousand dollars. The following year there was a report that the mill had begun mixing feed and required more capital. MFA sent two thousand dollars more and changed the mill's name to Missouri Farmers Association Purchasing Department.

By 1927 it was apparent that the mill was not large enough to handle the steadily growing volume, so it was decided to advance another ten thousand dollars for purchasing a new site. In 1928 the MFA executive committee recommended that earnings from the mill be invested in a new mill, provided exchanges and members bought enough certificates to finance the venture.

Early in 1929 the Springfield Mill and Feed Company was incorporated under the Non-Stock Cooperative Act. Its board was to consist of the seven members of the MFA executive committee and four members to be selected by the South Missouri Managers Association. In June 1929 the board changed the name to MFA Milling Company and purchased the Meyer Milling Company of Springfield to house the new mill. J. A. Helvig was named manager. In 1934 John F. Johnson became manager, a position he held until his retirement in 1974.

For the north part of the state a brokerage operation called Farm Club Mill and Feed Company of Kansas City was supplying feed to farmers exchanges; however, this operation did not have satisfactory manufacturing facilities. In June 1924 the Kansas City operation was discontinued, and MFA Purchasing Department began operating state-wide out of Secretary Cowden's office in Columbia. In September, Frank Farnen of Montgomery County was hired to head the Purchasing Department.

The Producers Contract

Five thousand attended the seventh annual convention of MFA in Sedalia on August 27–30, 1923. The convention elected William Steiner president and George M. Kelley vice president. The program for the convention revealed a total of twenty speeches, with titles such as "Going to the Consumer's Door," "What the Ozarks Want," "Rescuing the Wheat Grower," "Get Your Neighbors In," "The Officers Need Support," and "Freight Rates and Farm Products."

Among the actions taken at the 1923 convention was the beginning of a ten-year struggle to sell the idea of a producers contract to MFA members. *The Missouri Farmer* first mentioned such a contract in an article in the August 1, 1923, issue. It described contracts that had been employed successfully for single commodities such as tobacco and cotton, requiring that the farmers who produced those items sell their products to a central agency.

A California attorney, Aaron Sapiro, is credited with having promoted the idea of using a contract for commodity marketing of farm products. He was involved with the first wheat pool in the United States, started in the state of Washington. In 1920 he offered a plan of commodity marketing to the annual convention of the American Cotton Association. Robert Montgomery, in his book *The Cooperative Pattern in Cotton,* had this to say about the attorney:

> Sapiro is a dynamic speaker. His ability to convince his audience of the soundness and importance of his proposals is almost incomparable. He is an able lawyer. He understands

the weakness as well as the strength of his case, but is able to present the latter without having the former embarrass him. As a matter of fact, he presents just enough of the difficulties to convince the hearer of his complete candor, and not enough to damage his cause in the slightest degree.

It is not sufficient to say that some of his arguments are very weak (though never weakly put), that his economics is faulty, that his arguments by analogy are not legitimate, and his knowledge of the cotton trade is superficial. To this must be added that his knowledge of cotton marketing is sufficient to satisfy any but the experts; his analogy is so cleverly presented as to be usually accepted; his economic position is unassailable in its major redoubts; and the virility and versatility of his address is inimitable. As an economist, he is usually right, rarely entirely wrong. As a dramatic speaker he is superb. As a logician he is diabolically clever. As an evangelist he is without a peer.[3]

In tobacco the commodity marketing contract perhaps had its greatest success. The prime mover was Judge Robert Bingham, the publisher of newspapers in Louisville. At the suggestion of his friend the financier Bernard Baruch, he invited Sapiro to come to Louisville; as a result, the Burley Tobacco Growers Association adopted a commodity marketing system.

In the speeches made at the 1923 MFA convention in endorsement of a producers contract, some of the terms used to describe disloyal farmers were "poisoned bait," "market bribe," "back sliders," "the old rail fence crowd," and "penny grabbers." A speaker from the Burley Tobacco Growers Association said that as a result of that group's contract for marketing tobacco, the price had risen to thirty cents per pound, an increase of twenty cents. Hirth stated that the purpose of the producers contract was "to pool the selling of farm commodities so they can be disposed of through great central Selling Agencies and thus place in the organized farmer's hands the power to have something to say about what he shall receive from the fruits of his yearly toil." In his usual no-holds-barred fashion, Hirth pointed out to the assemblage that farmers were being forced to dump their grain, cattle, and hogs on the market in competition with each other, demoralizing the market. "It should be apparent," he said, "that we cannot compel 'production cost, together with a reasonable profit,' so long as we sell to the private dealer and speculator, who is merely interested in his profit margin." In *The Missouri Farmer* for October 1, 1923, he wrote:

> And isn't it about time that the Old Guard should say to the bunch on the old rail fence and to the "penny grabbers" within our own ranks, "The hour has come when you fellows must either fish or cut bait—either you must pull up on your end of the doubletree or so far as we are concerned, the wagon can stay in the mud hole," and once the Old Guard delivers this ultimatum, there isn't much doubt in my mind as to what will happen—I believe that they'll scramble down off the old rail fence and I also believe that the "penny grabber," if he is a man of intelligence, will return to the straight and narrow path and forever after remain with it.
>
> In any case, I submit to the delegates of this convention that a situation under which 50% of the farmers of a community are climbing up over the backs of the other 50% in an effort to pluck the poisoned fruit—or to tear down what the other 50% are trying to build up—I submit that such a situation is intolerable, and as far as I am personally concerned, I am heartily sick and tired of it—and what I want this convention to do is to find out whether the farmers of this state mean business or not. If they do mean business, then there isn't a mother's son of them who will refuse to sign the producer's contract—and if they don't mean business, then at least we have the satisfaction of finding out where we stand.

The convention adopted the concept of a producers contract by an overwhelming majority. In his front-page editorial, "Afterthoughts," in the September 15, 1923, issue of *The Missouri Farmer,* Hirth called endorsement of the contract a declaration of independence. In the "Secretary's Department" of the same issue, Carl Williams, president of the American Cotton Growers Exchange, which had approximately three hundred thousand members, was reported as praising the MFA for its decision, saying, "Outside of Missouri, the MFA has the reputation of being the sanest, most fierce, and most powerful organization of its kind in the world."

The adoption of the producers contract at the convention in 1923 marked the beginning of a period that would test the very existence of the organization. Most of the leadership's efforts were toward getting a sufficient number of farmers signed up to put the contract into effect. Although the terms of the contract were amended in later years, the original provisions were as follows:

1. The contract was to remain in force for a minimum of three years, with those signing the contract to sell grain and produce through their local MFA cooperatives and to sell all livestock through their local livestock shipping associations. The penalty for selling on the outside was 12.5 percent of the value of grain and livestock and 20 percent on dairy and poultry products.

2. The contract would be put into effect in counties when 75 percent of the farmers in a trade territory had signed it.

3. A fee of one dollar was charged on each contract to defray expenses; to finance facilities, each member would loan MFA ten dollars at 6 percent interest.

4. Local cooperatives, including exchanges and livestock shipping associations, would sell only through major MFA agencies such as cold storage plants and terminal markets.

At its meeting on October 19 and 20, 1923, the MFA board of directors discussed the producers contract at length, delegating discussion of the contract's details to the executive committee. L. S. Hulbert of the U.S. Department of Agriculture in Washington, D.C., a well-known expert in cooperative law, was called on to help write the final provisions of the contract. Rubey Hulen, a Columbia attorney hired by the MFA board on a retainer fee basis, aided Hulbert. A report of an executive committee meeting in November 1923 stated that MFA would not need to pay Hulbert for his services; however, since he had married recently, the committee agreed to buy him a wedding present not to exceed eighty dollars in value. The present selected was a handsome silver water set that cost only thirty-five dollars.

In late 1923 the work to obtain members' signatures on the producers contract got under way. The first man to sign the contract was Aaron Bachtel, the organizer of the first farm club in 1914. Several fieldmen were hired for three dollars per day plus expenses to work on getting members to sign the contract. Numerous business groups and chambers of commerce endorsed the contract. The Honorable J. W. Allister of Clinton, a former congressman and secretary of commerce under Woodrow Wilson, signed the contract, as did F. X. Herr of Springfield, the owner of Herr's Department Store, and Stratton D. Brooks, president of the University of Missouri and a farmer.

In 1924 Hirth suggested the formation of a formal group called the "Old Guard" as a way of rewarding farmers for volunteer work done on behalf of MFA. His proposal included the creation of an Old Guard emblem, an idea that originated with Napoleon, who awarded his soldiers a medal immediately after they committed an act of bravery. The MFA Old Guard emblem had the militant face of Washington on the shield. Hirth explained the Old Guard and its emblem thus: "Therefore the 'Old Guard' of the MFA is not like unto the Old Guard of Napoleon, which lived and died for little else than military glory. On the contrary, it has adopted as its patron saint the great man who fought, not for conquest but for human right and whose contribution in these premises is the greatest of its kind in the troubled course of the world's history."[4]

Over the years, more than three thousand of these emblems were awarded at ceremonies held during the MFA conventions. Members of the MFA board of directors were also given Old Guard emblems, but Hirth opposed this practice after the board members voted themselves five dollars per diem compensation. To become an Old Guard, an MFA member must have done at least one of the following:

1. Brought ten new members into MFA in one year.

2. Organized one new farm club of at least ten members.

3. Obtained signatures of 75 percent of farmers in his school district on the producers contract.

4. Driven an MFA fieldman who was working on the producers contract for at least one week.

One of the first disagreements between Hirth and Howard Cowden resulted from the difference in approach to the signing of the producers contract. Hirth favored use of the Old Guard to encourage MFA members to sign the producers contract, whereas Cowden preferred the use of hired fieldmen. In an editorial entitled "An Appeal to the Old Guard," in the December 15, 1925, issue of *The Missouri Farmer,* Hirth told of an Old Guardsman who said, "We will get the influential in each community first—then they will help to get the rest of them." Hirth noted that the dollar contract fee was more than paying his expenses, and continued: "And now why in the name of common sense and the Great Horned Spoon can't we during the next six weeks repeat this performance in fifty other counties?"

Another disagreement with Cowden concerned Hirth's belief that fieldmen should be concentrated in only three or four counties at a time, so that as soon as they signed up 75 percent of the farmers in a trade territory, the contract would be thrown into effect. "However, Mr. Cowden, who as secretary was in charge of the fieldmen, . . . insisted that we should begin signing up the members throughout the state and finally succeeded in converting the state board to this view."

Hirth insisted that all the ten-dollar loans paid by contract signers be invested in government bonds. In other cooperatives, similar fees had been spent without tangible results. Hirth did not want to see that happen. In April 1924 Cowden reported four counties over the top on the contract drive—Franklin, Phelps, Gasconade, and Maries.

An interesting sidelight on securing signatures on the producers contract was the objection of Mennonites in Morgan County. They did not believe in signing contracts but did pay dues and even the contract fee. MFA and the Mennonites worked out an arrangement to accommodate members of the sect, who were unusually loyal in dealings with MFA.

Chapter Four

Politics and Conflict

The producers contract was not the only activity being conducted during 1923 and 1924. In the months following the
1923 state convention, there were reports of MFA meetings
with attendance of twenty-one hundred at Iantha and fifteen hundred
at Mansfield. An MFA picnic at Lebanon attracted three thousand,
with businesses in town closed from 11 A.M. to 3 P.M. According to the
January 1, 1924, issue of *The Missouri Farmer,* Hirth made a two-hour
speech before a crowd of ten thousand in Kahoka.

The MFA convention in 1924, with attendance of eight thousand,
elected George M. "Cotton Top" Kelley president and A. J. Crawford
of Macon vice president. Speakers included Milo Reno, president of
the Iowa Farmers Union; Congressman Thomas Rubey of Lebanon;
and Congressman Gilbert Haugen of Iowa.

The 1924 presidential election resulted in Calvin Coolidge's victory.
Soon thereafter, the entire Missouri congressional delegation, both
Democrats and Republicans, wrote President Coolidge urging him to
appoint Hirth secretary of agriculture. The *Columbia Daily Tribune*
of December 16, 1924, proclaimed: "Missouri has no man, and, in fact,
there is no man in the United States who has done more for the
American farmer than William Hirth. He has an immense following
among farmers of the country. He has fought their fights for them, and

if President Coolidge is looking for a man who understands agriculture from alpha to omega, he need go no further than William Hirth of Columbia." Responding to the Missouri congressional delegation, Hirth asked it to withdraw his name because of his disagreement with Coolidge on the gravity of the farm situation.

The April 15, 1925, issue of *The Missouri Farmer,* in the lead story, listed bills sponsored by MFA and passed by the state legislature, including a bill licensing feed dealers, an egg bill enforcing inspection, and a forestry bill permitting employment of a forester to begin restoration of Missouri's forests. Listed were the names of legislators who had helped and those who had voted against MFA.

In the summer of 1925, MFA president Kelley issued a challenge to the leadership of north and south Missouri in signing up new members. He named C. M. Stiles captain of the south team, and T. H. DeWitt captain of the north. The south won the contest by a narrow margin of 442 members. Captain Stiles and his men ate peaches and cream at the next convention, while Captain DeWitt and his men had mush and milk.

The 1925 convention, held in Sedalia, had an attendance estimated at twelve thousand, the largest in history. A. J. Crawford was elected president, and Stiles was elected vice president. The WPFA had 1,226 women registered.

The McNary-Haugen Bill

Without question, Hirth's fight for passage of the McNary-Haugen farm-relief bill in the U.S. Senate consumed the major part of his attention in the 1920s. The first McNary-Haugen Bill, introduced in 1924, would have authorized the creation of a federal agency to help to maintain domestic prices for farm products. Hirth described the way it would have worked in the June 1, 1924, issue of *The Missouri Farmer.*

> To illustrate its operation with reference to wheat, let us suppose that we will produce a crop of 750,000,000 bushels during the present year and that 600,000,000 bushels of this will be needed for consumption within the United States, leaving

150,000,000 bushels for export; next, let us suppose that the Agricultural Export Corporation fixes the "ratio price" on #2 wheat at $1.70 f.o.b. Chicago, while the world price is only $1 per bushel, or 70¢ per bushel less; applying this loss of 70¢ per bushel to the 150,000,000 bushels of exportable surplus, this would entail a total loss of $105,000,000 and applying this loss on a bushel basis to the 600,000,000 bushels needed for home consumption, would reduce the domestic price to the extent of 17½¢ per bushel; in other words, the wheat grower would receive $1.70 per bushel, less 17½¢ per bushel, his share of the loss on the exportable surplus and to this would be added the cost of operating the Export Corporation.

Hirth's contention was that farmers could ill afford to pay fifty cents to a dollar an hour for what they purchased and then receive only twenty-five cents an hour for what they sold.

In 1925 the Corn Belt Committee was organized in Des Moines, with Hirth as chairman. This committee became the principal sponsor of the McNary-Haugen Bill. At a Senate committee hearing on the bill, Hirth spoke for nearly two hours, during which time hardly a person left the hearing. When his speech ended, he received an ovation even from many enemies of the bill. Senator John Benjamin Kendrick of Wyoming said to Hirth, "Mr. Hirth, I have served in the Senate for a long time, but I want to say that I consider the address you have just delivered as the ablest I have ever heard presented to a committee of congress, and I say this though I am against the bill."

Several days later both the House and Senate committees reported the bill to the floor by an overwhelming vote, but the full Senate rejected it. The March 1, 1927, issue of *The Missouri Farmer* carried the story of the passage of another McNary-Haugen Bill, with a dramatic description of the battles of the previous four years, and the following issue contained Hirth's attack on Coolidge for his veto of the bill.

In May 1927 Hirth was again unanimously elected chairman of the Corn Belt Committee. In that meeting Milo Reno had this to say about Hirth:

> It would be unfair if I did not give a large measure of credit for
> the united front that agriculture presents where it belongs—

to William Hirth, editor of THE MISSOURI FARMER, who organized the first Farm Clubs of Missouri and who has been the
inspiration of that great organization and who has presided
over the sessions of the Corn Belt Committee with a broad-
mindedness and tact that would have shamed the efforts of
lesser men. Mr. Hirth was the author of surplus control. It was
he who first wrote and gave to the public Agriculture's Declaration of Independence at Kansas City on February 9, 1923. He
it was who made far and away the most effective presentation
of the principles behind the McNary-Haugen Bill, at the committee hearings in Washington. But never did he rise to greater
heights than at the conference last week. His unanimous reelection as head of the Corn Belt Federation later was but
poor recognition of the service that he has rendered the
farmers of the country.[1]

In the William Hirth Papers, 1925-1934, in the Western Historical
Manuscript Collection at the University of Missouri in Columbia is a
letter to Hirth from Congressman Clarence Cannon, dated July 1, 1929,
in which Cannon tells Hirth that he was glad to note his reelection as
chairman of the Corn Belt Committee. "It is true, it is an imposition
on you personally, but you are the outstanding farm organization man
of the nation both in your ability to report the cost and in the success
of the cooperative agencies under your direction, and this is no time
to 'send a boy to the mill.'"

In 1928, the McNary-Haugen Bill passed the House again by a
majority of eighty-three votes—its previous passage in the House
had been by a majority of thirty-six—and it passed the Senate by
more than a two-thirds majority. Hirth's comment was, "Agriculture
has won the greatest victory in history, a victory so compelling
that the issue of effective farm relief is certain to overshadow the
coming National Political Convention." Again, Coolidge vetoed the
bill.

Although the McNary-Haugen Bill did not become law because of
the Coolidge vetoes, its passage through Congress twice was undoubt-
edly Hirth's crowning achievement. While the Corn Belt Committee
was the primary sponsor, most farm organizations, including the Mis-

souri Farm Bureau Federation, backed the bill. Unlike MFA's legislative accomplishments in later years, the McNary-Haugen Bill was not the work of the organization but was almost solely that of Hirth. He did keep the membership informed through the pages of *The Missouri Farmer* and thus exerted pressure on Missouri congressmen. But there were no MFA legislative committees or board members who participated in the political arena during the Hirth era. It was his personal influence that extended beyond state lines.

MFA Operations

While Hirth was in Washington, D.C., and in meetings of the Corn Belt Committee, the day-to-day operations of the Missouri Farmers Association were in the hands of Secretary Howard Cowden. Much of Cowden's work involved promotion of the producers contract. The business of organizing new farmers exchanges continued as well, but not at the fast pace of previous years. A news item in the November 15, 1925, issue of *The Missouri Farmer* noted that three new farmers exchanges had been organized recently at Bagnell, Meta, and Ethel, bringing the total to 399 exchanges. Another news item reported that Farmers Livestock Commission Company, of National Stockyards, Illinois, had returned $480,000 in patronage dividends in four years. A branch of the company had been established in Springfield, with Carl Gates as manager.

The August 15, 1926, issue of *The Missouri Farmer* reported that ten thousand people attended an MFA picnic of Henry County members at which Congressman Gilbert Haugen spoke. And on September 1-3, 1926, the tenth annual MFA convention was held in Sedalia. The assembly elected C. M. Stiles president, and Tom DeWitt vice president.

The size of the business operations of the Missouri Farmers Association was reported in *The Missouri Farmer* from time to time. For example, in 1926, MFA poultry and egg processing plants—all bearing the same name, Producers Produce Company—shipped 1,528 cars of eggs and 936 cars of live and dressed poultry with a volume of $9.5

million, thereby leading the nation in the value of poultry products marketed cooperatively.

At the MFA convention in 1927, the secretary reported that there were now 415 livestock shipping associations, 13 central plants, and 404 farmers exchanges affiliated with MFA. Among the locations are names not well known, including Bedison, Bois d'Arc, Bolckow, Boynton, Brookline, Charity, Clark, Creighton, Dutzow, Dunlap, Fillmore, Galt, Iconium, Ladue, Liege, Livonia, Longlane, Peers, Pollock, Reeds Spring, Santa Rosa, Squires, Stoutland, Stahl, Vista, Violet, Wilcox, Wisdom, and Worthington.

A mass meeting was held in Springfield on July 19, 1927, to vote for incorporation of Producers Creamery Company, which later became the largest creamery in the United States. Bill Hirth and other MFA leaders were active in the organization of Producers Creamery, but unlike MFA Milling Company, the soon-to-be-formed MFA Oil Company, and some other MFA cooperatives, all of whose board members were selected by the MFA board of directors, the Producers Creamery board was elected by member-owners. The original board of directors of Producers Creamery Company of Springfield consisted of C. E. Lane, president; D. C. Preston, vice president; T. D. McDonald, secretary; S. A. Nordyke, W. B. Rogers, Brick Wade, John Davison, N. H. Triplett, and G. M. Alford. Before the year was over, dairymen in the Clinton and Cabool areas had also organized creameries.

In late 1927, the exchange managers of southwest Missouri formed an association. Officers were Frank Clyde, Phillipsburg; J. C. Joyce, Carthage; Bob Dennis, Lebanon; and T. D. McDonald, Walnut Grove. At the organizational meeting in Herr's Tea Room in Springfield, they were hosted by the Missouri Farmers Association Purchasing Department and Producers Produce Company. A statewide meeting of managers was held in St. Louis in December 1928.

Recognition of outstanding MFA exchange managers was mentioned in the "MFA Department" of *The Missouri Farmer* in early 1929. Those names included Thomas Fitzpatrick, Argyle; R. O. Yowell, Kirksville; Henry Rapps, Union; W. S. Miller, St. James; A. W. Payne, Brookfield; D. W. Lehman, California; John Fleming, Rolla; A. M. Roderick, Halfway; John F. Johnson, Marshfield; George Wyss, Russellville; Clarence Whittington, Ozark; W. A. Beal, Ash Grove; E. L. Boss, Morrison; John Kreutzer, Owensville; Charles Brucks, Glasgow; O. J. Browning, Leonard; A. F. Heidbreder, Lohman; John Love, Lincoln; H. O. Woodard, Jasper; J. R. McNeill, Lockwood; F. H. DeMott, Adrian; Ben Grantham, Walnut Grove; George Renshaw, Branson; Earl Burt, Gifford; Ed Schelp, Emma; Guy Rose, Conway; J. C. Branscomb, New Cambria; G. L. Rauch, Billings; C. H. Lawrence, Golden City; and Claud Ferguson, Tipton.

Conflict between Hirth and Cowden

In July 1940, Hirth recounted the highlights of his controversy with Cowden in an article in *The Missouri Farmer* entitled "Know the MFA." Hirth stated that for several years he and Cowden had "worked together in harmony, but once he got in charge of the fieldmen he gradually began to assume increasing authority, and since their jobs were dependent upon him, they soon began to carry out his schemes and to end in ignoring my wishes. In order to increase his hold on the directors of the State Association, he placed a number of them on the field force payroll." Cowden also proposed consolidating the Missouri Farmers Association with the Missouri Farm Bureau Federation and Farmers Union, an idea that Hirth bitterly opposed, since it would have involved giving up the MFA name and emblem and giving joint control of the vast MFA business organizations to the Missouri Farm Bureau Federation.

During 1926 and 1927, when Hirth was chairman of the Corn Belt Committee and leading the fight on the McNary-Haugen Bill, he did not attend many MFA board of directors' meetings. At a board meeting in August 1926, immediately preceding that year's convention, the board passed a resolution prohibiting board members from becoming fieldmen. The vote was seventeen to eleven in favor of the resolution, and even though it passed, a sizable number of the directors saw nothing wrong in the practice of directors becoming fieldmen. As a matter of fact, a majority of the board members were already more in agreement with Cowden than with Hirth, although the depth of the conflict was never brought to the surface. Hirth became convinced that Cowden was trying to assume leadership of the organization, which would have meant the ouster of Hirth and *The Missouri Farmer*. At another board meeting later in 1926, Hirth tested his support by asking that *The Missouri Farmer* be withdrawn as the official organ, but the majority voted against this proposal.

With two strong leaders such as Hirth and Cowden beginning to develop difficulties, there was little hope of reconciliation. In early 1927 Hirth wrote a letter to the executive committee accusing Cowden of not doing a good job, of spending too much money, and of not spending enough time out in the field. Finally, at a state board meeting in March 1927, Cowden tendered his resignation as secretary to take effect not later than the next annual convention.

On August 17, 1927, just before the convention, Hirth issued a statement in which he charged that Cowden had refused to carry out the instructions of the MFA board of directors; that Cowden was incompetent and incapable of administering the duties of secretary of the association; and that Cowden had drawn up and sponsored the consolidation proposal with the Missouri Farm Bureau Federation and the Farmers Union. In his *Beyond the Fence Rows: A History of Farmland Industries, Inc., 1929-1978,* Gilbert Fite writes: "These charges of inefficiency were only a smoke screen for Hirth's real objection to Cowden. . . . Feeling that he was being pushed out of his position of leadership and power, Hirth concluded that 'in plain words, the time is come when the board must choose between Mr. Cowden and myself.'"[2]

The election of officers at that 1927 convention offered further proof of the division in the ranks. It had been customary for the president to be elected without opposition, but T. H. DeWitt, a strong Cowden supporter, was opposed by J. R. Meek of Daviess County. DeWitt was elected by a vote of 751 to 546. Ray Derr states, "No campaign was made for Meek's election, but the undercurrents of discontent with the executive committee's leadership were evident."[3] The vice presidency was won by J. Wiley Atkins of Lebanon, a Hirth supporter, over R. T. Pence by a vote of 757 to 489.

Some years before, *The Missouri Farmer* had reported that at an

MFA board of directors meeting in St. Louis on December 24, 1924, "young Ned Ball stated that a baby boy had been born to Mr. and Mrs. R. T. Pence and that Mr. Pence requested that the board of directors give him a name. Motion was made by Mr. Crawford, duly seconded and carried, that he name the boy William Hirth Pence." Now, Pence, as a Cowden supporter, was on the opposite side of the fence from Hirth. It would be interesting to know if Pence changed his son's name!

In November 1927, Frank Scott of Newtown, a former state legislator, was employed as secretary to replace Cowden. Scott was a board member of the Producers Produce Company of Chillicothe and had been active in MFA for several years. According to Derr, "Cowden's resignation did not materially affect the attitude of the executive committee, apparently, for a majority of its members favored Cowden's policies. Scott was known to be in sympathy with them and the situation was not changed by Cowden's resignation."

For several years MFA had a contract with Standard Oil Company which was to expire on July 15, 1927. At an executive committee meeting in June 1927, Cowden proposed to the committee that he would like to take over the furnishing of petroleum products to MFA. In a meeting the following month, Cowden again stated that he would probably get into the oil business and would like to have the MFA contract, and he presented a proposal. "After some discussion, motion was made by Mr. Kelley and duly seconded and carried that Howard A. Cowden be given the contract on oil."[4]

The Cowden Oil Company was incorporated on January 27, 1928. Its office first opened in Columbia and then later moved to Kansas City. Shareholders in Cowden Oil Company included some members of the MFA board of directors as well as T. H. DeWitt, president of MFA. In January 1928, in spite of objections by attorney Rubey Hulen, the MFA board approved the Cowden oil contract by a vote of seventeen to twelve.

In an editorial in the June 15, 1928, issue of *The Missouri Farmer,* Hirth pointed out that at the next convention the members of MFA would need to decide the question of leadership in the state association. "We are drifting like a ship without a rudder." A suggestion was made by A. J. Crawford that all the directors of MFA resign.

During 1928 both Hirth and the executive committee made a barrage of charges and countercharges, and mailed lengthy discourses to MFA leaders. In the March 1, 1928, issue of *The Missouri Farmer,* Hirth answered charges made by the executive committee.

> As to the statement that I have quit working with the committee because I cannot work with the secretary—I didn't say this—I said I had quit working with it because it was stacked against me, and I repeat this. When a new secretary was being selected, they went so far as to ask the applicants whether they would allow themselves to be influenced by a particular individual. Under these conditions, I have not and will not sit with the committee—I will not assault my self-respect to this extent.

Hirth also made the accusation that Cowden had "made a proposition to [Milo Reno] at Kansas City to organize a branch insurance agency in Missouri, which he, Cowden, should control. . . . in other words, the oil deal is not the first instance in which Mr. Cowden has sought to profit at the expense of the cooperative movement." Hirth closed out his article with a recount of his sponsorship of a motion in an MFA board of directors meeting in Sedalia in August 1926 that no member of the board should draw a salary from the state association.

In the August 15 issue of *The Missouri Farmer,* Hirth wrote that after having been away for six weeks, he had returned to his office to find a copy of a letter sent out by President DeWitt on July 28, devoted to the proposal for consolidation of MFA, Missouri Farm Bureau Federation, and Farmers Union, with the suggested name of Missouri Agriculture Association. In another editorial Hirth said he was not surprised that the executive committee and certain employees were trying to drive him from MFA. "For they know perfectly well that should I be restored to my old position of influence there will be a house cleaning from top to bottom. Also, I will not stand for board members to be on the payroll."

The showdown came at the next MFA convention, held August 26–28, 1928. The largest representation of voting delegates ever was present, 1,740 out of a total of a little more than 1,800 authorized delegates. Total attendance was more than 8,000. *The Missouri Farmer* reported:

> Evidence of the great interest in the 1928 MFA Convention reached its first high tide when the gates of the Missouri State Fair Grounds swung open to the vanguard of delegates and visitors on Sunday evening, August 26, 1928. All day Sunday, hundreds, yes thousands of automobiles from all sections of the state from north to south, and east to west, headed for Sedalia, told the World that the greatest militant organization of farmers in the Corn Belt was about to go into annual session. Delegates from many Clubs came in big motor trucks often belonging to the local Exchange, seated with chairs and a tarpaulin stretched over wagon bows or a stock rack to protect from sun or rain. Rich or poor, large operators or small, "Hill Billies" from the land of a million smiles, and pompous cattle feeders from the "big red barn" country up the state, met and mingled together sociably and earnestly, determined to solve their mutual problems cooperatively.
>
> Tents for temporary homes in "White City" were chosen by many where meals might be cooked from provisions brought from home and early morning serenades of hog calling were part of the program. Others slept on cots located in various buildings about the grounds while hundreds of people took advantage of Sedalia's hospitality, whose citizens generously opened their homes to the visitors at rates that were most liberal. It would be hard indeed to conceive of a more ideal place to hold such an overgrown affair as the MFA Convention than the State Fair Grounds. Plenty of shade, water, parking space, buildings, rest rooms, large Coliseum, and in fact every need supplied at the very reasonable charge of $1.50 for all three days. The livestock pavilion, which consists of a large arena completely circled by two galleries seating many thousands of people, was converted into a temporary Coliseum. This was accomplished by seating the tanbark arena with chairs facing a large stage which was erected in the north end. Naturally the acoustic properties of a building of this construction would of course be poor, but this was overcome by placing two microphones just up front of the speaker's stand and an arrangement of amplifying horns di-

rectly above them in the steel work of the roof. Others were located at other points about the building. This made it possible for those in the back seats to hear just as perfectly as those close to the speaker's stand. It really formed a miniature broadcasting system for the building.

It was at these microphones that President DeWitt called the Convention to order at 9 o'clock Monday morning, and through these that speakers and officials addressed and directed the proceedings of the Convention during the three days of its deliberations. Seventeen hundred and forty delegates presented their credentials to the committee and press reports estimated an attendance of 5,000 people the opening day. The same source again estimated an attendance of 8,000 the second day with the third day at about the same figure. In his opening address President DeWitt dwelt largely upon the growth of the Association since its beginning and spoke of its excellent financial condition.

Mayor Poundstone of Sedalia welcomed the gathering to the city in a duly appropriate manner and prompted a literal tumult of applause when he spoke of Mr. Hirth as the man who helped him to get through the University of Missouri and expressed his high regard for him. It was the first mention of Mr. Hirth's name in the Convention and the roar of approval that went up literally shook the foundation of the Coliseum. The saying that "A Prophet is not without honor save in his own country" did not hold good in the MFA Convention of 1928. Caustic ones, in hopeless minority, gathered about the sidelines in small groups and told one another that the popularity of "Bill" Hirth as a leader had become a thing of the past. It was not as they wished. In fact, we doubt if any previous Convention has ever defended him so stoutly nor so crushingly touted the opposition to his leadership. Cool headed, clear thinking men and women in whose breasts rankled the accusations of those who said that Mr. Hirth had been untrue to his trust, came to Sedalia this year to route [*sic*] the opposition to the man whom they loved and admired and to proclaim him as the greatest Farm Leader of them all. Each time Mr. Hirth appeared upon the platform, if but only to make a passing remark, the audience roared its approval. At the mere mention of his name they cheered and when nominated for the Presidency the entire audience came to its feet with a shout like the roar of Niagara and when elected straw hats soared high in the air while the Convention shouted itself hoarse. It was overwhelmingly a Hirth crowd and the opposition was like the fallen leaves of Autumn before a windstorm.

Besides electing Hirth for the first time as president of MFA, the convention elected J. Wiley Atkins as vice president and, by an overwhelming majority, elected board members favorable to Hirth.

At the convention Hirth proposed an amendment to allow the delegates instead of the MFA board of directors to choose the executive committee. This amendment carried, and the names of Hirth, Atkins, and W. S. Miller were placed in nomination by C. E. Lane. Lane, known as "Chart," was raised in Monett and worked on the railroad in his early years before engaging in lead mining in Kansas. In 1916 he moved to a farm near Ozark, where he was active in the early organization of Missouri Farmers Association, working with farm clubs and exchanges and later the big central plants of MFA in southwest Missouri. He served as president of Producers Produce Company in Springfield and on the board of MFA Milling Company and Producers Creamery Company. Following the nominations by Lane, Miller, in turn, nominated Lane, John J. Griffith, John Lindner, and Chris Ohlendorf. In Hirth's account of the 1928 convention, he mentioned that, in every vote, he received the support of every single delegate from Polk County, Cowden's home county.

A resolution adopted by the delegates stated that some of the members of the board of directors had

> during the past year utterly ignored the will of the overwhelming majority of the farmers who compose the membership of this Association and used their efforts to block and oppose the will of the membership even to the extent of engaging in a personal statewide campaign of vituperation and abuse and whereas this convention has once again, in language and by action that no man can misunderstand, expressed its will and chosen its policies, therefore, the board members thus referred to who have not abided by the will of the members of this Association as here expressed have

served their usefulness as board members and their resignation as board members is requested in order to promote the best interest of this great farm organization.

At a board meeting in St. Louis following the convention, the vote ratifying Hirth as president of MFA was twenty-five for, two against, and two not voting. Voting no were Ball and DeWitt. Ball went on record as having voted against Hirth and explained at length why he did not consider him the man to preside over an elective body. He felt that Hirth was more of a boss than a leader, one who wanted others to bow to his will.

In *Missouri Farmers in Action,* Derr had this comment:

> Judged from a public relations viewpoint, Hirth's policy of keeping the membership of the Association informed through the official organ was a major factor in his ultimate victory. The tremendous loyalty which was evidenced could not have been built up over the years by a leader who had failed to take his followers into his confidence. Hirth's every move was a public one; his every act was clearly delineated to his followers, and in this way he kept their confidence and their respect. As the convention closed, the Association was perhaps more completely united than at any time since the first meeting in 1917, when the new farm movement had been launched.[5]

Following the 1928 convention, the MFA board of directors appointed Russell J. Rosier to replace Frank Scott; he was to begin work on February 1, 1929. Rosier was the son of the late A. C. Rosier of Bates County, who had been one of the "wheelhorses" during the early days of the farm club movement. The new secretary's first experience with MFA had been as manager of the MFA elevator in Adrian, and he served for seven years as an MFA auditor. In the March 1, 1929, issue of *The Missouri Farmer,* Hirth described him thus: "In demeanor, Mr. Rosier is quiet and modest. There is no flash about him. He never wastes words, but is business to his finger tips." George McCarthy, chief auditor, told the story that Rosier called him wanting to take a day off from auditing the MFA exchange at Centertown. McCarthy did not ask him why he wanted a day off but learned later that Rosier had gotten married on that day and then returned to work in Centertown the next day.

The bitter fight between Hirth and Cowden had its influence on MFA for many years, particularly in north and west Missouri. Cowden converted his oil company into a cooperative, Union Oil Company, later called Consumers Cooperative Association and now Farmland Industries, Inc., of Kansas City. He was highly successful in organizing a multistate farm-supply operation that became the largest in the United States. Farmland made a great effort to sell its co-op products to MFA exchanges, but with little success. Without question, competition from Farmland has had an influence on business activities of MFA, including pricing policies, amount of patronage refunds paid, sale of bonds, and marketing strategies, among other activities.

In later years MFA and Farmland worked together in joint business enterprises that included the Farmers Chemical Company of Joplin; the Cooperative Farm Chemicals Association of Lawrence, Kansas; the Kansas City Terminal Elevator Company; and the National Cooperative Refinery Association (NCRA) of McPherson, Kansas. I can recall difficulties MFA Oil Company had in becoming a part owner of NCRA. In the early 1960s NCRA was not operating at capacity, and MFA Oil Company needed products. Ralph Booker, president of NCRA, and Ralph Hofstad, then with Illinois Farm Supply (now Growmark) and later president of Land O' Lakes, carried on the fight for allowing MFA Oil Company to become a part owner of NCRA. After considering the matter for about two years, the member-owners of NCRA agreed to sell 6 percent of their stock to MFA Oil Company over the objection of Farmland. Involvement in NCRA proved to be extremely beneficial to MFA Oil Company and also to the other owners, because NCRA increased its throughput, which resulted in lower-priced products for all owners.

The Founding of MFA Oil Company

Following Cowden's departure as secretary, the MFA immediately got serious about organizing a cooperative to supply petroleum products to MFA members, a move that leaders had been considering for many years. The first mention of an MFA oil company was in a board meeting in 1921, with several more references before 1928. Farmers were becoming more dependent on petroleum products as use of tractors increased. Farmers exchanges were selling petroleum products, including motor oils, axle grease, cup grease, floor oil, and kerosene. MFA had a contract with Standard Oil for lubricants, including Polarine Motor Oil, and Standard Oil advertisements appeared regularly in *The Missouri Farmer.* Before MFA Oil Company started, a few farmers exchanges—in Freeburg, Morrison, and Bronaugh—were in the bulk oil business.

In an executive committee meeting on March 23, 1929, A. D. Miller of St. Louis, formerly the Missouri sales manager of Pierce Pennant Petroleum Company, discussed the possibility of establishing bulk oil plants. The committee employed him for thirty days to assist in making a survey, with the understanding that his employment would continue if the survey justified starting a cooperative oil company.

At the next executive meeting, in April, Miller was hired for an additional thirty days, and in June the MFA Oil Company was incorporated for one hundred thousand dollars under the 1919 Cooperative Stock Act, with eleven members of the MFA board and the secretary of MFA as stockholders and trustees. From 1929 to 1946, the executive committee of MFA served on the board of directors of MFA Oil Company. Originally each bulk oil plant had its own board of directors, while the umbrella company provided management, purchased products, handled the accounting, and supervised operations. The organization and financing of bulk oil plants were done largely by MFA fieldmen. For example, F. L. Cuno of Franklin County devoted most of his time in 1929 and early 1930 to the start of MFA Oil Company. The expense of this organizational work was charged to MFA Oil Company and paid to MFA over a period of years.

In the fall of 1929 and early 1930, twenty-four bulk oil plants were financed, constructed, and put into operation. These were located in Boonville, Bucklin, California, Clinton, Crocker, Exeter, Hermann, Higginsville, Lebanon, Lincoln, Macon, Marshall, Marthasville, Maysville, O'Fallon, Owensville, Rolla, Russellville, Ste. Genevieve, Shelbina, Springfield, Union, Windsor, and Wright City. Agent Walter Bruning made the first delivery from the Wright City bulk oil plant to William Wisbrock on October 26, 1929, the date recognized as the beginning of MFA Oil Company. The home office was in St. Louis until 1934, when it was moved to Columbia because of the apparent need for closer supervision by MFA officers. A. D. Miller was replaced in early 1930 by Leonard F. Broach, who had been employed as assistant manager. From Meridian, Mississippi, Broach had been associated with Pierce Pennant Petroleum for several years.

The first several years of operation for MFA Oil Company were tough. Hard times hit just as the company started; the farm depression was most severe during the 1930s. The company did well to increase volume of business each year, though earnings were low. It quickly became apparent that having separate corporations at each bulk plant was not workable; some plants were making money and others were not. A few bulk oil plants paid patronage refunds in the early years, but the majority lost money. In order for all the plants to survive, it was decided to put them into one corporation, the umbrella company. (Appendix 1 herein provides a short history of the MFA Oil Company.)

Looking to the Future

During the twenties and thirties, the overwhelming amount of work done by Hirth and the stress caused by the conflict with Cowden began to take a toll on Hirth's health. Following the 1928 convention, his doctors ordered him to bed, and before the end of the year he made the first of many trips to the Mayo Clinic in Rochester, Minnesota. Frequently he made the clinic a meeting place for friends such as Milo Reno and A. B. Drescher.

At the last convention of the 1920s, held in Sedalia on August 26–27, 1929, the following resolution was adopted: "RESOLVED that we recognize William Hirth as our leader and consider him one of the greatest leaders the farmers of this state and of the entire nation have ever known." Hirth was reelected president, and J. Wiley Atkins was reelected vice president. Several new directors were elected, thus removing most of the Cowden supporters from the board. One of the new board members, who played a leading part in MFA for several years, was Roy D. Hatcher of Shelbyville, later a vice president of the association.

Now that Hirth was again in charge, he outlined his plans, including revival of the signing of producers contracts, creation of a sales agency to handle marketing for all produce plants, and reorganization of operations of the MFA Purchasing Department. In addition, he stated his opposition to using brokerage for general operations, insisting that brokerages should be refunded to farmers exchanges. The upcoming years were not going to be easy ones.

Chapter Five

MFA in the 1930s

D issension within the ranks continued through much of the
1930s, particularly in regard to the operation of some of the
poultry and egg plants. There was opposition to the use of
the John M. Shawhan Agency in Chicago as a selling agent for eggs
and poultry. Lee Farnham, manager of Producers Produce Company in
Springfield, was a strong advocate for Shawhan agency, which helped
Farnham's plant become the most successful and the largest plant of
its kind in the country.

A real battle occurred between MFA and Producers Produce Company of Chillicothe, where F. G. Peters was manager. The Chillicothe organization refused to let the MFA Auditing Department conduct audits there. In August 1929 a revealing letter to Hirth from
A. B. Drescher, an associate of Shawhan, reported that the Chillicothe plant was paying different prices to different exchanges
and that it bought produce from other dealers at higher prices than
paid to exchanges. That was why it did not want MFA to audit its
books.

Another letter from Drescher, to Joe Goeke at *The Missouri Farmer,*
told about "insurgents" in north Missouri who supported a merger
with the Missouri Farm Bureau Federation.

I fear for the future of the MFA, Goeke—these men do not give a damn about the Farm Bureau nor about hooking up with it. What they want is to WRECK Mr. Hirth and his friends so they will wreck the MFA to "get" us. I consider the situation VERY dangerous—I think the time for ACTION is right here—What I mean is to either buy or lease or take over in some way the BUSINESS of the MFA—Its CENTRAL plants FIRST, especially those in North Missouri.

From the early days of the organization, Hirth's enemies were quick to believe that he was getting rich from suppliers of MFA agencies. Hirth ignored most of the stories, but on one occasion when an inquiry came from an MFA member, he secured affidavits from supplier companies, including Washburn Crosby, Peppard Seed Company, Anthony Salt Company, Hoover and Allison Company, Cornell Seed Company, Darling and Company, Springfield Seed Company, and Success Mills. The affidavits stated: "For a number of years the report has been circulated by certain enemies of the Missouri Farmers Association that William Hirth, president of the Association, has received, or does receive, a commission or 'rake-off' on various commodities contracted for by the Association. We cheerfully make affidavit that all such reports are maliciously false."

In April 1932, in a letter to H. J. Blanton, editor of the Paris, Missouri, paper, Hirth asserted:

> The facts are that I have never drawn a dollar in salary from the Missouri Farmers Association, and until a year or two ago, I never charged up my traveling expenses, and they have run into thousands of dollars. During the last three years I have incurred a heavy penalty on my taxes because I couldn't pay them when they were due, and yet the story that "Hirth is getting rich" has been peddled from one end of the state to the other.

In the Hirth Papers there are letters from creditors asking for payment of delinquent bills, including one from a clothing company in St. Louis for $12.75. In 1929 Hirth was solicited by Stephens College for a donation of one thousand dollars. In his reply Hirth said, "I never was much harder up for money, but I subscribe $200." In 1932 a letter from Stephens College requested payment of the two-hundred-dollar pledge, and another letter from M. F. Thurston, cashier of Exchange National Bank, requested payment of a note.

In the December 15, 1927, issue of *The Missouri Farmer* is a picture of the publication's linotype shop in a wooden shack in Columbia. In the accompanying article Hirth pleads for payment of delinquent MFA dues, which included subscriptions to *The Missouri Farmer.* "Often as I look at the array of advertising that other papers carry and then compare it with the meager amount that appears in 'The Missouri Farmer,' I wonder whether I have been warranted in the sacrifices I have made in time and money . . . for I have no salary and thus every dollar I spend for railroad fare and hotel bills must come out of my own pocket." Yet there were those who appreciated what Hirth was trying to accomplish. In April 1929, Hirth received a letter from Concord, California, which declared: "Have just read excerpt from a telegram from Mr. Hirth to Senator McNary giving his ideas on farm relief. Judging from this telegram, I am almost convinced that I have at last found something unique in editors of agricultural papers[—]one that holds the interests of his farmer subscribers above that of his advertising patrons."

According to Karl Pfahl, who worked for Hirth on his farm during the 1930s, Hirth constantly received items at the farm that were sent in payment for ads in *The Missouri Farmer.* One example was a shipment of raccoons that arrived from Illinois, for which Karl had to build pens and crates. At other times various kinds of farm machinery would appear that had to be assembled.

Hirth was very tight with money, especially that of the MFA. In 1929, while A. D. Miller was manager of MFA Oil Company, he drew the wrath of Hirth by sending him three separate letters in one day. Hirth told Miller he could have sent all three letters for two cents postage instead of six. According to H. E. Klinefelter, longtime editor of *The Missouri Farmer,* Hirth was very generous, however, in picking up the tab for meals or other expenses for personal guests.

At the 1930 annual convention, with six thousand in attendance, Hirth was again elected president, and John Schindler of Columbia was elected vice president. This convention marked the beginning of increased legislative activity by MFA.

The fight by the Missouri Farmers Association to shift the state tax burden to intangible property was highlighted at the convention by E. Sidney Stephens, president of Stephens Publishing of Columbia. The publisher of the *Columbia Herald,* Stephens was active in community and state affairs and had been a leader in establishing the State Conservation Commission. He explained how tangible property, such as farmland, personal property, and dwellings, constituted only 20 percent of the state's wealth and yet accounted for 96 percent of the taxes. He argued that a good deal of hidden wealth, consisting largely of money, notes, and bonds, had been escaping taxation almost entirely. Stephens also complimented the directors of MFA on a questionnaire they had recently sent to candidates for the state general assembly, saying that it demonstrated that the Missouri Farmers Association had become the most powerful factor for sound government policies in Missouri.

The following year, in an article in the May 1, 1931, issue of *The Missouri Farmer,* Stephens listed the accomplishments made by the legislature during that year with the help of MFA, as follows:

1. The enactment of a graduated income tax, shifting a portion of the burden of public taxation from property to net profits.
2. Establishment of a 20¢ school levy throughout the state as the basis for state support to the public schools.
3. Guarantee of eight months of school to every child in Missouri.
4. The provision for a high school education, together with transportation, for each child in the state desiring such advanced public school instruction.
5. Provision for the rehabilitation and adequate support of the state's penal, eleemosynary, and educational institutions.

In an editorial in the same issue of *The Missouri Farmer,* Hirth commented on action taken by the 1931 legislature.

The passage of the new graduated income tax and the new school law easily constitute the greatest legislative accomplishments in the history of our state. Through the enactment of the graduated income tax we have definitely established the principle of shifting the burdens of taxation from tangible property, such as farm lands and real property in our towns and cities, to intangible property, or net incomes which consist chiefly of money, notes, and bonds. . . . Through the school bill we have established a 20¢ levy for rural school purposes throughout the state, and infinitely more important, we have guaranteed eight months school, and placed a high school education within the reach of every farm boy and girl in Missouri.

In the fall of 1931 MFA established the Committee on Taxation and Government Reform for the purpose of "presenting to the next session of the General Assembly a program of retrenchment and reform and tax reduction where possible."[1] The committee of ten members was equally divided between Democrats and Republicans, three from the state senate and seven from the house. The senators were D. L. Bales, A. M. Clark, and J. G. Morgan, and the representatives were Langdon R. Jones, Jerome M. Joffee, Jones H. Parker, James W. Armstrong, O. B. Whitaker, Rush H. Limbaugh (the grandfather of the Rush Limbaugh of radio talk show fame), and W. E. Freeland.

The members of the group served without pay, with their expenses of seven thousand dollars paid by MFA. Senator Bales was named chairman, and meetings were held throughout the state to make sure that the voters had an opportunity to participate in the legislative reform discussions. In addition, meetings were held in Jefferson City to allow the governor and the heads of various state organizations to contribute. The meetings resulted in several constitutional amendments. One limited the number of staff members for the legislature to 150, whereas in previous sessions staff had numbered between 800 and 900. Another amendment required preparation of a budget and gave the governor the right to veto any item in the appropriation bill. Both these amendments were passed in the general election in November 1932.

The work by the Committee on Taxation and Government Reform also led to laws passed by the 1933 legislature creating a state purchasing agent, consolidating county offices, requiring the state auditor to audit the books of county officials at least once during their terms, and abolishing numerous boards, bureaus, and commissions.

In spite of Hirth's strong interest in legislation, both state and federal, he had his feet on the ground in balancing this activity with business operations. Henry Wallace, editor of *Wallace's Farmer* and later secretary of agriculture and then vice president under Roosevelt, told of a visit to Hirth at his second-story office and of seeing Hirth writing in longhand. He noticed flowers in Hirth's office and re-marked: "Somehow I had never thought of Bill as a lover of flowers, but my friend told me that he is a specialist in the growing of peonies and iris. I am listing these things because it is rather unusual to find a man who can think part of the time in intensely political terms and part of the time in a clean-cut business way, and who liked to grow peonies and iris for a hobby."

Several years later, in an editorial in the November 1, 1936, issue of *The Missouri Farmer* entitled "The Big Problems of Farm Organiza-tion," Hirth described his philosophy about the relation between legislative activities and business operations.

> Every farm organization should take a keen interest in sound legislative policies for agriculture, in Washington and in its home state, but farm leaders must ever bear in mind that "money makes the mare go," and that no organization can long maintain the interest of members with mere oratory and long-winded resolutions that "whereas" and "therefore," etc. And this is why the MFA has weathered the depression better than any other Corn Belt organization—its first objective is to put money into the pockets of its members, and then to use the power of the Association on behalf of sound public policies.

Another example of Hirth's down-to-earth business acumen was his observation that "what you pay a man isn't nearly as important as what he can earn, and if a farm organization doesn't pay a man what he is worth, some private concern will."

At the 1931 convention, Hirth was reelected president and Schin-dler was reelected vice president. Attendance was between seven thousand and eight thousand, a surprise because of adverse farm conditions. The principal speaker was Governor Gifford Pinchot of Pennsylvania. One of the resolutions at the 1931 convention called for greater control by MFA over the operation of affiliated agencies. Russell J. Rosier, MFA secretary, reported that business activities of all MFA agencies in 1930 amounted to about $100 million, on which dividends were paid of $1 million.

The 1931 audit of the association showed a net gain for the fiscal year of $1,678.94, with a net worth of $42,839.54 and a membership of 20,306. In a lead article in *The Missouri Farmer* of June 1931, Hirth talked about building a new home for MFA and *The Missouri Farmer*, noting that dues from 15,000 new members would pay for the building. He also spoke of the great interest in starting an MFA radio station.

A landmark event occurred on October 1, 1931, when H. E. Klinefelter joined the MFA staff as general office assistant. Kline, as he was known, was born in Illinois and had come to Franklin County, Missouri, as a young man and worked as a telegrapher for the railroad. He also operated a farm near Labadie and wrote articles for a Franklin County newspaper that caught the attention of Hirth. Soon thereafter he became a regular contributor to *The Missouri Farmer* and active in the Franklin County Farmers Association. In 1938 he was hired by Hirth to work full-time for *The Missouri Farmer*. In 1939 he became editor. One of the most influential men in the MFA, Kline was also one of the organization's wittiest and deepest thinkers.

In one of Kline's early columns in *The Missouri Farmer*, he told of writing a play to be used at farm club meetings, and he suggested topics for debate, including:

> RESOLVE that every farmer in Missouri should belong to MFA
> RESOLVE that farmers should quit voting straight tickets
> RESOLVE that it is more profitable to ship livestock by rail
> RESOLVE that the wife has a harder time on the farm than her husband
> RESOLVE that women have as much right to smoke and chew as men.

The 1930s saw farm prices plummet to extremely low figures. Lee Farnham, manager of Producers Produce Company in Springfield, reported that the average price of eggs in 1929 was 28.55¢ per dozen, whereas by 1932 the average price had dropped to 11.93¢. The average poultry price in 1929 was 23.28¢ per pound, which by 1932 had dropped to 10.81¢. In 1933 the average per-hundred-weight price of cattle was $4.65 and of hogs $4.30; corn was $.32 per bushel. The U.S. Department of Agriculture estimated cash income from farm marketing to have declined from a high of $10,479,000,000 in 1929 to a low of $4,328,000,000 in 1932. Since 1920, the value of farmland had decreased by 50 percent. The farm share of the national income was 17 percent in 1928—and only 7 percent in 1932.

By 1932 the farm depression was acute. A letter from Klinefelter to Hirth, dated August 20, 1932, is more dramatic than statistics. "Many farmers do not drive cars, and one farmer, a Club secretary, said he had not been to town since spring. Many of their cars have 'given up the ghost!' Others cannot buy licenses. All seem to be nearing destitution in everything except food. Money is exceedingly scarce, and their sales of poultry, eggs, and cream appear to be their only source of income."[2]

MFA continued to encourage farmers to help each other through the formation of new exchanges. The May 15, 1932, issue of *The Missouri Farmer* carried a story of the organization of an MFA exchange in Grandin, on the Current River, with Rev. F. G. Wangelin as manager. In 1936 and 1937, after I had left my first MFA job at Producers Produce Company and had become a traveling auditor for MFA, I audited the records of that exchange. The volume of business was very small; the Reverend Wangelin provided most of the capital, and he received no salary. He was interested solely in helping out farmers in a very poor section of the state. Later, Wangelin was elected to the board of MFA and served eight years, from 1936 through 1943.

Overall, however, in 1932 MFA membership dropped to a low of 15,132. The association showed a net gain of only $1,114 for the year. Attendance at that year's convention was five thousand, with Hirth and C. E. Lane elected as president and vice president, respectively. Rubey Hulen made a "powerful address," and other speakers included Congressman Clarence Cannon.

During 1932, Hirth, who saw Franklin D. Roosevelt as the only salvation for farmers, jumped into the presidential election with both feet.

He became acquainted with Roosevelt and reported in a letter to Judge Xemophom Cavermo, dated February 26, 1932, "I am just back from Washington. . . . Incidentally, I took supper with Governor and Mrs. Roosevelt night before last." Hirth took an active part in the campaign, speaking in several parts of the Midwest. His expense account, sent to Jim Farley, the Democratic national chairman, was $1,072.07.

On November 8, 1932, immediately following the election, Hirth sent a four-page, single-spaced letter to Roosevelt at Warm Springs, Georgia, giving his views on the economy, the farm situation, and other issues.

> In my opinion human beings are a thousand fold more important than the dollar, and yet during the last dozen years as a government we have worshipped at the shrine of the latter.
>
> The nation cannot endure under a system of special privilege under which the masses more and more become hewers of wood and drawers of water, nor can we compromise on the score . . . either the masses must definitely become the first concern of government, or in a little while we will find ourselves back in the same economic morass in which we are now floundering.

There was some backing of Hirth to be Roosevelt's secretary of agriculture. J. R. Danball, secretary of the Wood Farm Club in High Hill, sent a letter of endorsement to Hirth. In his reply, Hirth said:

> I have your letter about endorsing me for Secretary of Agriculture, and while I deeply appreciate this attitude on the part of your members, I hope you will not pursue this matter further . . . my one desire is to help formulate a real farm bill when Gov. Roosevelt gets on the job, and if I was begging for any kind of a political position, I might weaken myself in this respect. I have spent the best years of my life in fighting the farmers' battles as effectively as I know how, and now there is a chance to "cash in," I want to strip to the waist for this fight.

In 1933 MFA membership dues were reduced from $2.50 to $1.00, and the association showed a net loss for the year of $1,817. Early in 1933, Rosier reported that a general across-the-board salary reduction of approximately 20 percent had been put into effect during the month of October 1932.

The producers contract was abandoned in 1933 after a ten-year struggle to secure sufficient signers to put it into effect. Approximately fifty thousand farmers signed the contract and advanced the ten-dollar fee or signed a note for that amount. Refunds amounted to $487,240 plus interest of $24,500. In a series of articles entitled "Know the MFA," written shortly before his death in 1940, Hirth reminisced about the experience of the producers contract.

> The adoption of the producers contract by the MFA back in 1923 marks one of the highlights in the Association's history, and one that involved many heart throbs filled with hope, and others that led to deep disappointment. It was a period which might easily have presaged the dawn of a new day in American agriculture, but, as it was, it turned out to be a beautiful dream that came to nothing.

At the 1933 annual convention, attended by approximately seven thousand, Hirth and Lane were reelected as president and vice president. One of the planned speakers, who was unable to speak because of time restraints, was Fred Victor Heinkel, president of Franklin County Farmers Association.

In spite of poor farm conditions, interest in the organization remained strong. The third annual Lafayette County picnic held in August 1933 was attended by several thousand, with two thousand members' cars in a parade miles long. John Simpson, president of National Farmers Union, made the main address. And a report in the September 15, 1933, issue of *The Missouri Farmer* told of a big MFA picnic in Shelbina, with five thousand to six thousand people attending. Hirth and Lane were the principal speakers.

The Producers Creamery Company of Chillicothe, which had pulled away from MFA two or three years earlier, held a membership meeting in November 1933 and voted unanimously to rejoin and work with the association. Hirth remarked: "And thus ended the chapter. Once more our battle flags unitedly face the enemies of agriculture throughout the length and breadth of Missouri."

When the MFA Oil Company moved its headquarters from St. Louis to Columbia in 1934, it located one block north of the main entrance to the University of Missouri campus. On April 15, 1934, *The Missouri Farmer* reported, "The new quarters are exceptionally well suited for the general offices of the Oil Company and present an appearance of which every MFA member would feel justly proud." That same year, MFA Oil's largest investor, Casper Stauffacher, of Dunnegan, started returning 1 percent of the interest paid him on his $4,700 certificate, contending that 8 percent was too much.

By the middle of the decade things were starting to look up once again. MFA membership increased from 18,000 in 1933 to 24,000 in 1934 and to 25,000 in 1935. The annual conventions in 1934 and 1935 were held in Sedalia, with Hirth and Lane reelected president and vice president, respectively, each year.

Before becoming editor of *The Missouri Farmer,* Klinefelter often contributed human-interest stories. In the August 15, 1935, issue he described the annual Franklin County picnic. "The band is playing and the various concessions are running full blast. 'Dutchmen' of all ages and statures are gathered around the beer stand where they, with the help of townspeople, drank 25 half-barrels and 42 cases of beer, and someone else drank 109 cases of soda pop, not to mention lemonade, etc." Reporting on a meeting of MFA managers that same year, Klinefelter wrote: "One of the most delightful and inspiring talks was made by a lady manager, Miss Dowell, of Mountain View, whose celibacy, Mr. Hirth held, was a reflection upon the young men of the Ozarks." Lois Dowell, later manager of the farmers exchange at Fordland, was not the only woman manager in the MFA. Others included Naomi Walker of California, Irene Maples of Marionville and Aurora, and Dorothy Brown of Neosho, whose exchange, by the early 1940s, had over two thousand members, the largest membership of any exchange in the state.

The year 1936 started with an announcement from Hirth at the annual managers meeting in January that he would run for governor of Missouri. He announced that he would immediately place his resignation in the hands of Secretary Rosier, "as I have no desire to use the prestige of our great organization in my candidacy for a public office."

And he admonished managers at the meeting not to become involved, saying, "This is my fight." Hirth knew he had no chance to win, yet he thought he could put the spotlight on the corrupt Pendergast political machine in Kansas City and thereby bring about reforms.

> I shall not complain if I am compelled to travel over the most lonely road I have yet encountered, and my only hope is that when the battle has ended, and regardless of the outcome, I will have rendered a degree of public service. . . . So long as [Tom] Pendergast rules Missouri, what chance will we have to evolve a fair system of taxation? . . . Under existing conditions the voters of Missouri are practically disenfranchised . . . not only does Mr. Pendergast select our U.S. Senators, Governors, and other high official forces, and dictate our policies of state government, but Democratic candidates for the Supreme Court and State Superintendent of Schools must likewise have his approval if they hope to be nominated.[3]

One issue in the campaign was Pendergast's involvement in the dispersal of insurance funds. In the summer of 1935, the following had appeared in the minutes of an MFA executive committee meeting:

> Mr. Hirth stated that since 1930 the old line fire insurance companies operating in Missouri had, without the state's approval, increased their rates 16⅔% . . . that the fund which had been impounded in the meantime now totals approximately $11,000,000, over which there has been much legislation, and, as a result, Mr. [R. Emmett] O'Malley, State Insurance Superintendent, has recently ruled that this huge sum would be disposed of by permitting the insurance companies, their attorneys and agents to retain 80% of it and refund only 20% to the policyholders.

A January 1991 article in the *Missouri Historical Review* detailed the connection between O'Malley and Pendergast, and described at greater length the extent to which Pendergast had manipulated the 1933–1937 administration of Governor Guy Park.

> He [Park] appointed R. Emmett O'Malley, a loyal member of the Pendergast machine, as State Superintendent of Insurance

and approved a deal granting 80% of $9,000,000 impounded insurance dollars to grieving companies and 20% to the policyholders. Although Park may not have known about the proposed $750,000 payoff O'Malley arranged for Pendergast through A. L. McCormack, the president of the Missouri Association of Insurance Agents, the scandal certainly besmirched his administration and later became part of the evidence that helped send the Kansas City "boss" to prison.[4]

Hirth's opponent in the Democratic primary was Lloyd Stark. Stark, from the town of Louisiana, Missouri, was a member of the Stark Brothers Nursery family, well known for its apple trees. He had the backing of the Pendergast machine and won the primary by a large majority, carrying Kansas City and St. Louis overwhelmingly. In Pendergast-controlled Jackson County, Stark won by a vote of twenty-nine to one. Hirth carried several rural counties. In the general election Stark defeated his Republican opponent and shortly thereafter reversed his previous stand and joined Hirth in attacking Pendergast.

The primary election was over by the time of the 1936 MFA convention. C. E. Lane, who replaced Hirth as president while he was campaigning, nominated Hirth for president, but Hirth declined and nominated Lane for president for the ensuing year. Lane was elected, and Fred Victor Heinkel, of Franklin County, who had become a member of the MFA board of directors in 1935, was elected vice president. At the annual conventions in 1937 and 1938, Hirth was again elected president, with Heinkel serving as his vice president. Attendance at the conventions in 1936, 1937, and 1938 was low—approximately 4,000, 5,000, and 6,000, respectively.

The business operations of MFA continued to grow. A report in 1937 about the three largest MFA operations in Springfield stated, "Producers Produce Company, Producers Creamery Company, and the MFA Milling Company, under the strikingly able management of Lee Farnham, William T. Crighton, and John F. Johnson did a combined business last year of $9,420,000, with net earnings of $364,000."

It was a constant battle to keep exchange managers from buying on the outside. At a managers meeting in the middle 1930s, John F. Johnson likened the Missouri Farmers Association to a huge football game with each manager a player. "Buying outside the Association is fumbling the ball and leads to defeat." In late 1935, Lane, as vice president of MFA, made a powerful appeal, expressing his belief that the association's greatest flaw was the managers' weakness of yielding to the temptation to buy outside the organization. "It's hard to make converts when there are sinners inside."[5]

In 1937 a name appeared in *The Missouri Farmer* that would be heard from in later years—that of Maurice Maze, manager of the farmers exchange at Sullivan. The old exchange building there had burned, and at the dedication of the new building on January 15, 1937, speakers were Frank Young, manager of Farmers Livestock Commission Company, and W. S. Miller, manager of the exchange at St. James. Another name that popped up was that of Marvin Young, who played a piano solo at the MFA picnic in Franklin County in July 1937. Young later became both an attorney and an executive with MFA.

In early 1938 new wholesale cooperatives in Springfield included an egg hatchery and a grocery company. The hatchery was acquired by Producers Produce Company and MFA Milling Company, who hired Fred Hoelscher as manager. In the early 1940s Earl Johnston, a former exchange manager at Mountain View, became manager of the hatchery. By 1943, when Johnston left to join the armed services, the business was reporting fiscal year sales of $123,000, with earnings of $18,000. Johnston was succeeded by Perry Martin, who stayed until 1957, when MFA Milling Company took over the operation and John F. Johnson became supervisor. Dale Benton was transferred from MFA Milling Company to serve as office manager of the hatchery that year and stayed until 1961, when Charles Berry took over as manager. The hatchery closed down in the mid-1960s when broiler production in the Ozarks was phased out.

Some groceries had been merchandised by the Producers Produce Company of Springfield to farmers exchanges since the early 1930s, including sugar in hundred-pound bags and some canned goods in case lots. In 1938, the Producers Produce Grocery Division was organized to handle the grocery business, and in 1941 a separate cooperative, the Producers Grocery Company, was formed. Its first manager was Harold Kidd; he was replaced by John Scott, who became manager in 1941. Scott stayed until 1960, when Del Scroggins, who had been with Producers Produce Company since 1935, became manager. In 1971, Dale Benton took over as manager and served in that capacity for the next ten years, until Jim Gargus, a former MFA auditor, was named manager in 1981.

At one time the Producers Grocery Company had 150 exchanges as patrons, and for a short time it operated retail stores in Camdenton, Warsaw, Monett, and Houston. There was much talk in the 1940s of starting another wholesale grocery company in northern or central Missouri to supply farmers exchanges that could not be reached from Springfield, but nothing happened. Until the 1980s the Producers Grocery Company showed a profit every year. In 1961, for example, sales were $4 million with net savings of $100,000. In 1978, when sales were over $9 million, the company was the only surviving farmer-owned grocery cooperative left in the United States. Seven years later the grocery company closed its doors, because farmers exchanges had for the most part gone out of the grocery business.

A cooperative creamery in Emma, organized in 1900, adopted new cooperative bylaws and affiliated with MFA in 1938. Also in 1938, the MFA Grain and Feed Company of Kansas City was incorporated, partially to secure a seat on the Kansas City Board of Trade. The company had formerly been operated as a part of the MFA Purchasing Department. The new corporation was under the control of the MFA executive committee with an advisory committee of managers, an arrangement that would cause some contention in later years.

The year 1939 marked the twenty-fifth anniversary of the first farm club meeting held at the Newcomer School House on March 10, 1914. Hirth was not able to be as active as he had been on previous occasions; his health was beginning to fail, and he was spending more time at home and at the Mayo Clinic. To celebrate the anniversary, however, farm clubs were urged to hold meetings on March 10 and "listen in via a good radio" as Hirth told the MFA story on station KERA of Del Rio, Texas.

Chapter Six

The End of an Era

Leonard Broach, who had been manager of MFA Oil Company since 1930, died on August 7, 1939, and I was selected by the board of directors to replace him. The only other applicant was MFA Oil Company fieldman B. R. Adams of Higginsville. I think the fact that he told the board he would not remain with the company if he was not selected as manager was instrumental in my selection. Of greater importance, however, was a telegram from Hirth, who was in the Mayo Clinic at the time. His telegram stated, "Young is the only one I will vote for." Hirth's familiarity with, and respect for, my work as an auditor most likely accounted for his support of me.

The delegates attending the 1939 annual convention in Sedalia re-elected Hirth and Heinkel as president and vice president, but Hirth was absent for the first time because he was still at the clinic. The MFA's net gain for the year was $11,800, its net worth was $89,700, and its membership was 26,659—a decline from the previous year. Counties having more than 1,000 members included Greene, with 1,932; Polk, 1,569; Christian, 1,135; Webster, 1,129; and Texas, 1,056. All these counties are in southwest Missouri, where membership was favorably influenced by the patronage refunds paid by the three large MFA institutions there. Sales from all MFA agencies, including central plants and exchanges, totaled $49 million, with net savings of $835,000.

The year 1940 saw many significant changes in the operation of the Missouri Farmers Association, including the method by which farmers became MFA members. The old practice of soliciting annual dues had become the job of the exchange managers, bulk plant agents, and other employees. In 1939 membership had grown to only 26,659 from the 1932 low of just over 15,000.

The MFA board of directors appointed a committee of central plant managers to work on better ways to collect annual dues. On May 2, 1940, the committee met and worked out a tentative plan to be voted on at the upcoming convention. Members of that committee were: John F. Johnson of MFA Milling Company, William T. Crighton of Producers Creamery in Springfield, Lee Farnham of Producers Produce Company of Springfield, Frank Farnen of MFA Grain and Feed Company, Frank Young of Farmers Livestock Commission Company, John Cook of Producers Creamery of Chillicothe, Fred Heinkel as vice president, and I, representing MFA Oil Company.

Under the new "earned membership" plan, local exchanges, elevators, bulk oil plants, creameries, and livestock cooperatives solicited membership applications, and when a farmer completed twenty-five dollars' worth of business, the local MFA agency would send half his dues to Missouri Farmers Association. The remainder of the dues was allocated to the major agencies as follows: 12.82 percent each for the Springfield companies, MFA Milling, Producers Creamery, and Producers Produce; 10.25 percent each for MFA Oil Company, MFA Grain and Feed Company, and Producers Produce Company of Shelbina; and smaller allocations for eight other agencies. Heinkel thought that this plan could result in as many as sixty thousand members the following year. The next convention adopted the plan, which remains in effect today with some changes.

Another important event in 1940 was the founding of MFA Central Cooperative. In the late 1930s some farmers exchanges suffered financial losses, and the MFA Purchasing Department took over their operation. By 1940 there were five such exchanges, in Marshall, Versailles, Barnett, Eldon, and Moberly, and MFA appointed a committee to recommend a solution to the exchanges' problems. Committee members included Heinkel, Rosier, Klinefelter, and me. The outcome was the organization of MFA Central Cooperative, which would own and operate farmers exchanges that were in financial difficulty. The board of directors of MFA Central Cooperative had two classes of membership, each making up half the board: Class A members were selected from the MFA state board of directors, and Class B board members were elected by MFA members who belonged to farmers exchanges owned by MFA Central Cooperative. In 1969 the MFA Central Cooperative was merged into Missouri Farmers Association and became an operating division overseeing eighty-five exchanges.

The first general manager of MFA Central Cooperative was Jack Silvey. Silvey, originally from South Gifford, was a traveling auditor for MFA when I joined the auditing staff in 1935. My first job as auditor was working with Silvey at Producers Produce Company in Shelbina. Silvey was with MFA Milling Company for a short time and then became assistant secretary in the late 1930s. He played a big part in expanding the business activities of MFA, including work on the formation of the Farm Supply Department and the Insurance Department. After serving as manager of MFA Central Cooperative for several years, Jack played an important role in starting MFA Mutual Insurance Company and was its first president. He was highly intelligent, with great drive and great ambition, and his contribution to MFA was enormous.

Another significant happening in 1940 was the decision to construct a home office building at the corner of Seventh and Locust Streets in downtown Columbia. Heinkel and Rosier broke ground for the building on October 16, 1940. Simon Construction Company had the contract on the building, which was completed in the middle of 1941 at a cost of approximately fifty-six thousand dollars.

The 1940 convention in Sedalia was the second consecutive convention that Hirth missed because of ill health. The convention re-elected Hirth and Heinkel president and vice president, and membership stood at thirty-two thousand. Governor Lloyd Stark, Hirth's opponent in the race for governor in 1936, delivered a eulogy of Hirth.

It would have been enough for an ordinary man to have attained success as a farm leader and as the head of a great business organization, but William Hirth is no ordinary man.

He is a fighter and a crusader for the things he knows are right. He is a scourge of evil-doers and an undying enemy of the things he knows are wrong. So I am paying William Hirth no light tribute when I say that he stands out in Missouri history as one of the most patriotic and gracious citizens who ever battled the forces of corruption.

On September 18, 1940, George McCarthy, chief auditor of MFA since October 1919, died in Columbia. Known for his keen sense of humor, McCarthy had been one of the few men who could "kid" with Hirth, and his work with MFA played a big part in the early success of the organization. I was especially close to McCarthy, having worked for him for three years as a traveling auditor. For most of that time, I worked with him on audits of the major agencies of MFA, including MFA Oil Company, and I grew very attached to the lovable Irishman. He was visiting me in my office in Columbia when he became seriously ill, and he died later that same day.

One month later, on October 18, C. E. Lane, longtime member of the MFA board of directors, MFA vice president for four years, and for a short time MFA president, died in Springfield. I was fortunate to have known Lane, particularly while I worked at Producers Produce Company. He had a reputation as a peacemaker and frequently met with board members of farmers exchanges to iron out difficulties. I remember that his favorite expression was "By the gods!"

On October 24, 1940, William Hirth died of a cerebral hemorrhage. He was sixty-five years old and had been ill for much of the preceding two years. Occurring just one week and one day after the groundbreaking for the new MFA building, an event that marked the start of a new era for the association, the death of Hirth marked the end of a major era in MFA's history. Hirth was a giant. A man of lesser strength would not have survived, nor would he have been able to pull MFA along with him.

Hirth was an extremely hard worker, putting in seven days a week with long hours every day. Russell J. Rosier reported that he went to Hirth's second-floor office in the Miller Building every Sunday morning. Hirth always kept that day available for fieldmen to come to Columbia to discuss plans for the coming week. On the occasion of the fiftieth anniversary of MFA in 1964, a letter from Hirth's longtime secretary, Idalee L. Woodson, stated that "he worked between twelve and sixteen hours every day six days per week and sometimes seven." She also spoke of the tough financial binds that haunted Hirth. She said that he would call his good friend Edward J. White, vice president of Missouri Pacific, and say: "Hey, Ed, I need you again. I'm all the way down and in disgrace over at the bank. Send me a check for a couple thousand so I can get it to the bank in the morning. Otherwise can't pay for a carload of paper and can't publish on time."

Hirth had only a few close friends with whom he enjoyed visiting and discussing problems and plans. One of those was J. A. Hudson. Hirth described his feeling for Hudson in an article in *The Missouri Farmer* on August 15, 1922, following Hudson's death.

> It is with a heavy heart that I chronicle the death of Col. J. A. Hudson, chairman of the executive committee from the first session it ever held. . . .
>
> In the early days we fought the battles of the Columbia Commercial Club side by side . . . and rare were the occasions when we lost a struggle for community progress or betterment. . . .
>
> When I began the publication of THE MISSOURI FARMER and often when the paper houses wouldn't give me enough credit to get out the next issue or when the time had come to write the checks on the Saturday afternoon payroll and when there was no balance in the bank—in those dark hours I would go to Col. Hudson and say, "Well, I am up against it again," and then with a laugh he would reply, "Well, then, we will have to go to the bank and fix it."
>
> As I watched them lower the casket of my old dear friend into the grave the other day, unconsciously my lips murmured, "God, what a man!" And to the end of my days, the beautiful friendship that existed between us and the thought that such a man could see something of good in even me— Oh! how precious this will be!

Friction frequently arose within MFA because of Hirth's personality. Theodore Saloutos wrote in the *Mississippi Valley Historical*

Review that "Hirth was domineering, blustering, positive, arrogant, and often devoid of humility. His stinging rebukes were felt by many with whom he differed. His correspondence reveals a proprietary air in his demands to speak for agriculture." The conflicts with the Missouri Farm Bureau Federation, the Extension Division, and Howard Cowden had roots in Hirth's domineering ways.[1]

In spite of his rough manner, Hirth was a good listener. In board meetings he would listen until everyone had his say, and then he would cut through to the heart of the problem being discussed and announce his recommendation. Usually he was right, and most directors did not fancy an argument with him.

H. E. Klinefelter, who knew Hirth as well as anyone, said:

> When he liked a person, he loved him, and, by the same token, when he disliked a person, he hated him. Also when he became angry, he was mad indeed, and when he was amused, he laughed heartily. When some person befriended him, he never forgot, and he never forgot either when someone betrayed him or worked against him. He was a very learned man, not only had he had many and varied experiences, but he was an avid reader, having read much history and biographies. I was always amazed at his unlimited vocabulary. . . . He was attached to his old office, which he occupied 25 years and wherein he had fought his battles with "The Missouri Farmer" and in building the MFA. He was attached also to a big unkept roll top desk and to his squeaky chair and his dilapidated guest chair. He held on to those old relics, not because he could afford none better, but because he loved them. Once he owned an old Dodge touring car, long out of date, but he became attached to it and would have no other. One night someone stole it, and he went forthwith and bought another just like it and drove it until it was past going.

Later, Klinefelter also observed:

> One of the qualities that set Mr. Hirth apart from most men was his capacity to think and to work hard. His keen mind was never idle, and he didn't simply wonder about things, he thought about them. He was born with both the capacity to think and

to work hard. Blessed with good health and having inherited a determination that knew no bounds, he worked like a Trojan, taking only a half-day off on Sundays. To have known this great man intimately was indeed a privilege. He was an exceptional person, a genius such as nature only occasionally produces.[2]

Karl Pfahl, the German immigrant who worked on Hirth's farm for a few years, told me that Hirth was very difficult to work for but that he was also a kind man. Hirth went to the farm every morning, seven days a week, and laid out the work to be done that day—usually enough work to take a week. He would want to know why more work was not being done, but he would also tell Pfahl he was working too hard. Hirth was at the farm one day when the workers were dipping sheep, and he ordered Pfahl not to do that work any more because he thought it was too hard for him.

There was never any question that Hirth had a sincere love for the underdog, particularly the farm family. Despite Hirth's rough exterior, he was loved by the vast majority of Missouri farmers. His attack on the steel barons, the meat-packers, major oil companies, and corrupt politicians provided a rallying point for farmers whose income was well below that of other segments of the population. The dramatic success of MFA in the early days of farm clubs, farmers exchanges, livestock shipping associations, cold-storage plants, creameries, and all the other associated businesses, was concrete evidence that Hirth's leadership had paid off in dollars and cents.

An article by Klinefelter in the November 15, 1940, issue of *The Missouri Farmer* listed Hirth's four greatest achievements as: the founding and building of MFA, the promotion of the McNary-Haugen Bill, the fostering of legislative reform in Missouri, and the fight against bossism in Missouri. "Behind his rugged exterior," Klinefelter continued, "there beats the greatest of hearts. He had friends among the high and the low. Probably the finest tribute ever paid him came from a lowly negro who was profoundly shocked at his death. He said, 'He never let me go hongry [*sic*] when the snow was on the ground.'"

After Hirth's death, a few of us attended a wake at Hirth's home, as was customary in those days. Goeke, Klinefelter, Silvey, Rosier, and I were at the house on Westwood Avenue in Columbia most of the night before the funeral. Although he had been my idol since grade-school days, I did not realize at the time what a great man he was. As an inexperienced country boy, I was frightened by his shaggy eyebrows, his stern demeanor, and his piercing eyes. I recall visiting him in his upstairs bedroom in the spring of 1940, after MFA Oil Company had just paid its first companywide patronage refund. He asked how business was, and I told him that because of wet weather, our business had not increased over the previous year. He pulled his eyebrows down, looked a hole through me, and said, "God damn it, Young, if we can't do any better than that, we had better sell out to Standard Oil and go home." But before I left, he was agreeing that the weather had indeed been bad and had given me a pat of encouragement.

The momentum of the large and successful business organization Hirth had founded, with sales of approximately $50 million per year, continued. In addition, a group of veteran MFA business leaders aided in the transition to new leadership after Hirth's death. Included in this group were such men as Russell J. Rosier, Jack Silvey, H. E. Klinefelter, Lee Farnham, John F. Johnson, William T. Crighton, John Cook, Frank Young, and Earl Burt, manager of Producers Produce Company in Shelbina, to name but a few. As manager of MFA Oil Company, I also assisted during this transitional period.

William Hirth, founder of both *The Missouri Farmer* and the Missouri Farmers Association. He served as editor of the magazine and as leader of the organization until his death.

The Missouri Farmer's original linotype shop, shown in the magazine's December 15, 1927, edition with "new" addition on the left.

The Newcomer School House in Brunswick, "birthplace of MFA." The first farm club was organized here on March 10, 1914.

Founding members of the first farm club.

Top, left to right: George Heisel, Aaron Bachtel, W. J. Heisel;

center, left to right: John Kohl, Thomas Penick;

bottom, left to right: Will Armstrong, Earl Smutz.

State fairgrounds in Sedalia at an early MFA convention.

An early farm club exchange, Owensville.

Frank B. Young. Hired by MFA in 1921 as manager of the Farmers Livestock Commission Company, he became an important contributor to the success of MFA.

Howard A. Cowden. He played a major role in the development of MFA during the twenties, serving as MFA secretary. He and Hirth parted ways in 1927 in a policy and power struggle.

John F. Johnson, manager of MFA Milling Company from 1934 to 1974.

MFA Milling Company of Springfield was begun in the early 1920s as a wholesale feed operation called the Farm Club Mill and Feed Company. It received these new quarters and a new name in 1929.

Producers Produce Company consisted of a group of several MFA poultry and egg processing plants. It led the nation in 1926 in the value of poultry products marketed cooperatively.

Lee Farnham,
manager of Producers
Produce Company in
Springfield.

Russell J. Rosier, MFA secretary and the son of A. C.
Rosier, one of the early MFA
leaders. He was known for
his business acumen and
his quiet dedication to the
association.

William T. Crighton,
the able manager of
Producers Creamery
Company of Springfield
and the Dairy Products
Company.

Raymond A. Young,
author of this volume. He
had his first MFA job with
Producers Produce Com-
pany, followed by three
years as a traveling MFA
auditor, before becoming
president of MFA Oil Com-
pany. In 1968 he had the
added responsibilities of
becoming vice president
and executive vice presi-
dent of the Missouri
Farmers Association.

120

Fred V. Heinkel and Russell J. Rosier breaking ground for the
new MFA office building in downtown Columbia, 1940.

The home office of the MFA, Columbia.

Fred V. Heinkel.
He succeeded Hirth
as president of MFA,
a position he held
from 1940 until
1979.

A. D. Sappington.
He succeeded Rubey
Hulen, MFA's earliest
legal adviser, in 1943.
He later served as
general legal counsel
for MFA Insurance
Companies before
becoming its presi-
dent in 1964.

Left to right: William Beckett, who followed Sappington as MFA's general counsel and was later MFA vice president and executive vice president; F. V. Heinkel; Raymond A. Young; Russell J. Rosier.

The annual MFA convention was held at Stephens College auditorium, shown here, from 1958 to 1972.

Clell Carpenter, former state commissioner of agriculture and later MFA director of public affairs.

Ormal Creach. He was secretary-treasurer of MFA, MFA Oil Company, and MFA Livestock Association, and president of the MFA Foundation.

Senator Hubert Humphrey, *left,* with the author. Humphrey and Kansas senator Robert Dole were speakers at the 1966 MFA annual convention.

Orville Freeman, *left,* and Heinkel. President John F. Kennedy considered both men for the position of secretary of agriculture before choosing Freeman.

128

Jim Halsey,
former manager of MFA
Livestock Association.

Pete Moles, manager of MFA
Livestock Association in Marshall.

Jack Silvey, first president
of MFA Mutual Insurance
Company.

Dale Creach,
president of MFA
Oil Company from
1981 through the
present.

Eric Thompson,
president of MFA,
1979–1985.

Bud Frew,
president of MFA from
1986 through the present.

II.

The Heinkel Era, 1940-1979

Chapter Seven

Expanding Business Ventures

The 1940s

Vice President Fred Victor Heinkel became the new president of Missouri Farmers Association. Heinkel was born on September 22, 1897, on a farm near Oermann, in Jefferson County, Missouri. His grandfather, a German immigrant, came to America on a sailing ship. He landed in New Orleans after a seventy-two-day voyage from Hamburg and then traveled up the Mississippi River to settle in Missouri. Fred Heinkel's parents, Cora Bell McDaniel and William G. Heinkel, moved to Franklin County in 1904. Fred attended public schools there but never went beyond the sixth grade. In 1914, he passed the county examination to become a teacher and received his certificate at age sixteen, but he never taught. He was farming in partnership with his father when, in April 1917, he heard Hirth speak in nearby Jeffriesburg. He joined MFA that year and was soon elected secretary-treasurer of his local farm club and of the local livestock shipping association. In 1926, he helped organize the MFA exchange at Catawissa, and in 1931 he became president of the Franklin County Farmers Association. He ran for the state legislature once but lost the election.

H. E. Klinefelter was a longtime friend of Heinkel's. During the time that Heinkel was president of the Franklin County association, Klinefelter served as secretary-treasurer, and they were both instrumental in the development of MFA there. Soon after Heinkel's ascension to the presidency of MFA, Klinefelter reported in *The Missouri Farmer:*

> Under President Heinkel's leadership it is expected that the MFA will become more democratic than before. He believes there should be more state board and executive board meetings; that the board and managers of our major agencies should be consulted more; that meetings with employees and local boards should be held over the state; that a legislative committee [should] be named; that closer cooperation be done with other organized groups in the state; [that] closer cooperation [should exist] between MFA and other farm organizations and cooperatives; and [that] a school for MFA employees [should] be established.

One of those goals, a school to help teach employees more about the history of MFA, its business operations, and the philosophy behind the establishment of agricultural cooperatives, was realized in April 1941 and was continued for the duration of Heinkel's presidency. Roy Reed was in charge of the first school, and among the instructors were Dean M. F. Miller of the University of Missouri College of Agriculture; the Extension Division director, Jim Burch; Professors O. R. Johnson and Herman Haag; and officers of the St. Louis Bank for Cooperatives and the Farm Credit Administration in Washington, D.C. Students included Bill Conboy, later an executive with MFA Insurance Companies; Travis Harris, later manager of MFA Milling Company; and Carlos Bradley, later manager of MFA Grain Divisions, Kansas City.

Heinkel had just assumed the presidency when he and the executive committee had a visit from a committee of farmers exchange managers—A. Mortenson of Higginsville, Ed Schelp of Emma, Hadley Butts of Slater, Charlie Brucks of Glasgow, and Ora Collier of Sedalia. The exchange managers made the following suggestions: that MFA buy *The Missouri Farmer;* that MFA Grain and Feed Company be reorganized and, together with MFA Milling Company, be allowed to contract directly for goods; that all fieldmen be abolished; and that the new membership plan be scrapped as premature.

Only some of these were issues that Heinkel would be able to resolve quickly.

When Hirth died, his son, William V. Hirth, had inherited his ownership of *The Missouri Farmer.* Early in 1941, he sold the magazine and printing plant to MFA, but negotiations did not go very smoothly. The original asking price for *The Missouri Farmer* and for a formula owned by Hirth known as the Square Deal Stock Tonic was seventy-five thousand dollars. The main point of contention was whether goodwill should be a part of the price. Because the journal's mailing list belonged to MFA rather than to *The Missouri Farmer,* the only value of the journal to MFA was in the printing equipment, which MFA finally bought for twenty-five thousand dollars. MFA paid another five thousand for the Square Deal Stock Tonic formula.

In *The Missouri Farmer* issue of April 1, 1941, young Hirth expressed his disappointment at the outcome.

> It is with deep regret that I announce the sale of "The Missouri Farmer," and I say with deep regret for I had hoped that circumstances might have been such that I could continue editing of "The Missouri Farmer." . . . At one time during the negotiations, I offered to give the Association "The Missouri Farmer," including its press, good will and name, for not one cent of cost if the Association will but allow me to continue to operate it for ten years on the same basis my father had for 27 years.

Young Bill Hirth, an only child, was a journalism graduate of the University of Missouri and had worked at a radio station and an advertising firm in St. Louis, where he met and married Mildred Orr of Wichita, Kansas. They returned to Columbia, and Hirth worked for his father on the staff of *The Missouri Farmer.* During World War II, he enlisted in the Naval Air Corps, and he died shortly after the end of the war. The Hirths' only child, Susan Orr Hirth, was born while Bill Hirth was in the service and now lives in southern California.

In the summer of 1941 the new MFA home-office building was completed. The entire basement and four rooms on the first floor were occupied by the printing plant and personnel of *The Missouri*

Farmer; the remainder of the first floor was rented to MFA Oil Company. Space on the second floor was for Missouri Farmers Association, including offices for Heinkel, Rosier, Silvey, and Glen Denham. Denham was head of the Insurance Department, which had started in 1939 with a premium volume of $25,000 and would grow to $104,000 by 1943.

The original plan was for Hirth's office to be in the southeast corner of the first floor. A plaque was placed in the vestibule reading, "In memory of William Hirth, founder of the Missouri Farmers Association. He loved Agriculture and everything beautiful." During a remodeling of the MFA building many years later, the plaque was removed. In 1980 it was reinstalled and rededicated with his son's widow, daughter, and granddaughter present at the ceremony.

During his first year in office, Heinkel called on farmers to march on Jefferson City in opposition to House Bill 565, which was an attempt to set up soil conservation districts with undue control over farmers. About two thousand farmers showed up, and the bill was defeated. In 1941 Judge J. W. Armstrong of Pulaski County, who had represented MFA in Jefferson City for the previous six years, commented, "I have never known the MFA to ask for or support legislation that was unfair to the people of Missouri."

Before Heinkel had been in office a year, the association's elections approached with opposition to him coming from the western part of the state. An unidentified clipping from a Sedalia newspaper reported:

> F. V. Heinkel will have a hard time on his hands to be re-elected president of MFA next week, it developed yesterday. About twenty managers and delegates held a meeting last Friday in Sedalia and decided definitely Heinkel must go. The group claimed support all over the state and will throw its influence back of George "Cotton Top" Kelley for president and Charles Fuller, of Odessa, for vice president.

Heinkel got wind of what was happening and on August 19 mailed a two-page letter to MFA leaders, asking for their support at the upcoming convention.

Six thousand members attended the twenty-fifth annual convention in Sedalia in 1941. The results of the election for president gave Heinkel 1,047 votes and Kelley 457. Opposition came largely from those dissatisfied by the manner in which MFA Grain and Feed Company was organized. Exchange manager Mortenson of Higginsville spoke for the group after the election, stating that he believed the election had been conducted fairly and the group's grievance had been heard, and he moved that Heinkel's election be made unanimous. Roy Hatcher of Shelbyville was elected vice president, a position he would hold until his death in 1952. Hatcher was an important leader in north Missouri, having served as chairman of the board of Producers Produce Company of Shelbina for several years.

Under Heinkel's leadership, farmers exchanges remained the backbone of MFA, just as they had been under Hirth's. In addition to the statewide convention, each exchange held its own annual meeting. These meetings were the big event for most exchanges. Either an MFA auditor or the exchange manager gave the financial report; members of the exchange voted to dispose of the year's earnings through cash payments or retention in net worth; members elected board members for the coming year and selected delegates to the annual MFA convention; and generally a speaker from one of the MFA agencies would talk to the gathering. In the case of exchanges that had been absorbed into MFA Central Cooperative or were owned and operated by MFA, advisory board members were elected at annual meetings. Local entertainment, such as old-time fiddling, and refreshments, singing, movies, and drawings for prizes enlivened the meetings. After television came along, attracting crowds became more difficult. Some exchanges now substitute a simple open house, where members are served refreshments and ballots are available for election of board members and delegates.

Occasionally disputes arose between farmers exchanges and major wholesale agencies such as MFA Milling Company and Producers Produce Company. In 1942 the Bolivar Farmers Exchange began selling eggs to outside buyers, and the West Plains Farmers Exchange established a private dealer in Oregon County, which was outside its territory. It was relatively easy to discipline those exchanges by refusing to do business with them, thus cutting off the sizable patronage refunds paid by the major agencies. Shortly after both Producers Produce Company of Springfield and MFA Milling Company quit doing business with the West Plains and Bolivar exchanges, they both came back into the fold. In later years both the Crane and the Monett exchanges got into similar difficulties. The Crane Farmers Exchange was reinstated, but the MFA License and Service Agreement was canceled for the Monett Farmers Exchange, and it was never reinstated.

In 1942 the MFA convention was postponed indefinitely because of the war. Clyde Morwood was named chief auditor to succeed George McCarthy. Net savings for the year were $32,800 and net worth was $157,000. A few more exchanges joined MFA Central Cooperative. Combined MFA business agencies in 1942 had a volume of over $100 million with net savings of $2.6 million. MFA creameries at Chillicothe, Kirksville, Emma, Cabool, and Springfield had sales in 1942 of $10.9 million, with earnings of over $1 million.

Because of the war, MFA Oil Company experienced difficulty in obtaining petroleum products. To insure a supply of fuel for farmers, a small refinery at Chanute, Kansas, was purchased in May 1943, with 115 miles of pipeline and a capacity of fifteen hundred barrels per day. Certificates of indebtedness to aid in the purchase were oversubscribed.

Rubey Hulen, the Columbia lawyer who had worked for MFA on a fee basis since the early days of the organization, became a federal judge in 1943. A member of Hulen's law firm, A. D. Sappington, replaced him as MFA counsel. His new duties included lobbying for MFA in Jefferson City and Washington, D.C. Sappington, a native of Columbia, had worked his way through the University of Missouri Law School as an employee of his father's business, Central Dairy. In addition to working for Hulen's law firm, he had served as Columbia city attorney for three terms. Sappington was familiar with MFA and had represented the organization in legal matters. He served as general counsel from 1943 until he became general counsel of MFA Insurance Companies in 1957 and then president of MFA Insurance Companies in 1964.

On May 28, 1943, the president of each of the twelve district branches of the Bank for Cooperatives and of the Central Bank for

Cooperatives visited Springfield as guests of MFA. D. M. Hardy, who dealt with MFA and was president of the St. Louis Bank for Cooperatives, was instrumental in getting his associates to attend the meeting. *The Missouri Farmer* printed a special edition for the Springfield visitors. Because of the large volume of business done by MFA agencies in Springfield, it was called the "cooperative capital of the United States." At that time, Producers Creamery Company had sales of $8.1 million, Producers Produce Company sales of $6.4 million, and MFA Milling Company sales of $9.5 million. Branches of Farmers Livestock Commission Company, MFA Oil Company, MFA Hatchery, and three farmers exchanges were also located in Springfield. I attended the meeting and recall vividly the visitors' surprise at, and complimentary remarks about, the size and efficiency of MFA's Springfield operations. John Brown, president of Louisville Bank for Cooperatives, commented, "Never in our experience throughout the country have I seen a more thorough and sound cooperative than here."

In 1943 the MFA convention was again postponed. Heinkel was the principal speaker at the annual meeting of the National Cooperative Milk Producers Federation, which represented 350,000 dairymen. During that year, eighteen major MFA agencies had sales of more than $1 million each. Total sales of all major agencies were $83.5 million, with savings of $2.35 million. As just one example of the size of business operations at this time, the plant at Producers Produce Company of Springfield had two acres of floor space, feeding capacity for fifty thousand birds, and killing capacity of fifteen hundred birds per hour, and it employed 425 people.

In an editorial in *The Missouri Farmer* of January 1944 entitled "Is the MFA Being Penalized?," the federal Farm Credit Administration (FCA) was criticized for not appointing someone from MFA to the Farm Credit Board in St. Louis. The appointees to the board were Howard Shirkey of Richmond, a farmer and a Missouri Farm Bureau Federation leader, and Fred Groves of Cape Girardeau, described as an "agriculturist" and "one of the largest automobile distributors in the Delta section of Missouri."

The editorial pointed out that these appointments were made in spite of the fact that the Missouri Farmers Association comprised the largest federation of cooperatives in the nation and was by far the biggest borrower from the FCA in Missouri. Congressman Clarence Cannon took the matter up with Albert G. Black, governor of the FCA, who had promised MFA the next appointment, but Missouri's Senator Harry S Truman objected. The editorial questioned, "Is Senator Truman sore at the M.F.A. and if so why? The only way we can account for it, if it is actually true, is because of an old feud between himself and the late William Hirth. Mr. Hirth once called him 'Pendergast's bellhop.'" (A story circulated at that time about Truman and Hirth meeting in a men's rest room, where Truman told Hirth that he did not like his characterization of him as "Pendergast's bellhop." Hirth's reply was, "Well, goddamnit, that's what you are!")

In 1944 MFA voted to join the National Council of Farmer Cooperatives, sponsored by the Grange League Federation (GLF) of New York. The organization consisted of nearly five thousand cooperatives, most of them part of large regional groups or federations of cooperatives similar to MFA. The Missouri Farmers Association was the third largest member cooperative of the National Council, surpassed only by GLF and the California Fruit Growers Exchange. The organization served as the spokesman for cooperatives at the national level and played an active part in legislative and regulatory matters. Thus membership in the National Council would provide MFA with more of a national voice on issues important to farmers and with increased representation on political issues in Washington, D.C. In January 1948 Heinkel would be elected vice president of the group at its annual meeting in Memphis, Tennessee.

In 1944, after a lapse of two years, the MFA held its annual convention in Sedalia with twenty-five hundred in attendance. It was only a one-day affair. The association had net savings for the year of $115,000, bringing its net worth up to $342,000. Heinkel and Hatcher were reelected president and vice president, respectively.

It was at this time that MFA undertook a major change in the means by which it provided merchandise to member exchanges, allowing for the direct purchase and sale of a variety of items. Previously, all sales had been through a brokerage arrangement, with MFA contracting with suppliers, who in turn sold their products directly to farmers exchanges. In 1944, for example, brokerage fees received amounted to $39,000, with sales of only $325,000. By 1948 sales exceeded $6 million.

From the founding of the association until the middle 1940s, all sales of MFA, for accounting purposes, were in a single category, with no breakdown into commodity divisions. In 1945 the Farm Supply Division was established, with Jack Silvey as its manager. As additional commodities became important, other divisions were formed, including the Seed Division, Feed Division, Plant Foods Division, and Grain Division.

As early as 1936, the MFA executive committee had decided to sell roofing materials and had urged that additional lines of merchandise be carried, including hybrid seed corn and paint. Roy Reed, a salesman for Amalgamated Roofing Company of St. Louis, became acquainted with Hirth and Rosier in 1936, and in 1939 MFA hired him to put it into the lumber and hardware business. For the next forty years, Reed was closely associated with the growth of MFA. Besides running the first school for employees, he became director of sales and organization in 1947. He was one of the best-known and best-liked employees in the MFA family.

Before the advent of farm supply warehouses, merchandise such as roofing or steel products was sold to farmers exchanges through MFA wholesale agencies—produce plants, MFA Milling Company, and MFA Oil Company. The first farm supply warehouse was built in Springfield, and others were built later in Sedalia, St. Joseph, and Maryland Heights. Longtime warehouse managers included Thurman Evans at Springfield, Glen Warren at St. Joseph, Ralph Lohman at Maryland Heights, and Lloyd Neill at Sedalia.

On January 1, 1945, Herman Haag, professor of agricultural economics at the University of Missouri, was hired to fill the new post of research director of MFA. A native of Poplar Bluff, Haag received his bachelor's degree from the University of Missouri with the highest grades ever in the School of Agriculture, and then earned a Ph.D. from Cornell University. He was a hard worker and seemed to be "on the run" continually. Before the year was over, the results of Haag's work were being felt. Producers Produce Company of Sedalia bought the

Armour Poultry and Egg Processing Plant there following a study by Haag. He headed another study committee that resulted in the establishment of additional dairy plants and implementation of plans to build a soybean processing plant in the city of Mexico.

Creameries affiliated with MFA were doing an outstanding job in the 1940s. Producers Creamery Company of Springfield, managed by William T. Crighton, had sales of $10 million in 1945, with net savings of $750,000. Milk production in the area had doubled since 1940, and expansion was underway to process 1.2 million pounds per day. At Cabool, the Producers Creamery Company managed by Fred Edwards had sales in 1944 of $2.5 million, with savings of $150,000.

At a meeting in 1945 Haag presented a research report to MFA creamery managers concerning expansion of creameries through a new cooperative, MFA Dairy Products Company. The cooperative's new plants were later built at Monett, Lebanon, and El Dorado Springs. Managers at that meeting were Crighton and Edwards; R. O. Yowell, Kirksville; John Cook, Chillicothe; and H. H. Dierking, Emma. William T. Crighton became manager of the new enterprise, and his right-hand man in starting the plants was Clarence Gonnerman.

Gonnerman had gone to work for MFA in the home office in Columbia in 1937, where he, Rosier, Katheryn Deering, Ida Mae Jones, and Carolyn Wayland composed the entire staff. At first, Gonnerman's job was to work on getting MFA into the insurance business. Later, he entered the University of Missouri to obtain a degree in business while working full-time for MFA typing audit reports at night. Gonnerman graduated at the top of his class and then entered the navy. It was after his discharge in 1946 that he went to Springfield to work for William T. Crighton in the MFA Dairy Products Company.

In 1948, MFA Dairy Products Company was merged into Producers Creamery Company of Springfield. Farmers who were on a milk route and were therefore members of Producers Creamery enjoyed an increased value of their farms. Patronage refunds from the creamery were large enough to have that impact.

At the convention in 1945 Heinkel and Hatcher were again reelected president and vice president. In his speech, Heinkel summarized the organization's recent accomplishments: the hiring of a full-time attorney; the creation of the research and farm supply departments; the addition of eight new bulk oil plants and two new farmers exchanges; the purchase of produce plants in Clinton and Sedalia; and the organization of MFA Dairy Products Company. He also told of the organization of MFA Mutual Insurance Company, to begin operations on January 1, 1946, and of plans for a new milk plant at Clinton and a new soybean plant in Mexico. Heinkel also mentioned a number of other divisions, departments, and cooperatives that would be formed in the upcoming years.

MFA leaders had dreamed of starting an insurance company for many years. In a board of directors meeting as early as 1923, Secretary Cowden stated his opinion that an MFA mutual company should be organized, and he was instructed to investigate possibilities. In 1937 the board made another effort to get such a company started, and again in 1940 the board moved to proceed with organization of an auto insurance and casualty company. At a meeting on July 6, 1945, Haag, Silvey, and Sappington explained to the board the need for an MFA mutual insurance company, and the board authorized an advance of one hundred thousand dollars to get such a company started. On October 15, 1945, the MFA Mutual Insurance Company was organized. F. V. Heinkel was president; Roy Hatcher, vice president; Russell J. Rosier, secretary; and Jack Silvey, executive vice president; and board members were John Meisner, C. C. Collins, L. O. Wallis, D. E. Ellis, and Arthur Neuenschwander.

It was the board's original intention to organize the insurance company as a capital stock corporation, with MFA owning the stock. Had this occurred, MFA would have been able to receive dividends and thus would have enjoyed substantial financial benefits and been assured of maintaining ownership and control. Because of income tax considerations, however, it was made a mutual company, with ownership and control in the hands of the policyholders. Financial benefits to MFA included payment for use of the MFA name, the coverage of a portion of MFA officers' salaries, the supplying of food at MFA conventions, and the loaning of money for building facilities. In the beginning most MFA agencies switched their casualty insurance to the new insurance company. Many exchange and bulk oil plant managers became part-time MFA Mutual Insurance Company salesmen. This proved so lucrative that many of them became full-time salesmen.

Under the able management of Jack Silvey, the company grew rapidly and expanded into other states. Silvey also continued as manager of MFA Operating Divisions until 1956. In spite of the success of MFA Mutual Insurance Company, internal dissension eventually arose between the board of directors and Silvey. The final straw was Silvey's dismissal of one of the department heads, which aroused the ire of Heinkel and some of the other board members. In a confrontation on February 20, 1964, Silvey resigned and was replaced by general counsel A. D. Sappington. At that time, MFA Mutual had assets of $48 million, a surplus of $11.8 million, and premium income of $32 million per year.

Following our initial meeting in 1935, when we were both traveling auditors with MFA, Silvey and I remained close friends for the next twenty years. He was a tough administrator with lots of ambition. The fact that he started up his own insurance company after leaving MFA was an indication of his talent and drive. Before Silvey's death in 1988, he had built a company worth several million dollars. Incidentally, he purchased Hirth's Sunshine Farm at the west edge of Columbia and lived there until his death.

During the 1940s and 1950s, Silvey was one of the leading forces in building MFA. Under his management, MFA Central Cooperative had grown from five to twenty exchanges by the end of 1945. Sales for that year were $4.6 million, with savings of $35,000. When Silvey resigned on January 1, 1946, to assume control of the insurance company, Bob Morrow took over. Morrow came from Barnett and had managed various exchanges in the MFA Central Cooperative. He did not get along well with Heinkel, however, and resigned in 1948. I hired Morrow as a fieldman in MFA Oil Company for a short time and helped him obtain the position of manager of a large cooperative in Osceola, Arkansas, where he did an outstanding job until his death in an automobile accident.

Otto Schulte replaced Bob Morrow as manager of the MFA Central Cooperative. Schulte began work for MFA in the 1930s at the Eugene and Henley exchanges as a truck driver, bookkeeper, and helper. He became manager of the Eugene Farmers Exchange in 1940, and in 1946 he went to Green City as manager of the exchange there, which was a part of the MFA Central Cooperative. Slightly more than one year later, he moved to Columbia as manager of the Boone County MFA Exchange, and on June 1, 1948, he became general manager of MFA Central Cooperative, with twenty exchanges. Sixteen years later Schulte left MFA Central Cooperative, which had grown to include seventy exchanges, and became vice president of the Grain Division of MFA. He retired sixteen years after that, in November 1980. Schulte was widely known and highly respected in the grain trade. He was a director of the U.S. Feed Grain Council and a member of the boards of directors of Farmers Export Company, St. Louis Grain Company, and Kansas City Terminal Elevator Company. In 1967 he was named by the U.S. secretary of agriculture to a grain mission to seven European countries.

Schulte developed an early friendship with Jerry Litton of Chillicothe, whose brilliant political career was cut short by an airplane accident on August 3, 1976, just after he had won nomination to the U.S. Senate. He was serving as a U.S. congressman at the time. Through a common interest in Charolais cattle, Schulte secured Litton as a speaker at an annual meeting of MFA Central Cooperative in 1960 while Litton was still a student at the University of Missouri.

Late in 1945, Judd Wyatt was hired to head up a new information department of MFA. He had worked for the Farm Credit Administration in its public information area. After several years working for MFA and then MFA Oil Company, Wyatt moved to MFA Mutual Insurance Company in advertising and communications. He produced several prize-winning movies for MFA Oil Company and MFA Mutual Insurance Company. He was known for his great sense of humor and became nationally known for his preseason football rankings contest.

The star performer in MFA Oil Company films was Jack Taylor, alias Timothy Hays. Taylor was hired by Missouri Farmers Association and MFA Oil Company in 1946 as editor of the MFA Oil Company's magazine, *The MFA Oilogram,* of MFA's *The MFA Cooperator,* and of MFA Milling Company's magazine. Taylor, a talented writer, speaker, and

actor, was with the MFA organizations for only three years but during
that time became widely known and respected. He appeared as the
"little character" in three MFA Oil Company movies and in other MFA
agency films. For many years, Taylor has entertained throughout the
country as Timothy Hays.

On December 6, 1945, the board of MFA met in the Colonial Hotel
in Springfield and authorized purchase, effective January 1, 1946, of
the Springfield Packing Company on East Mill Street, just east of the
old MFA stockyards. The plant was located on fifteen acres and had
forty employees. In 1945 it processed 18,000 hogs and 7,250 cattle,
with total sales of $1.5 million. Frank Young, manager of Farmers
Livestock Commission Company, of National Stockyards, Illinois, was
named manager of the new venture. A new cooperative, MFA Packing
Company, was formed with two classes of members: MFA members
and livestock producers. Cost of the plant was $232,000, and financ-
ing was provided through sale by mail of $200,000 in certificates of
indebtedness. One year later, the MFA Packing Company was merged
into MFA and became the MFA Packing Division. The successor to
Frank Young as manager of Farmers Livestock Commission Company
was S. P. Knowles, a longtime employee.

In the early 1940s artificial insemination for dairy cows was a
growing practice in Missouri, partly because a world authority, Harry
Herman, was a professor of dairy husbandry at the University of Missouri. Producers Creamery Company of Springfield and MFA Milling
Company organized the Artificial Breeding Association with investments of forty thousand dollars each. In addition, certificates of indebtedness were sold to dairymen. The cooperative began business
on January 1, 1946, with L. O. Wallis serving as president and John
Fawcett, formerly with the School of the Ozarks in Hollister, as manager. By 1947 the association had forty-eight employees, largely technicians scattered throughout the territory. In the early years of the
cooperative, delivery of semen was made by airplanes that dropped
capsules by small parachutes.

In the middle 1950s, the Artificial Breeding Association purchased
a farm on South Campbell Street in Springfield and built a barn large
enough to house over fifty bulls. F. G. Stevenson succeeded Fawcett as

manager, and by June 1955, the association covered seventy counties with eighty-one technicians. The Artificial Breeding Association became a division of Missouri Farmers Association in 1956. It was sold to a large multistate breeding association several years later.

Early in 1946 MFA created its Seed Division, with headquarters in Marshall and Harold Swinger as manager. A seed-corn processing plant was completed late that year, capable of processing 100,000 bushels annually. The production, processing, and marketing of hybrid seed corn and other seeds was an important and interesting activity in MFA for the next few decades. The division was not always profitable, but the seed-corn sales contests and corn growing contests generated a good deal of excitement.

In 1950 Herman Schulte became manager of the Seed Division, a position he would hold for the next ten years. Herman, a brother of Otto Schulte, had an interesting and varied experience in MFA. He became manager of the Henley exchange in 1943 and later served as manager of several other exchanges, including Boone County MFA Exchange in Columbia. After leaving the Seed Division, he became manager of the MFA Grain and Feed Division in northern Missouri for three years. In 1964, he replaced Otto as manager of the MFA Central Cooperative when Otto became manager of the Grain Division. Bob McDonough replaced Herman as manager of the Seed Division and served in that capacity from 1964 to 1967. Under McDonough's management a seed processing plant was built in Chillicothe. In 1967 Herman became manager of the MFA Seed Division again. He resigned in 1970 to go into the seed brokerage business and became the largest seed broker in the United States and Canada.

Also in 1946, the city of Mexico, Missouri, became the site of one of the first cooperative soybean processing plants in the nation, owned and operated by MFA. MFA had bought the Pollack Feed Mill in 1943 with the intention of converting it to a soybean plant. After delays caused by a shortage of materials and a fire in 1944, the plant finally started operation in late 1946 with a capacity of eighteen hundred bushels per day, later enlarged to three thousand bushels per day. Maurice Maze, who had managed farmers exchanges at Sullivan and Washington, became manager of the Mexico operation in 1943.

After the Pollack Feed Mill burned in 1944, MFA purchased the Famo Feed Mill in St. Joseph to supply feed to MFA exchanges in northern Missouri. To aid in the purchase of the mill, the Missouri Farmers Association loaned MFA Grain and Feed Company fifty thousand dollars, to be repaid through the sale of certificates of indebtedness. Art Loutch, formerly with the St. Louis Bank for Cooperatives, was hired to manage the mill.

It was also in 1946 that MFA made the first move to become involved in ownership of an interregional cooperative, Central Farmers Fertilizer Company. The term *interregional cooperative* applies to enterprises, such as fertilizer manufacturing plants, oil refineries, and grain elevators, that are owned and operated by two or more regional cooperatives such as MFA. During the following year, MFA bought one hundred thousand dollars' worth of capital stock in Central Farmers Fertilizer Company for the purchase of phosphate deposits. The same year, Darling and Company, from which MFA had bought fertilizer for several years, canceled MFA's contract.

A research report conducted by Haag showed that farmers in Missouri had used 226,000 tons of fertilizer in 1946. MFA had bought nearly a fourth of that, obtaining 26,000 tons from Darling and 26,000 tons from other sources. Haag's report showed that the cost of building a plant capable of producing 25,000 tons of fertilizer per year would be about $140,000 plus $110,000 in working capital. The board of directors authorized management to proceed with building a plant in Springfield. Later the plant was enlarged, and the total cost, including working capital, was $420,000; the fertilizer operation became known as the Plant Foods Division.

At the annual convention in 1945, MFA Oil Company had officially been changed from a stock cooperative to a nonstock cooperative with two classes of membership. The MFA board of directors constituted one class of membership and selected one-half of the oil company board of directors; MFA Oil Company members, who constituted the other class of membership, elected the balance of the company's board.

In the fall of 1946, MFA Oil Company membership meetings were held in the territories of the forty-six bulk plants. Data processing manager Lloyd Rosson and I attended all those meetings, where I had specified that only coffee, soft drinks, and doughnuts would be served. But the following year, at the conclusion of the Ste. Genevieve meeting held in Zell, members of the local advisory board rolled out a barrel of beer. They said they were afraid we would never get an audience again at one of their meetings unless we served beer!

Five thousand members attended the 1946 annual convention in Sedalia. Speakers included Congressman Clarence Cannon and John Brandt, president of Land O' Lakes Creameries. Heinkel and Hatcher were reelected to their respective positions. And for the first time, MFA membership exceeded 100,000—the total for the year was 113,073.

Indication that, in spite of all the successes, some dissension in the MFA ranks persisted during the middle 1940s was a message sent out on the letterhead of Farmers Elevator of Clinton. Signed by A. Mortenson of Higginsville and W. S. Herring of Clinton, it called a meeting of the "lately organized Cooperative League." Those in attendance, in addition to Mortenson and Herring, included Howard Cowden, president of the Consumers Cooperative Association (CCA); Frank Farnen, manager of MFA Grain and Feed Company of Kansas City; R. W. Ballew, an employee of Farnen's; H. L. Beezley, manager of the Bolivar Farmers Exchange; and Elmer Welty, manager of the Versailles Farmers Exchange. According to the letter, the meeting was to deal with questions involving income taxes.

Officers of the MFA learned of the meeting, and Jack Silvey asked Wilbert Stone, a longtime manager of exchanges, to attend. Stone told me that after he dined with the group at a Sedalia hotel, he was asked to leave. Having done so, he then climbed out a window in his room at the hotel and found a listening post at a ventilation opening on the roof. From there he was able to hear most of the proceedings, which did not involve income taxes. The underlying reason for the meeting was to discuss weaning farmers exchanges from MFA to CCA.

In his history of CCA, *Beyond the Fence Rows,* Gilbert C. Fite describes the struggle between Union Oil and the Farmers Union State Exchange of Omaha, a regional cooperative—a struggle that was reminiscent of the friction this meeting caused between CCA and MFA.

As the Union Oil Company intensified its field work in Nebraska, the editor of the *Nebraska Union Farmer* expressed the home organization's opposition. He sharply attacked Cowden and referred to him as a "cuckoo Cooperator." The editor explained that a cuckoo was a bird that laid its eggs in the nests of other birds. . . . Why proselyte, he asked, when there was so much territory in the United States where cooperatives needed to be organized?[1]

In a letter to the executive committee dated July 2, 1946, Rosier related that "Mr. Heinkel was married at 5:00 p.m, last Saturday evening, to Dorothy Riley and left about 9:00 p.m. that night for points unknown—at least to us. Don't know when he will return, but expect him to be gone about three weeks." This marriage was a partnership that lasted until Dorothy Heinkel's death in 1989. She participated in many MFA activities and played the organ at MFA conventions as well as at church. She was friendly and good at public relations, and she assisted Fred Heinkel in many ways.

During these years of business growth, MFA was also busy on the legislative front. In the July 15, 1946, issue of *The Missouri Farmer,* a lead story reported:

> Probably for the first time in the history of MFA we scored one hundred per cent at Jefferson City in the past session of the legislature. Every bill we supported was passed, and every bill we opposed was killed. We supported an amendment to the sales tax law, which provided exemption to feeds, seeds, and fertilizer. We opposed the medical school bill, which would have split up the University's Medical School by taking two years of it to Kansas City.

Early in 1947, the research director Haag presented a report to the MFA board of directors on the status of rural roads in Missouri. Sappington drew up a constitutional amendment (known as Joint Resolution 6), and Senator J. E. Curry of Ava introduced it to the state legislature. Under the terms of the amendment, the state gasoline tax would increase from two cents to three and a half cents per gallon, with one cent of the additional tax to be shared equally by cities and counties on the basis of vehicle registrations, and the remaining one-half cent to be allocated to counties as grants for maintaining and surfacing roads. Although the amendment passed the legislature, voters turned it down, large majorities in Kansas City and St. Louis proving unwilling to share funds for rural roads.

In 1947 the MFA convention, at which Heinkel and Hatcher were reelected, was moved from Sedalia to Brewer Field House on the campus of the University of Missouri in Columbia. It would continue to be held there until 1958, when it was moved to the auditorium of Stephens College, also in Columbia, where it remained until 1972. MFA officers called the 1947 convention "our greatest convention, with 1,860 delegates registered, the most ever." Attendance was 5,000; membership, 117,000; savings, $135,000; and net worth, $654,000. During the year, the sale of certificates of indebtedness was authorized for the first time for the Missouri Farmers Association itself, to furnish funds for a building to house *The Missouri Farmer,* for a seed plant at Marshall, and for the fertilizer manufacturing plant in Springfield. The authorized amount of the certificates was $500,000 at 5 percent interest.

During the 1940s one of the outstanding MFA leaders was Ed Schelp, manager of the cooperative elevator for the Emma and Sweet Springs area and one of the group of exchange managers that had visited Heinkel when he first assumed the presidency. In 1947 the Emma Cooperative Elevator Company had sales of almost $2 million and savings of $80,000, each probably a record for a farmers exchange. Schelp was offered bigger jobs in MFA, including management of MFA wholesale agencies, but he always turned them down because of his affection for the folks around Emma and Sweet Springs.

In the late 1940s a transportation section was started. Dale Janssen, an employee of the MFA Plant Foods plant in Maryland Heights, assisted Herman Haag in gathering information for establishing the department. Janssen came to Columbia in 1952 to work full-time in that area, and in 1955 a separate MFA Transportation Division was started with George Ross of St. Joseph as manager.

Ross had been with the Burlington Railroad for eighteen years, and his first big assignment with MFA was securing boxcars for the shipment of grain. This was before hopper cars were available, and grain losses en route were plentiful; thus filing claims was a major function of the Transportation Division. Other functions included obtaining reduced rail rates and opposing abandonment of branch lines serving MFA exchanges and elevators.

In 1965 MFA hired another experienced transportation expert, Lowell Morse of Kansas City, who had worked sixteen years with Missouri Pacific. With his expertise in in-transit rates, one of Morse's first duties was the handling of traffic matters at the MFA Feed Mill in St. Joseph. He became head of the division in 1979 and vice president of distribution in 1980.

The Transportation Division not only dealt with railroads, trucking firms, barge lines, and steamship companies but was also responsible for purchasing and maintaining company-owned or -leased rolling stock. By the early 1990s, MFA had approximately seven hundred trucks and cars. It is difficult to quantify savings made by the Transportation Division (those savings appear in earnings of Operating Divisions), but they have been considerable. Much credit goes to the highly capable managers of that division, George Ross and Lowell Morse.

Evidence that MFA continued to grow throughout the forties was the borrowing of $800,000 from the St. Louis Bank for Cooperatives in 1948 and the authorized sale of certificates of indebtedness for up to $1.5 million. The money was to be used for a new fertilizer plant in Maryland Heights, stockyards in Springfield, an addition to the MFA office building, and a seed processing plant in Marshall.

Following World War II, petroleum products had become scarce, and MFA Oil Company had problems in securing an adequate supply. In 1948 the company purchased another refinery, Delta Refining Company, of Memphis, Tennessee, at a cost of $1.25 million. The goal of $500,000 in MFA Oil Company certificates was oversubscribed. In addition to supplying products for Missouri patrons, MFA Oil Company began to distribute products in the mid-South area, including portions of Tennessee, Arkansas, Alabama, and Mississippi.

At the 1948 convention, MFA dues, which had been lowered from $2.50 to $1.00 during the depression years of the 1930s, were increased to $2.00. Membership totaled 126,000, and the net gain for the fiscal year was $86,000, bringing net worth up to $740,000. During the year, $800,000 in certificates of indebtedness were sold, and Heinkel and Hatcher were reelected president and vice president. That convention saw the first presentation of the Distinguished Service to Agriculture Awards, which had been created by the MFA board to be presented each year at the convention. The first awards went to Congressman Clarence Cannon, Senator Arthur Capper of Kansas, and Dean Emeritus M. F. Miller of the University of Missouri College of Agriculture.

A significant addition to the staff of MFA occurred in 1949 with the employment of William Beckett as the number-two man in the Law Department. Beckett, a native of Boonville, was a graduate of the University of Missouri Law School and was teaching there when hired by A. D. Sappington, general counsel of MFA. Beckett had a quick mind and ranked first in his graduating class. He also had a brilliant record in the armored division during World War II. He would play an important role in MFA's business and legislative activities for the next nineteen years, eventually taking Sappington's place as MFA's general counsel. Later Beckett became vice president of MFA, as well as executive vice president.

At the 1949 annual convention, Heinkel and Hatcher were reelected by acclamation. Sales reported were $8.8 million, net savings were $196,800, and net worth was $936,000. The Plant Foods, Farm Supply, and Packing Divisions were leaders in volume of sales. Sales for all MFA agencies (including creameries, produce plants, feed mills, farmers exchanges) totaled $225 million with savings of $350,000 and net worth of $15 million. It had been a busy decade.

Chapter Eight

MFA in the 1950s

In the January 1951 issue of *The Missouri Farmer,* Heinkel looked back ten years and forward ten years. For the previous ten years he enumerated the following accomplishments: a fourfold increase in both volume of business and membership; four new milk processing plants; two additional feed mills; two oil refineries; a soybean processing plant; a livestock breeding association; a mutual insurance company; a new home office building; a modern seed processing plant; two fertilizer manufacturing plants; two tire recapping plants; two farm supply warehouses; a stockyard; and a packing plant. Then Heinkel listed his goals for the next ten years: one hundred additional farmers exchanges; terminal grain storage facilities; a revamped livestock marketing system; an additional fertilizer plant; a new supply warehouse; the appointment of county legislative committees; the conversion of *The Missouri Farmer* to a weekly magazine; and a training program for managers.

The 1950s would see a growth in membership from 120,000 to more than 150,000, a jump in sales from $11.3 million to more than $50 million, and an increase in net worth from just under $1 million to $9 million. Heinkel was elected president each year during the decade without opposition. Roy Hatcher served as vice president until his death on January 14, 1952. He was succeeded by L. O. Wallis of Springfield, who served until his retirement in 1967. Wallis, an MFA leader in southwest Missouri, had been president of Producers Creamery Company for many years and a board member of other MFA agencies.

Further centralization of major plants and wholesale agencies of Missouri Farmers Association continued in the 1950s. The Artificial Breeding Association of Springfield and Producers Produce Company of Shelbina both became part of MFA. MFA Grain and Feed Company of St. Joseph and Producers Grain Commission Company of St. Louis became a part of the MFA Grain Division. Also, ownership in interregional cooperatives continued to expand. MFA became a stockholder in Mississippi Chemical Corporation of Yazoo City and built a terminal elevator in Kansas City in conjunction with Farmers Union of Nebraska.

The business activities of the Plant Foods Division became increasingly important during the decade. Near the end of 1952 the MFA board of directors made a decision to raise $2.5 million through the sale of certificates of indebtedness, to be used to invest in Central Farmers Fertilizer Company, grain terminals, and another addition to the home office building. By the end of the decade, MFA had thirteen bulk fertilizer plants, with board authorization for twenty-five additional plants.

The certificates of indebtedness issued in 1952 were also used to finance a large fertilizer manufacturing plant in Joplin. In August 1953, a large group of MFA officials attended a cornerstone laying at that new plant. In the manufacturing process, waste smelter gases from Eagle-Picher's nearby plant would be made into sulfuric acid and then piped to MFA's unit to be mixed with rock phosphate, potash, and ammonia to produce more than 70,000 tons of complete and mixed fertilizers per year. The plant was estimated to cost $3.5 million, and Walter Horn, originally from St. Louis County, was hired to manage it. In 1959, the board of directors placed the Joplin plant in a new cooperative, Farmers Chemical Company, with Consumers Cooperative Association (CCA) owning 75 percent and MFA 25 percent. This division of ownership reflected the volume of products purchased from the plant. In coming years, the plant would expand to a capacity of 140,000 tons.

To operate more efficiently and to produce higher octane gasoline,

MFA Oil Company added a catalytic cracking unit at the Delta Refining Company in Memphis, Tennessee. An open house and dedication of the completed unit in September 1953 drew more than a thousand members and employees to the ceremony conducted inside a large tent on the refinery grounds. A few years later, MFA Oil Company sold both the Chanute, Kansas, refinery, which had been owned since 1943, and Delta Refining Company of Memphis, Tennessee, owned since 1948. Both plants were sold for slightly more than book value after having shown small earnings for the entire period of operation. Their chief value had been in their assurance of a source of supply as MFA Oil Company expanded through the building of bulk oil plants and service stations in Arkansas, Mississippi, Alabama, and Tennessee.

In 1959 MFA made a change in the method of delegate representation whereby local cooperatives such as farmers exchanges, bulk oil plants, and creameries—rather than the farm clubs that had served as the focus of the association for so many years—became the units for the election of delegates.

The Legislative Front

Throughout the 1950s, legislative issues remained an important focus of MFA. Early in 1950 MFA began to work through Congress to alleviate the squeeze play by major oil companies on independent and cooperative oil companies. MFA executives first called a meeting of cooperative oil companies in Des Moines, but after much discussion there was little action. MFA and MFA Oil Company, with the assistance of Congressman Clarence Cannon, then called on Congress for a Federal Trade Commission investigation of the major oil companies that were diverting profits from refining and marketing into their crude-oil production area, on which they enjoyed a 27.5 percent depletion allowance.

On May 23, 1950, a subcommittee of the House Interstate and Foreign Commerce Committee held a hearing on Cannon's resolution. Cannon was ill that day, but he appeared nevertheless and spoke for an hour and a half without notes. Then A. D. Sappington read a forty-five-minute prepared statement, after which he answered questions for about two hours. The subcommittee took no action on the resolution, but the hearing did attract a considerable amount of attention. Shortly thereafter, margins at the refining level were substantially helped by changes in the pricing practices of the major oil companies.

On May 22, 1951, John Carson, of the Federal Trade Commission, wrote to Klinefelter:

> I promised sometime ago to write to you for your personal information, or the information of your Board, a report on a conversation I had with one of the lawyers who represents a rather large investment in the oil industry.
>
> The lawyer came into the Commission to talk about another case that is before us and which is not related to the oil industry. After he concluded that business, I asked him what reports he was getting from his oil companies, and he told me that the re-adjustment in prices had assured his company and others of an opportunity to live, at least, and he thought that conditions were very good as of that date, which was only a few months ago. He then began to discuss the period prior to the readjustment and made one remark at least which indicated he wanted to relate his thought to the condition in the cooperative oil companies. He indicated some degree of sympathy with the cooperative groups. Then he said that he assumed that their financial situation had improved greatly, as had the situation of the other oil companies, particularly other independents. I asked him what caused the revision of the prices, and he looked at the floor for a few minutes, and then raised his eyes and said with a smile, and a little laugh, that "there was no doubt it was because of the Cannon Resolution." I asked him if he really thought that, and he said there was no doubt in his mind that that was true. He continued by saying that he thought some day the oil industry would begin to realize that the cooperatives could not be destroyed, and that they would become an increasingly important factor in the industry.
>
> I know that you and your associates believe that the Cannon Resolution had been most effective in saving your oil business

from red figures. I hope that other cooperatives will appreciate
how much was accomplished through your initiative.

In 1952 President Harry Truman appointed Heinkel to serve as a
member of the Missouri Basin Survey Commission. This commission
was a study group to determine if development and flood control
throughout the Missouri River basin could be achieved in a manner
similar to that of the Tennessee Valley Authority. Heinkel had been
critical of the work of the U.S. Army Corps of Engineers, its handling
of flood problems along the Missouri River, and its rivalries with other
federal and state agencies, and he believed that a more unified authority would better meet the needs of the region. Meetings of the committee required both rail and boat travel throughout the area adjacent
to the Missouri River. Heinkel enjoyed his work on this committee
more than any similar undertaking.

In 1953, Heinkel received another appointment, this one from the
governor of Missouri, to serve on the board of curators of the University of Missouri. At the same time, A. D. Sappington was appointed a
member of the State Highway Commission, where he would serve for
nine years.

By January 1951, MFA legislative committees with ninety-five hundred committee members had been established in seventy-two counties. MFA mailed out a flood of material to the committee members,
including a publication entitled *The Beacon,* and held regional meetings with members of the legislature. On a regular basis until his death
in 1956, Klinefelter sent out letters or bulletins detailing relevant
activities of the state legislature and Congress. Thereafter, William
Beckett replaced Klinefelter as secretary of the MFA state and national
legislative committee. And Randall Kitt, an attorney and former legislator from Chillicothe, was employed part-time to represent MFA in
Jefferson City.

Action by MFA in 1952 prevented election of Missouri congressmen
by voting conducted at-large rather than by districts. Ray Derr, in
Missouri Farmers in Action, described the issue.

Because of technicalities, a referendum petition submitted
to the Secretary of State would have forced all candidates for

Congress to run at large, and in the opinion of the MFA leaders, would have meant domination by St. Louis and Kansas City political machines.

The Association's legislative committee, President Heinkel, R. J. Rosier, J. M. Silvey, and H. E. Klinefelter brought suit in the Cole County Court to contest the legality of the referendum.

Upheld there, the case was carried to a higher court where the Association won a second victory, and in the August election, candidates were nominated in their respective districts.[1]

On another issue, a report from A. D. Sappington at the April 2, 1952, MFA board of directors meeting confirmed that the "MFA did much to secure an apportionment for a four-year medical school in Columbia." Herman Haag also contributed to this project through a research report, which pointed out the benefits that would accrue to rural Missouri if the medical school—in the process of being expanded from two years to four years—was located in Columbia rather than in St. Louis or Kansas City.

One of the most severe droughts in years struck Missouri in 1953. Extremely hard hit were livestock and dairy farmers because of the resulting shortage of hay. Through the efforts of Governor Phil Donnelly and L. C. "Clell" Carpenter, the state commissioner of agriculture, the State of Missouri appropriated $6.5 million to bring hay into the state. Further help came from the railroads, which cut freight rates in half. MFA Milling Company of Springfield played the largest role in the purchase and distribution of more than 480,000 tons of hay, without charging a dime for its services. Local farmers exchanges also engaged in the distribution process without charging a fee of any sort. In 1954 MFA gave its distinguished service awards to Governor Donnelly and to Clell Carpenter.

Carpenter, who had been both the state and national head of the Farmers Home Administration, ran for governor in 1954 but withdrew and shortly thereafter was hired by MFA. He aided the formation and management of the MFA Livestock Association but later spent most of his time as legislative representative in both Jefferson City and Washington, D.C. (Appendix 2 herein provides a brief history of the MFA

Livestock Association.) He became one of Heinkel's closest confidants and was very effective in legislative affairs.

On the national scene Heinkel and Sappington were in constant touch with legislators and other farm organizations about farm legislation. In November 1957 MFA held a series of seven regional legislative conferences that dealt with national farm policies, income decreases, and other farm problems.

The People

The decade of the 1950s saw the departure of many longtime MFA employees as well as the arrival of new employees who would be important leaders in the years to come. In 1951 Jack Hackethorn, a graduate of the University of Missouri School of Journalism, joined the staff of MFA as director of information. A colorful personality, Hackethorn had a background in photojournalism dating back to the Roosevelt presidency, and he had also worked for newspapers in Detroit and St. Louis. Before joining MFA, he served two years as executive secretary of the Missouri Democratic Party, and he had a large number of friends in both the newspaper business and the political arena. Hackethorn was skilled in getting newspapers and radio and television stations throughout Missouri to carry stories and pictures of MFA activities. An avid reader of many newspapers, he kept a flow of clippings moving through the mail to MFA officials and to political contacts.

At the MFA Milling Company annual meeting in 1951 Alex Drier, NBC news commentator, was the principal speaker. In his remarks, Drier, whose network commentary was sponsored by Skelly Oil Company, praised MFA Milling Company and the cooperative way of doing business. Before the day was over, we learned that he had received a "dressing down" from his sponsor, Shell Oil Company, which did not think too highly of cooperatives.

MFA lost one of its outstanding early leaders when W. S. Miller, "the Fighting Farm Club leader of St. James," retired as manager of the St. James Farmers Exchange in 1952. He died in 1956 at the age of seventy-eight. Miller was an imposing, dignified figure, but always friendly. I had come to know him when I attended and spoke at several annual meetings of the St. James exchange. A hands-on manager, Miller always knew the volume of sales of each department for the preceding day.

In September 1953, Frank Young, manager of MFA Packing Division in Springfield, attended the dedication of the catalytic cracking unit in Memphis and the following day suffered a fatal heart attack. Young had played an important role in the early history of MFA as manager of Farmers Livestock Commission Company, and both Hirth and Heinkel called on him frequently because of his extensive knowledge of livestock and of other matters. He was succeeded as manager of the Packing Division by Jack O'Bryant, a longtime employee of the Springfield plant. In the early 1960s the Packing Division opened a plant in Macon, but a prolonged strike hampered its operations, and MFA sold that facility in 1969. O'Bryant retired from the Springfield plant in 1970, and Ron Walser, an experienced manager in the meat-packing business, replaced him. Ron retired in 1974 and was succeeded by Robert Feyen, who managed the plant until it closed in 1977 because of continued losses in the slaughter operation.

A well-known MFA employee, Harold Brooks of Macon, got his start in the Farm Supply Division in 1953. He began as salesman for the division in north Missouri. Shortly thereafter, the new Commodity Division combined sales of all items—feed, seed, fertilizer, and farm supplies—under each of the twenty-one salesmen. Brooks later became the program's supervisor. During his career he was also manager of the MFA Tire Division and later a field secretary. His competence and cheerful, friendly attitude made Brooks a valuable employee.

Another longtime employee, Albert Smith, worked his way up through the Supply Division and retired in 1992 after more than forty-five years with MFA. Smith started as an employee of farmers exchanges at California, Pilot Grove, and Sedalia. Like Brooks, he was a salesman for all divisions for a short time. Thereafter he worked for the Seed Division before becoming district manager and then sales manager in the Exchange Division, manager of Market Expansion, and sales manager of Field Crops. Both Smith and Brooks were talented musicians who often served after-hours duty as performers.

H. E. Klinefelter, editor of *The Missouri Farmer*, died in 1956. Klinefelter had been nationally known and respected by farm leaders and editors. News of his death prompted comments from many of them. Kit Haynes of the National Council of Farmer Cooperatives said:

> Through his keen insight into agricultural problems and his farsighted judgment he made an outstanding contribution to American agriculture and to activities of farmer coops. His outstanding work as editor of "The Missouri Farmer" and in the conduct of other affairs of MFA, with which he was directly concerned, will always be an inspiration to all of us.

Jim Patton, president of the National Farmers Union, noted:

> I am deeply regretful and sorrowed by the passing of H. E. Klinefelter. Kline made a great contribution during his life to the welfare of people and especially to the welfare of farm families. He will be missed by all of us, but his deeds will be a living memorial to a life of good and worthwhile effort.

Jerry Voorhis, executive director of the Cooperative League, summarized the feelings of many.

> The bad news has arrived. Kline's death leaves a big gap in the ranks of those men and women who constantly prod their fellowmen to greatness. He was forceful and effective, and he used those talents selflessly to promote a larger brotherhood. He was a great man.

In his honor, the cooperative editors established an annual H. E. Klinefelter Award for contributions in the field of cooperative writings.

Following Klinefelter's death, Glenn Hensley took over as editor of *The Missouri Farmer*. Under Hensley's leadership, the magazine enjoyed national recognition, winning first prize at the National Council of Farmer Cooperatives Information Fair for five years in a row.

In 1956, Jack Silvey resigned as general manager of MFA Operating

Divisions to devote full time to MFA Mutual Insurance Companies. He was succeeded by Homer Darby, a native of Buffalo, Missouri, who had worked for MFA Milling Company and for the MFA Auditing Department for two years before joining the navy in 1942. When he returned in 1946, he became assistant manager of MFA Central Cooperative, and then manager of MFA Farm Supply Division in 1949. When Darby became general manager of MFA Operating Divisions in 1956, Jim Heether replaced him in the Farm Supply Division. In Darby's new job, he reported to a newly formed management committee consisting of Heinkel, Rosier, Sappington, and Silvey.

Among other comings and goings, Maurice Maze, manager of the soybean plant in Mexico, was selected to head MFA Employee Training and was succeeded in Mexico by Kermit Head. William Beckett left MFA to join a law firm in Kansas City for one year, then returned to the MFA Law Department in 1957. He succeeded A. D. Sappington as general counsel of MFA when Sappington resigned to become general counsel for MFA Insurance Companies (which had been called MFA Mutual Insurance Company prior to 1957). Herman Haag resigned in 1957 to accept a position with the Ford Foundation in Burma. Jim Halsey, from the MFA Organization Department, moved into the position of manager of MFA Livestock Association in 1959.

Following the death of Clyde Morwood in 1956, Ormal Creach was named chief auditor of MFA in 1957 after having been an MFA auditor since 1944. A native of Mack's Creek, Creach encouraged auditors to become certified public accountants. He offered increased salaries as an inducement, and as a result most of the auditors became CPAs. Subsequently in his career in MFA, Creach became controller and then general manager of MFA Central Cooperative, and later secretary-treasurer of MFA, MFA Oil Company, and MFA Livestock Association. He was also president of the MFA Foundation, created in 1958, and served as president of the National Society of Accountants for Cooperatives. He was one of the best-known and most-respected officials in MFA.

The MFA Auditing Department played an important role in the success of MFA. It was a training ground for MFA leaders, including Russell J. Rosier, John F. Johnson, Jack Silvey, Joe Goeke, Ormal

Creach, Paul Keithley, George Kent, Gene Packwood, Larry Fick, Don Copenhaver, Dave Jobe, and me, to name just a few. Upon completion of an audit, the auditors always met with the board of directors to explain the financial statement and to offer suggestions for improvement of operations. As openings occurred in various positions in the MFA, the auditors could recommend persons to fill those vacancies.

In 1957, Clarence Gonnerman was named manager of MFA Poultry and Egg Division, which had begun in the early fifties, with the responsibility of selling its plants at Shelbina, St. Louis, Union, and Sedalia, all of which had been absorbed by MFA because of financial difficulties. And he did so successfully. He had previously worked several years for William T. Crighton in the MFA Dairy Products Company. Gonnerman then left MFA to run his father's business in Iowa; after selling it, he was offered jobs by both MFA and Producers Creamery Company. He went to Columbia to work for the Poultry and Egg Division and later became head of Management Services and then credit manager of the Exchange Division, where he remained until his retirement in 1981.

The other men who served as managers of operating divisions during the middle 1950s were Herman Schulte, continuing as head of the Seed Division; Art Loutch, Grain and Feed Division; Loryn McQuerter, Plant Foods Division; Vern Lloyd, Tire Division; Henry Strid, Farm Supply Division; and F. G. Stevenson, Dairy Breeders Division (originally MFA Artificial Breeding Association, started in January 1946). Under their leadership, a large team of employees saw to the day-to-day operations of all the divisions of the association.

Chapter Nine

Reorganization

The 1960s

There was much excitement around the MFA offices in Columbia during the third week of December 1960. At the request of President-elect John F. Kennedy, Heinkel made two quick trips to Washington, D.C.—his first airline travel—to discuss the prospective appointment of Heinkel as secretary of agriculture. Kennedy had had his eye on Heinkel during his election campaign, as a letter he wrote Heinkel on August 16, 1960, reveals.

> I have heard many fine things about you, about your knowledge of agriculture, and about the eminent position you hold in the minds of all who are interested in and knowledgeable about agriculture policy in our country. . . . I hope you will attend our meeting of the midwestern states in Des Moines on August 21, and sometime when you are in Washington, I hope you will give me a call.

According to Hilton Bracey, a later MFA employee who was at this time executive vice president of the Missouri Cotton Producers Association, Missouri senator Stuart Symington was instrumental in arranging for the December meeting between Heinkel and Kennedy. I have heard it said that for forty-eight hours Heinkel actually was secretary of agriculture. When Heinkel was not appointed, Symington asked

Kennedy the reason. Kennedy's reply was, "He is a little too old for this administration." It was also rumored that Robert Kennedy advised against Heinkel's appointment and in favor of that of Governor Orville Freeman of Minnesota, largely because Freeman had been defeated as a candidate for senator and thus deserved an appointment. *The Missouri Farmer* reported, "When asked by reporters about the cabinet post, Heinkel stated that he was not seeking nor campaigning for the spot, and that is the way it was. He was neither anxious for the job nor disappointed when Orville Freeman was named to it. Missouri Senators and Congressmen left no stone unturned in their support of Heinkel for the position."[1]

At the annual MFA convention in 1960, during the election campaign, Congressman Clarence Cannon had indicated his high esteem for Heinkel.

> I tell you there is no farm organization man in the U.S. who stands higher [than,] or has the confidence of the Congressional Committees in both the House and the Senate [more than,] Mr. Heinkel. In the first place, he knows what he is talking about. He has been all along the road himself, and he speaks from first hand knowledge. He has the best trained men anywhere working on these problems and keeping up with the times. And most important of all, you can depend on what he says.[2]

In 1961 Secretary Freeman appointed Heinkel chairman of the Feed and Grain Committee of the Department of Agriculture. In an article in the March 1961 issue of *The Missouri Farmer,* Heinkel explained that he had accepted the position because of his concern about declining feed grain prices and their effect on farm prices in general. Serving on the committee allowed him to promote his belief "that food should be more effectively used both here at home and abroad—in this country, through direct distribution to the needy and through a food stamp plan; abroad, by more realistic recognition of the aid which could be contributed by our agricultural abundance in the battle for peace."

During the early 1960s, new and expanded facilities were the order of the day for the Missouri Farmers Association. The number of bulk fertilizer plants and anhydrous ammonia plants each quickly grew to thirty-five. A joint venture of the Missouri Farmers Association and MFA Oil Company was the Newcomer Corporation, designed to supply seeds, fertilizer, and pesticides to seed and garden stores. After a few years the company was merged into MFA Oil Company to take advantage of its loss carryforward.

The following comparative figures emphasize the growth of all MFA agencies between 1939 and 1961:

	1939	1961
Assets	$ 6,800,000	$ 99,500,000
Net Worth	4,600,000	46,300,000
Sales	49,000,000	352,600,000
Savings	835,000	6,400,000
Members	26,659	160,717

Savings for the entire period amounted to $104 million for all agencies. Elevators at 165 locations had twenty-four million bushels of storage capacity. MFA Milling Company of Springfield continued its growth. In 1961, feed production there totaled 12,375,000 hundred-pound bags, the largest in history. This translated into sales of $34 million, with savings for the year of $1,325,000. For the previous twelve years MFA Milling Company had paid cash refunds in excess of $1 million per year. The cost of producing a hundred-pound bag of feed was $.16, the lowest in the nation.

MFA Oil Company at its 1962 annual meeting announced that for the thirty-third consecutive year sales volume had increased over the previous year. Missouri Farmers Association transferred its wholesale tire operations to MFA Oil Company, which also began handling propane, with plants at Sweet Springs, Maysville, Stockton, and Willow Springs.

A new solvent extraction soybean plant began operation in Mexico, Missouri, during 1962 under the management of Kermit Head. The capacity of the new plant was fifteen thousand bushels per day. The old expeller plant had been crushing three thousand bushels per day.

In addition to the new facilities, there was, as Heinkel stated, "the matter of influence in state and national affairs. The MFA is respected because it has been consistent in objectives and because it speaks with the weight of over 160,000 members. The state sales tax exemption of 2 percent means $5,000,000 per year for farmers; gasoline tax exemption of 5¢ per gallon amounts to $6,000,000 per year." In early 1962 Heinkel called a conference of farm leaders to meet in St. Louis and consider proposed national farm legislation; 127 representatives of fifty organizations from twenty-two states attended. In 1965 there was a similar meeting in Kansas City, and on March 20, 1966, more than 400 attended a meeting in St. Louis called by Heinkel "to develop fruitful communication among farm organizations through the nation."

Heinkel's election in 1962 to the executive committee of the National Council of Farmer Cooperatives gave further evidence of his recognition as a national farm leader. Before the decade was over, he again served as vice president of the organization.

The early 1960s was also a time for looking back. In 1960, Producers Produce Company of Springfield turned forty years old. In *The Missouri Farmer* of April 1961, the long-term manager of the company, Lee Farnham, told of the early days of the cooperative, which opened for business on July 10, 1920, and was originally called the Farm Club Cold Storage Company.

> Our goal has been to transform poultry and eggs into whatever will make the most possible money for the farmer producers. Our aim during the past forty-one years has not been to see how cheap we could buy poultry and eggs from the farmers, but, instead, to see how much we could pay for these products. Poultry was shipped live to New York City, Boston, and Philadelphia. The plant began dressing poultry in the late 1930s, but continued to ship live poultry until 1935. When we first started dressing poultry, we just killed and removed the feathers. This was known as "New York dressed." From 1935 to 1940, eviscerated poultry started coming into style. We didn't do much with eggs in the beginning except [accumulate] them in carload lots of 400 cases and ship them to market. By 1927 it was necessary for us to open up an egg-

breaking department to handle the dirty and checked eggs that wouldn't go out as number-one eggs. The plant today has facilities to break from 3,500 to 4,000 cases of eggs per day.

Four years later, in 1964, MFA celebrated its own fiftieth anniversary. In the December 1962 issue of *The Missouri Farmer*, reflecting on the upcoming event, Heinkel wrote:

> When the MFA first began to take shape, the idea behind its formation was not a new one. Its premise was simple—that by joint effort farmers could better their economic position. The significant thing was that dedicated men, beginning with William Hirth, a skillful writer and a practical philosopher, and going on down through the years with many hard-working and honest-to-goodness farmers, had enough forethought in this idea to make it work.
>
> And work it has. Today MFA members own plants to manufacture feeds and fertilizer; plants to process milk, meat, poultry, and eggs; facilities through which to market livestock and grain; an insurance company operating in twelve states; a complete distribution system to supply themselves with petroleum products, tires, seeds, and other farm supplies.
>
> The assets of these MFA cooperatives exceed $90,000,000. Their combined sales now top $350,000,000 annually, and the savings resulting have been as much as $8,000,000 a year.
>
> In fact, the MFA is commonly recognized as the largest business in the state and the most diversified cooperative in the nation. In 1962, there were more than 160,000 MFA members who owned and operated 250 cooperatives, which make up the MFA family.

In 1964, Governor John M. Dalton proclaimed March 5–12 as MFA Week in celebration of the association's golden anniversary. A highlight of the anniversary celebration was the unveiling of an oil painting entitled *Genesis: MFA* by Sid Larson of Christian College in Columbia. The painting, depicting the first farm club meeting in the Newcomer School House on March 10, 1914, includes the likenesses of the seven men who attended that meeting, a copy of *The Missouri Farmer*, and the Great Seal of the State of Missouri, with the wording

"United We Stand." The painting now hangs in a meeting room in the MFA headquarters building in Columbia. Thirty-six hundred farmers purchased a special anniversary MFA membership for ten dollars.

The balance of the decade saw a focus on organizational changes in MFA. A letter from the MFA's auditing firm, Arthur Andersen and Company, to Secretary Russell J. Rosier in 1961 reveals that the management structure was a problem.

> Lines of authority and reporting responsibility, as shown on the organization chart, may appear for the most part to be clearly defined. It is our impression that these lines are not all clearly defined.
>
> As an example, the division managers of grain and feed, packing, and state exchanges reportedly report to the general manager. In actual practice, they generally report direct to the management committee.

The auditing firm also pointed out that even though volume of sales had increased, net savings after 1955 presented "a grim picture. Per cent of savings to assets employed is regarded as unsatisfactory." Year after year losses occurred in certain profit centers, including the poultry and egg operations at Sedalia and Shelbina, the Tire Division, and State Exchanges. By 1963, sales of MFA itself were $88 million, with savings of $820,000, of which $225,000 constituted patronage dividends paid back in cash to members. In 1964 the gain was only $408,000. The Grain Division showed a loss of $43,000, the Packing Division a loss of $100,000, and the Poultry and Egg Division a loss of $115,000. Patronage dividends paid were $544,000.

In 1963, Homer Darby resigned as general manager of Operating Divisions of MFA in order to join Mississippi Chemical Corporation in Yazoo City. Following his departure, the position of general manager was abolished, and the managers of the individual divisions reported to the management committee, the executive committee, and the board of directors. In the middle 1960s Operating Divisions consisted of MFA Breeding Service, Farm Supply, Feed, Grain, Packing, Plant Foods, Seed, Poultry and Egg, and State Exchanges.

In 1964 First Missouri Corporation was formed to replace MFA

Facilities Corporation, which owned the fixed assets leased to MFA agencies. The original capital for First Missouri Corporation, $375,000, was furnished by MFA Insurance Companies, MFA Oil Company, and the Missouri Farmers Association. Two of the principal assets were *The Missouri Farmer* building and a travel agency operated by the MFA Transportation Division. MFA gained ownership of the travel agency as the result of a debt owed to MFA.

In the same year, MFA purchased a 25 percent interest in Cooperative Farm Chemicals Association (CFCA) of Lawrence, Kansas, from Central Farmers Fertilizer Company for $6 million. The remaining 75 percent was owned by Consumer Cooperative Association. This highly efficient plant, producing one thousand tons of nitrogen daily, was an excellent investment.

The staff of *The Missouri Farmer* in the middle 1960s consisted of Richard Collins, editor; David Bryant, associate editor (he would later be editor); and Mike Graznak, managing editor. Jack Hackethorn also contributed articles in his capacity as director of information. In 1964 an article by Leslie Stice, a grain marketing specialist at the University of Illinois, summarized the importance of Midwest farmers to national and international food production. "Last year, twelve midwest states accounted for 73% of all grain marketed in the U.S.; 85% of corn; 75% of wheat; 82% of oats; 55% of beans. Foreign markets for U.S. grain have boomed in recent years, and are of such importance that farmers and the grain trade in the midwest must take steps to serve and compete in these markets." He also pointed out the increase in grain moved by water and predicted that the volume of grain produced would increase; that farmers would demand more of the grain marketers; that country elevators would expand and modernize; and that the Mississippi River Valley would be an ideal location to capitalize on these predictions.

Taking advantage of the trends identified by Stice, MFA joined Farmers Union of St. Paul and Illinois Grain Company to form St. Louis Grain Company, with elevators on both sides of the Mississippi River. Later in the decade MFA joined with Farmers Union, Farmers Grain Dealers, Far-Mar-Co, Illinois Grain, Tennessee Farmers Coop, and Mississippi Federated in building the Farmers Export Company elevator in Ama, Louisiana, near New Orleans. The plant started operation in June 1969, and Heinkel served as chairman of the board for Farmers Export Company for several years.

MFA also expanded into grain marketing in southeast Missouri through the purchase of a grain elevator at Caruthersville with a capacity of 850,000 bushels and an elevator at Hayti with a capacity of 200,000 bushels. Later, the elevator at Caruthersville was expanded by 1 million bushels. Local managers included Delmar Stockton, Al Cravens, and Melvin Dowling.

William T. Crighton, manager of Producers Creamery Company in Springfield since its beginning in 1928, retired in 1964. The volume of sales that year was $40 million. Later that decade a Des Moines dairy cooperative merged with Producers Creamery. The directors of Producers Creamery, Sanitary Milk Products of St. Louis, and Square Deal Milk Producers of Highland, Illinois, voted to merge. The effective date of the merger, July 1, 1968, resulted in the formation of a large dairy cooperative, Mid-America Dairymen, known as Mid-Am. To provide capital, Mid-Am adopted a system of retaining four cents per hundredweight from all Class A milk producers. The first president and chairman of the board of the association was Bill Powell of Princeton. Crighton's successor at Producers Creamery, Wes Johnson, was the first general manager. Johnson retired in 1970 and was replaced by Jim Baldi, who served until 1975, when Gary Hanman became manager.

Before its incorporation into Mid-Am, Producers Creamery Company of Springfield had become the leader among dairies in research and development of products. For example, it had worked closely with Mead-Johnson on infant foods, and from 1958 to 1963 Producers Creamery Company manufactured a liquid diet product, Metrecal, at the Cabool plant. In his book, *First Twenty Years: The Story of Mid-America Dairymen,* Jim Reeves, former sales manager at Producers Creamery, writes: "The Mid-Am Research and Development (R&D) activity was inherited from one of the constituent coops (Producers Creamery Company) that was a party to the original Mid-Am merger. Looking back to the roots of the program, Burdett Heinmann would have to be remembered as the father of Mid-Am's R&D effort."[3]

The affiliation of Producers Creamery with MFA ended with the formation of Mid-Am. It had become a multistate operation, and the contribution to farmers in other states from affiliation with the Missouri Farmers Association was not important. In the early days all dairy farmers who were members of Producers Creamery were also members of MFA and received *The Missouri Farmer,* and the creamery employees were part of the MFA retirement plan. Leadership in legislative activities affecting dairymen was handled by MFA, and I can recall the time when MFA attorney William Beckett was regarded as one of the nation's experts on milk marketing orders.

A new sister cooperative, Midcontinent Farmers Association, was organized by MFA in 1965. The major reason for this action was to make expansion into neighboring states more acceptable by substituting *Midcontinent* for *Missouri* in the name of the organization. Another reason was the possibility that membership dues and insurance commissions received by MFA would be regarded by the Internal Revenue Service as nonmember income and thus subject to income tax. Transferring that income to Midcontinent would alleviate the problem, because the expenses of the new organization would be large enough to offset the income.

Membership in Missouri Farmers Association automatically included membership in Midcontinent Farmers Association. The boards of directors were identical, and the annual meetings were simultaneous. Income from dues, however, transferred to Midcontinent, as did the MFA emblem and the Insurance Department. Midcontinent also became the publisher of *The Missouri Farmer,* though the magazine remained the official organ of MFA.

In 1965 the MFA legislative committee consisted of Heinkel, William Beckett, A. D. Sappington, Russell J. Rosier, and Clell Carpenter. Delegate meetings were held annually for the purpose of discussing legislative matters and formulating policies. Field secretaries, along with Carpenter and Heinkel, conducted the meetings, which had a total attendance of three thousand to four thousand delegates. *Field secretary* was the term applied to traveling employees who helped farmers exchanges hold their annual meetings, met with local boards, planned and assisted in holding delegate meetings, had responsibilities at the annual convention, and "put out fires" in their territories. Field secretaries included Harold Brooks, Claud Bowles, Jim Evans, Jim Halsey, Guy Patton, and Art Wood. After Midcontinent Farmers Association was organized, the fieldmen became employees of that organization. Roy Reed and later David Thomas also worked for Midcontinent. Making sure that the right board members and officers in MFA were elected was one of the duties of the Midcontinent staff. But this group of MFA employees had no line responsibility in business operations, and so it was not surprising that some friction occurred.

In early 1966, the MFA board of directors named Clell Carpenter vice president of Midcontinent Farmers Association, and he also continued as director of public affairs for the Missouri Farmers Association. Carpenter served on the National Advisory Committee on Rural Area Development, the Governor's Committee on Watersheds and Flood Protection, the Advisory Committee of the Missouri College of Agriculture, and the Missouri Rural Areas Development Committee.

For the fiscal year 1965, savings totaled $1,548,000—the first year savings exceeded $1 million. The Plant Foods Division made $2.1 million, but State Exchanges lost $220,000, and the Poultry and Egg Division lost $65,000. Total sales for MFA were $91 million, and net worth was $10,575,000. Patronage dividends paid were $220,000. The audit report for the following year, 1966, showed sales of $113 million, savings of $1.5 million, and patronage refunds of $2.5 million received from interregionals. Patronage dividends paid were $600,000.

The top twenty farmers exchanges and managers in the mid-1960s, based on volume and earnings, were: Albany, Dale Gillespie; Bernie, Wayne Mitchell; Bolivar, Howard Hayter; Browning, Harley Hawkins; Buffalo, Lonnie Pitts; Centralia, Wendell Mustain; El Dorado Springs, George Barker; Greene County, Perry Martin; LaBelle, Sammy Day; Lebanon, Lawrence Wheeler; Lexington, Ranie Thompson; Marshall, Shelton Cunningham; Maryville, Hubert Gumm; Memphis, Gerald Porter; Neosho, Lyle Shorter; Perryville, Dave Kephart; Salisbury, Leroy Magruder; Shelbina, Kenneth Dolbeare; Unionville, Jack Johnson; and Vandalia, Leon Dempsey.

In 1965 the MFA board of directors organized Agricultural Money (AGMO) to provide credit to farmers through MFA agencies. Missouri

Farmers Association owned stock of $200,000, MFA Milling Company $100,000, and MFA Oil Company $100,000. Harold Baker was the first manager. Earlier, MFA had made an attempt, ultimately unsuccessful, to provide production loans to farmers in conjunction with Production Credit Association. AGMO was organized for the purpose not only of providing funds to farmers exchanges and other MFA agencies but also of encouraging better credit practices. In the first five years AGMO loaned $21 million through 158 exchanges.

An important step for expansion in southeast Missouri and northeastern Arkansas in 1966 was the formation of Planters Fertilizer Company and employment of Hilton Bracey as general manager. Bracey, of Portageville, had been executive vice president of the Missouri Cotton Producers Association for fourteen years and, prior to that time, chairman of the Missouri Agricultural Soil Conservation Service.

When Bracey joined MFA, the organization owned stock in Mississippi Chemical Corporation, giving MFA call on a certain tonnage of fertilizer. Planters Fertilizer Company was to be the vehicle for distributing that MCC fertilizer in southeast Missouri and northeast Arkansas. Shortly thereafter, MFA organized a network of more than fifty private fertilizer distributors known as MFA Delta Dealers, which became the avenue for moving plant foods to farmers. The use of fertilizer was new in that area, having reached large-scale use only in the 1960s. By the end of 1970, the MFA Delta Dealers in the area distributed over 50 percent of the fertilizer used in northeast Arkansas and southeast Missouri. In Pemiscot County, Missouri, MFA supplied 85 percent of the fertilizer. MCC owned a fertilizer warehouse in Hayti, in the Missouri bootheel, which Missouri Farmers Association purchased. Investment by MFA in Delta Dealers was small, and thus the return on investment was high. In one of the best years, the net return was more than $3 million on MFA Delta Dealers operations.

In 1966 speakers at the MFA convention were Senator Robert Dole of Kansas and Vice President Hubert Humphrey. Distinguished Service to Agriculture Awards were presented at the convention to Elmer Ellis, president of the University of Missouri, and Ovid Martin, a correspondent for the Associated Press and a native Missourian.

At the 1967 annual convention William Beckett was elected vice president, replacing the retiring L. O. Wallis, who had served for fifteen and a half years. At the convention, the sales for all MFA agencies were reported at $500 million, savings at $11.5 million, net worth at $78 million, and assets at $133 million. MFA itself showed sales of $127 million, with savings of $683,000.

In October 1967 a special board meeting was called to ratify several management changes. Bob McDonough resigned as manager of the Seed Division and became manager of Midcontinent Seed Company to handle outside sales. Herman Schulte resigned as vice president of MFA Central Cooperative and became vice president of the Seed Division. Ormal Creach resigned as chief auditor and controller and became vice president of MFA Central Cooperative. Marvin Young resigned as attorney and became vice president of operations of MFA Central Cooperative; Paul Parker became chief auditor; John Ekstrom became controller; Steve Lay became manager of MFA Farm Supply Division, following the death of Jim Heether; and Bill Ballew became vice president of the Fertilizer Division.

Among the activities of 1968, the city of Palmyra agreed to build a fertilizer plant and lease it to Missouri Farmers Association to replace the Maryland Heights plant, which was to be closed. And in July, Heinkel stated that the management committee had decided to give Beckett full responsibility for MFA Operating Divisions and the related staff of the controller's office, central accounting, and data processing. Also in July, Marvin Young, vice president of operations of MFA Central Cooperative, resigned to become vice president and chief counsel of Peabody Coal Company. He was replaced by Shelton Cunningham, manager of the farmers exchange at Marshall.

In early November 1968, I was called to meet with Heinkel, Rosier, and Sappington, who surprised me by offering me the position of executive vice president of Missouri Farmers Association. I was also surprised to learn that Beckett had resigned the position to engage in private practice and resume teaching at the University of Missouri Law School, which he would continue to do until his sudden death in 1975. I agreed to take the job, provided I could continue as the president of MFA Oil Company. My duties and salary were to be divided equally between MFA and MFA Oil Company; however, because of MFA's financial situation, the majority of my salary was paid by MFA Oil Company for a few years. As a logical austerity measure, I requested that the portion of my salary paid by MFA be halved.

The board of Missouri Farmers Association met on November 7, 1968, to confirm me as executive vice president. I became vice president of MFA and Midcontinent Farmers Association, as well as a board member of several interregionals, including CF Industries (as Central Farmers Fertilizer Company was then known), Farmers Export Company, and Cooperative Farm Chemicals Association.

The successor to William Beckett as general counsel was Alfred Hoffman, a veteran of twenty years with the organization. Hoffman, a native of Germany, was reared in St. Joseph and attended the University of Missouri. He finished his law degree in 1946, ranking second in his class, just behind Beckett. Hoffman joined MFA Mutual Insurance Company in 1948 and Missouri Farmers Association in 1950. He retired from MFA in 1982 but continued as counsel for MFA Oil Company until 1990. Hoffman "covered the waterfront" in legal matters for the organization and was particularly skilled in labor negotiations for MFA and most of its affiliates.

One of the first knotty problems to confront me was the operation of American Press, which had the primary function of printing *The Missouri Farmer.* The 1968 audit report had commented on an accumulated loss in American Press of $351,000. In the early part of December 1968, I was contacted by Jim Black of Lawrence, Kansas, inquiring about a position with American Press and the possibility of purchasing the operation. Black had several years experience in the printing business, and it was apparent that something needed to be done. There was a considerable investment in the plant with a negative return, and MFA simply could not afford that luxury. After considerable negotiations, I agreed to hire Black and give him an option to buy 49 percent of the capital stock of American Press.

Before I left on a two-week vacation in late December, I notified MFA officers of the arrangement with Black and asked for their approval. On returning, I found that the request had stirred up a hornet's nest, the chief concern being that MFA needed to retain control of the printing plant to make sure *The Missouri Farmer* was printed on time. I felt that perhaps I had been too optimistic about the freedom I would have in running the business affairs of MFA. Finally I received reluctant approval for this move, and in the first year American Press was profitable for the first time in several years. In a relatively short time the press secured much additional business, and the plant was operating at capacity. In 1971 the remaining 51 percent of the capital stock of American Press was sold to Black and his associates for $459,000, the approximate net worth.

When I became executive vice president in 1968, MFA Oil Company was ahead of MFA in areas such as management structure, salary and wage administration, and incentive plans for employees. One of the first moves I made was to hire Frank Stanton, a consultant from Minneapolis, to make a study of MFA's management structure and salary and wage administration, and to organize a personnel department. Within the first year, I had initiated changes that included establishing rigid controls on expenditures by utilizing a single purchasing facility; reducing operating costs through consolidation and streamlining of operations; and developing a sound wage and salary administration program.

To fill a void in management of MFA Supply and Marketing Divisions, I advertised for the position and eventually hired George Polly, of the fertilizer division of Standard Oil of Ohio, to be vice president of the MFA Supply and Marketing Divisions. Polly was responsible for the Plant Foods, Seed, Farm Supply, and Packing Divisions. Shortly thereafter, Bill Ballew, head of the Fertilizer Division, resigned, and Polly hired Al Lehmkuhl, who had also been with Standard Oil of Ohio, as manager of the Fertilizer Division. Two years later, in 1971, George Polly resigned under pressure from some quarters of MFA. Although highly competent in his field, Polly, as an outsider, was not able to fit into the organization. Since leaving MFA, he has enjoyed a successful career, and at the time of this writing, has completed a five-year assignment for M. W. Kellogg Company as managing director of a large fertilizer complex in Nigeria. Lehmkuhl left MFA shortly after Polly's departure and returned to Ohio, where he has been successful in operating his own farm supply business.

One of the department heads reporting to me when I assumed the position of executive vice president included John Ekstrom, vice president of finance. Previous to being employed by MFA, he had been with the Arthur Andersen auditing firm and had worked on the MFA audits. Other department heads who reported to me were: Otto Schulte, vice president of the Grain Division; Clarence Gonnerman, director of management services; Al Hoffman, vice president and general counsel; and Don Loso, director of employee relations. Loso came to MFA from FS Services of Illinois in 1969.

For fiscal year 1968, MFA had showed a loss of $400,000; patronage refunds received from interregionals were down to $1.9 million; net worth was $10.5 million; and long-term debt totaled $28 million. In contrast, for fiscal year 1969, MFA had a net gain of $100,000. This was in spite of patronage refunds from interregionals being down by $575,000. Beginning in 1970, the end of the fiscal year was changed from December 31 to August 31.

The overall growth in size of business activities in MFA during the 1960s was shown in the increase in total assets from $22 million to $60 million and in sales from $53 million to $104 million; however, net worth increased by only $1 million—from $9.6 million to $10.6 million. Perhaps the most significant factor in those increases during the decade had been MFA's increased participation in regional cooperatives.

Chapter Ten

MFA, a Good Neighbor

In addition to working for the financial benefit of cooperatives and their members, MFA has made being a good neighbor part of its mission from the beginning. Indeed, shortly after the formal organization of the association, Hirth called on MFA members to provide food baskets for the poor in St. Louis and Kansas City at Christmastime.

In a more general sense, the economic benefits of MFA extended not only to members but to nonmember farmers. For example, when a farmers exchange opened for business, the price paid in the area for produce such as chickens, eggs, and cream increased considerably. But at the same time, the cost of purchasing items such as binder twine, feed, and seed decreased, and competitors had to adjust their prices. Further, all Missouri taxpayers have benefited from MFA-supported legislation, including reductions in the numbers of courthouse employees, auditing of county records, and consolidation of county offices.

But perhaps the best-known public service activity of MFA is the MFA Foundation, a nonprofit Missouri corporation organized on February 3, 1958. The intriguing story of MFA Foundation begins with Robert O. Wurmb, a well-known union organizer in St. Louis who retired to a modest home and a few acres in St. Clair. There, Wurmb became acquainted with Vernie Emmons, the manager of MFA Farmers Elevator in St. Clair, and started attending MFA annual meetings. Wurmb became friends with many of MFA's top executives. So impressed was he with the organization and its people that he left most of his modest estate, twenty-eight thousand dollars, to MFA at his death. This became the seed money for the MFA Foundation.

For several years there was very little activity in the MFA Foundation. In 1964 Heinkel appointed a committee to develop a plan for the foundation and a program that all MFA agencies would be proud to sponsor. On the committee were Ormal Creach as chairman, Marvin Young, and William Toler of MFA Insurance Companies. Allan Purdy, director of Financial Aids and Awards for the University of Missouri, was asked to provide guidance in establishing a worthwhile program. The committee recommended that the foundation establish scholarships for high school seniors in areas where an MFA agency was willing to cosponsor the scholarship, which would allow a student to attend any accredited college or university of his or her choice.

The original scholarship was for $200, of which $100 was provided by the foundation and $100 by the local sponsoring MFA agency. As the fund grew, the amount paid to students increased to $1,000, with the foundation paying the entire sum and the local agency contributing $250 to the principal fund. Local committees of three to five persons were created to select the scholarship winners.

Whereas the MFA Foundation's main thrust is the college scholarship program, it also pursues other worthwhile projects. The foundation makes gifts to private colleges and contributes to schools for the handicapped and other programs consistent with the foundation's original purpose of providing educational opportunities for youth. Included in these programs are support for 4-H activities and for the Future Farmers of America, Young Farmers, and Young Farm Wives associations. The foundation has also made substantial contributions to the University of Missouri Medical School Library and School of Veterinary Medicine.

MFA Foundation funds have come from a number of sources, the largest of which has been unclaimed equities and refunds of MFA members. At the annual convention in 1974 a resolution was adopted to give the equities of members that could not be located at the end of ten years to the foundation. Other sources include surplus assigned by liquidating MFA agencies, contributions from MFA agencies and MFA employees, and bequests.

In 1992, scholarships to high school seniors totaled 253 (in 1994 they totaled 274). Virtually all of them were sponsored by farmers exchanges and MFA Oil Company bulk oil plants and propane plants. Since the beginning, more than six thousand scholarships have been provided.

Missouri Farmers Association has also played a role in helping to develop cooperatives in Third World countries around the globe. Unfortunately, most of those activities are not well known among MFA members. The largest single project was Cooperative Fertilizers International (CFI), involving MFA and other regional cooperatives. CFI was organized in 1967, with Don Thomas, a former employee of CF Industries, as president. American cooperatives donated $1 million to provide technical and managerial assistance in the building of a fertilizer complex in India. Thomas supervised building the complex at a total cost in excess of $100 million and within 5 percent of the original estimate. Completion of the project increased the capacity of Indian fertilizer production by 25 percent.

The Agricultural Cooperative Development International (ACDI) and the Volunteer Overseas Cooperative Assistance (VOCA) are organizations that contract with the Agency for International Development for projects involving cooperatives in Third World countries. As a board member of ACDI, I visited projects in Paraguay, the Philippines, Costa Rica, Egypt, Kenya, and Tanzania. After retirement, I had a six-week VOCA assignment as a consultant to FEDECOOP, a coffee cooperative in Costa Rica. A year later I did a four-week follow-up with the same cooperative. FEDECOOP had the reputation of being one of the best-managed cooperatives in Latin America, and in a number of respects it was well managed. In other respects, however, it reminded me of MFA back in the 1920s and 1930s, but progress was being made.

Other retired MFA employees who had assignments with VOCA were Al Hoffman, in the Philippines and Bulgaria; Harvey Strothman, also in the Philippines; and Hilton Bracey, in Hungary.

Chapter Eleven

MFA in the 1970s

For the short, eight-month fiscal year of 1970, there was a net gain of $937,000. In the December 1970 issue of *The Missouri Farmer,* Heinkel summarized the current state of the association's operations.

> During the first eight months of the year net savings from MFA supply and marketing operations amounted to about $1,017,000—it does reflect a sharp turn-around from the $620,000 loss experienced during the same period in 1969. Highly significant is the fact that savings were achieved despite the handicap of greatly inflated costs. If interest had been at the level of three years ago, MFA could have reported at least $600,000 in additional savings. . . .
>
> Sharing credit for the improved financial condition of MFA are two developments:
>
> > Increased sale of products and services—as a result of continued membership loyalty and stepped-up leadership effort. . . .
>
> > Improved efficiency—resulting from efforts initiated more than a year ago to streamline operations and upgrade services.
>
> Next year's farm program will provide less assurance of maintaining and improving farm income than we had hoped

for. But as a result of the coordinated efforts of MFA and other groups and organizations in the National Farm Coalition, hopefully the farm program for next year will be more helpful than would otherwise be the case.

A very important happening during 1970 was the merger of MFA Central Cooperative into Missouri Farmers Association. Ormal Creach, who had been general manager of that cooperative, was made treasurer of MFA. Farmers exchanges in MFA Central Cooperative were added to State Exchanges and became the Exchange Division. John Ekstrom, who had been vice president of finance, became the vice president of the Exchange Division.

Also during 1970, MFA sold its interest in Farmers Chemical Company in Joplin to Farmland Industries, Inc. The primary reason for the sale was to reduce indebtedness and to free up working capital.

In January 1970 MFA Oil Company purchased a twelve-hundred-acre farm near Marshall to be used jointly with Missouri Farmers Association as a research farm. MFA Oil Company could better afford to make the investment, although MFA would use the farm to a greater extent. In 1973 Senator Tom Eagleton was the featured speaker at the dedication ceremony for the farm.

Jim Claxton, formerly with the School of the Ozarks in Hollister, was named manager of the research farm, and Stuart L. Spradling was placed in charge of the operation. Spradling had roots in Franklin County, where his father was a friend of Heinkel's and Klinefelter's. I first hired Spradling to work in the MFA Oil Company laboratory while he was attending the University of Missouri. Largely through his efforts, MFA Oil products were leaders in quality in the company's marketing area. Besides his expertise in fuels and lubricants, Spradling was probably as knowledgeable in the field of agricultural chemicals as anyone in Missouri, and he could write and speak with clarity. The fact that he was a longtime friend of Heinkel's proved to be both an asset and a liability. When George Polly resigned in 1971 as president of the Supply Division, Spradling replaced him while retaining his position as vice president of research.

Each fall for several years, as many as seventy-five hundred farmers viewed test and demonstration plots at the research farm. The remainder of the farm was used for commercial enterprises consisting primarily of field crops, but that activity was also tied in with the testing of seed, fertilizer, pesticides, and other products. MFA Oil Company operated the farm and charged the other MFA agencies for the costs of the experiments conducted.

In the 1970s *The Missouri Farmer* introduced a new section in which technicians from Missouri Farmers Association and MFA Oil Company answered questions from farmers. Usually the feature, entitled "You Ask About," covered two pages in the magazine. Another experiment in providing technical information was the use of a "green telephone" installed at farmers exchanges. Members were invited to use the telephone to "Ask the Professionals." The intention was to provide information quickly to managers and patrons. It was a good idea, but it did not prove practical.

In January 1970 an advertising program was begun with the slogan "As you farm ask us." It was a takeoff on a Standard Oil promotion, "As you travel ask us." Standard Oil objected, but because of a close friendship between officials of Standard Oil and MFA Oil Company, there was no penalty, simply a request that MFA desist.

In the September 1970 issue of *The Missouri Farmer,* Heinkel wrote an article entitled "Two Fronts for Action: Cooperative Marketing and Purchasing and Effective Government Farm Programs."

> Both [cooperative and government programs] are proven tools in efforts to improve income for farmers, and both must be maintained, strengthened, and improved to keep abreast of the needs of a changing agriculture, Feeder pig Tel-O-Auction, initiated by MFA, has been termed the most significant livestock marketing innovation of this century [see Appendix 2 herein for more information on Tel-0-Auction]. Recently completed grain handling facilities, including the big terminal elevator at New Orleans, now enable MFA members to take product closer to overseas markets than ever before. MFA operations in plant foods, seeds, feeds, and farm supplies are being reshaped and streamlined in an all-out effort to provide the best possible service to farmers at lowest possible cost.

At a July 1970 board meeting, Ralph Hampton, with the St. Louis Bank for Cooperatives, emphasized the progress that MFA had made during the previous year. He said the relations between Missouri Farmers Association and the Bank for Cooperatives was good and that he deplored the increase in interest rates. At a board meeting in November, Harry Chlebowski, president of St. Louis Bank for Cooperatives, also commended MFA for improved operating performance as well as for preparation of an extensive budget.

In 1971, the first full year of operation with the farmers exchanges that had formerly constituted MFA Central Cooperative functioning as the Exchange Division of MFA, the loss for the Exchange Division was $2.4 million, contributing to an overall loss for MFA of $680,000. Grocery stores and franchised Coast-to-Coast stores were closed out in numerous Exchange Division units. Locally owned exchanges that merged into the Exchange Division included those in Hamilton, Warsaw, Beaufort, Greenfield, West Plains, Bronaugh, and Fair Play.

In the spring of 1971 John Ekstrom resigned as manager of the Exchange Division and was succeeded by B. L. "Bud" Frew, who had come to work for MFA a year earlier as the division's director of operations. Frew was born and raised on a farm in Illinois and had graduated from Bradley University in Peoria with a degree in mechanical engineering. From 1960 to 1970 he was with FS Services (now Growmark) in Illinois, where he worked in engineering, processing, and planning, as well as in operations. In 1981 Frew became executive vice president of MFA, and on January 1, 1985, he was elected as president and CEO.

In the March 1972 issue of *The Missouri Farmer*, Heinkel wrote an article, "With a Purpose, a Spirit and a Flag," that reminded readers of what MFA was all about.

> The broad foundation for this system was laid by the founders when they included this statement of purpose in the bylaws: "To promote and improve the economic and social position of farmers, to raise the plane of farm living to a higher level, to enhance the economic, social, educational, and religious opportunities of farmers and their families. . . ." Through the 58-year history of MFA and yet today, farmers have faced formida-

ble challenges. In that respect, I am reminded of the words of
Thomas Jefferson, who in the face of unlikely odds, declared:
"A people with a purpose, a spirit, and a flag can win." We have
a purpose—as defined by the founders of MFA. We have spirit—
as reflected by member loyalty and employee dedication. And
we have a "flag," the red, white, and blue shield of MFA.

District meetings of delegates continued through the 1970s, as they
had since Heinkel had become president. For example, in January
1971 thirteen hundred delegates attended thirteen district meetings.
They endorsed MFA's plan to buy $1 million in fertilizer-spreading
equipment; to develop a new program of livestock feeding and crop
production at the research farm; and to continue expansion of livestock marketing and grain storage facilities. Development of resolutions to be voted on at the annual convention began with more than
sixty local meetings in July attended by some fifteen hundred delegates. These delegates hammered out the resolutions, which were
then presented to a thirty-five-member resolutions committee that
met in advance of the convention.

At a new type of gathering begun during the 1970s, more than
three thousand delegates and managers attended fifteen regional
meetings. The exchange managers received cash-patronage refund
checks, and the delegates answered legislative questionnaires on
topics such as the updating of target and loan prices; inclusion of
soybeans as a basic crop; establishment of a national support price on
milk at not less than 85 percent of parity; and establishment of prior-
ity status for farmers in energy allocations.

During the 1970s the annual conventions continued the routine
of having prominent political and cooperative leaders as principal
speakers. In 1972 the conventions moved from Stephens College to
the Hearnes Multi-Purpose Complex on the campus of the University
of Missouri in Columbia. Heinkel and I were reelected president and
vice president, respectively, without opposition until the end of the
decade. There was little turnover in board members, with several
having served terms of fifteen years or more. These included Turpin
Youtsey; B. M. Seaman; Miller Hern; Sam Murrell; D. T. Weekley; Cecil
Letsinger; Lawrence Kullmann; Richard Miller; Edwin Sachs; Glen

Myers; R. L. Scroggins; Keith Meek; Dean Bolton; James Bess; Gene Nitsch; Forest L. Dohrman; and Donald Becker.

Fiscal year 1972 saw the beginning of a turnaround in operations. The Plant Foods Division, aided by some sizable refunds from inter-regionals, had a net gain of $2.4 million. After a bad year in 1971, the Exchange Division just about broke even in 1972, as 75 of the 105 exchanges reported a net gain for the year. Additional grain storage was authorized in 1972, including 375,000 bushels in Caruthersville, 290,000 bushels in Lamar, and one million bushels each in the Missouri cities of Mexico and Louisiana. In addition, a one-million-bushel facility at Hull, Illinois, was purchased.

Reviewing operations for the 1972 fiscal year, Heinkel commented:

> Complimenting the improved financial position of MFA Exchanges is a remarkable improvement in combined earnings of MFA seed, feed, fertilizer, farm supply, meat packing, and grain marketing operations. At the annual MFA Convention last summer, you may recall, we estimated net earnings of $1,750,000 for the fiscal year, which ended August 31. That was a big turn-around from the previous year. Final audited figures, however, show net earnings of $2,700,000.

On January 31, 1973, an era in MFA came to an end with the retirement of Russell J. Rosier, who had served as secretary-treasurer since February 1, 1929. Counting his early years as a bookkeeper and then manager at the Adrian MFA Elevator and as a traveling auditor, he had worked for MFA for more than fifty-two years. Rosier's tenure—more than that of any other MFA leader—had encompassed the entire history of the organization. In his first decade as secretary, he was at Hirth's service seven days a week. He played a major part in organizing MFA Oil Company, MFA Central Cooperative, MFA Mutual Insurance Company, and many parts of the association.

Most important, Rosier was the epitome of strength and integrity for more than four decades as secretary-treasurer. His signature on MFA certificates of indebtedness and bonds helped to sell them. One close associate of Rosier described him as "so honest he squeaked. He commanded greater confidence than any man I have ever known."

Another's appraisal was that he was "100% loyal, professional, frugal." A fitting tribute was a letter to Rosier from Heinkel presented at his retirement dinner.

> As I recall we first became acquainted when you audited our little MFA Exchange at Catawissa.
>
> During the more than 44 years that ensued since you became secretary-treasurer, MFA was confronted with many tough decisions, and you helped handle each one in an able and forthright manner. Moreover, on several occasions you helped make decisions that actually determined the continued existence and success of MFA Insurance Companies, the MFA Oil Company, and the Missouri Farmers Association itself.
>
> And, all the while you played a most important role in building a fine image for MFA. A good image is priceless and can only be built into an organization by people of sterling character such as you possess.

In 1965 Rosier had written a thirty-page analysis titled "Problems and Suggested Solutions of MFA, Inc." The paper was submitted to five top officials of MFA, but they took no formal action on his suggestions. However, a review of those suggestions reveals that his evaluation of the problems and solutions was correct in many instances. Several changes made in Missouri Farmers Association since that time were exactly in line with the suggestions in his report. Among other things, he suggested consolidation of many major agencies in MFA; organization of retail operations on a county basis, which would result in closing many farmers exchanges; and the closing of unprofitable operations such as the packing plant in Springfield. I had a close personal and working relationship with Rosier for over forty years. He deserves to be remembered as one of the giants in MFA, along with Hirth and Heinkel.

Bob Maupin succeeded Rosier as secretary of MFA. A native of Carrollton, Maupin had joined the MFA Law Department in 1959. Besides attending to legal matters, he worked closely with Heinkel and Carpenter on legislation. He was secretary of MFA Oil Company and other affiliated companies for several years. He left MFA in 1980 to become vice president and director of public affairs for MFA Insurance

Companies. He became the general counsel for MFA Insurance Companies in 1981, executive vice president in 1986, and president in 1988. Maupin was well acquainted with all operations of MFA and its affiliates and was highly effective in Jefferson City and Washington, D.C.

At the July 1973 board meeting, Wayne Sanders, director of Personnel and Management Training, introduced David Thomas, who gave a report on the Management Training program. Sanders had come to MFA in 1971 from the Ohio Farm Bureau Cooperative. Thomas, a native of Barry County, had joined MFA the same year, having just graduated from the University of Missouri, where he was president of the student body. He later became a vice president and director of member relations of Midcontinent Farmers Association and was a close associate of Heinkel's and Carpenter's. After leaving MFA in the fall of 1979, Thomas returned to the University of Missouri Extension Department, and he eventually received a doctorate in 1990. He also became an officer in a dairy cooperative in Ohio and was president of the American Institute of Cooperation until 1991, when he became executive director of the United Soybean Board.

Other department heads during the 1970s included Dick Cellar, manager of the Feed Division; John Gilbert, marketing manager for the Supply Division; Keith McLaughlin, coordinator of sales for the Exchange Division; Harvey Strothman, manager of the Plant Foods Division; Lloyd Satterwhite and Billy Streeter, managers of the Farm Supply Division; Ralph Bolzenius, manager of the Seed Division; and Chet Johnson, director of Management Training.

In 1973 sales were $317 million, versus $214 million in 1972; savings were $4.3 million, versus $2.7 million; and net worth was $17 million, versus $14.2 million. The Exchange Division acquired four more locations, in Barnard, Cowgill, Higginsville, and Norborne. Earnings at Caruthersville were dampened by a flood loss of $2.6 million, but the Exchange Division had an overall gain of $2 million. The Plant Foods Division by 1973 had storage at various locations approximating one-half of the yearly sales.

A considerable increase in investment in interregional cooperatives occurred during the 1970s. A big portion of this investment was in retained earnings, which were distributed in the form of capital stock. In the 1970s, fertilizer interregionals showed substantial earnings. Cooperative Farm Chemicals Association and Mississippi Chemical Corporation made substantial cash equity payments annually, while CF Industries made much smaller payments.

In the 1970s CF Industries became the largest producer of plant foods in the United States, accounting for approximately one-third of the total supply. By 1975 its volume of sales totaled 4.9 million tons, amounting to $468 million, with net savings of $158 million. Barney Baxter was president of CF Industries at that time.

In 1974 MFA joined a new interregional cooperative, Agri-Trans Corporation, organized to haul grain down the Mississippi River and return with fertilizer. Agri-Trans had 7 towboats and 200 barges, with plans to expand to 10 towboats and 400 barges. Besides MFA, other owners were St. Louis Grain Corporation, Illinois Grain Corporation, Iowa Farmers Grain Dealers Association, Farmers Union Grain Terminal Association, and CF Industries.

The mid-1970s produced the highest earnings in the history of MFA. Sales volume increased, refunds from interregional cooperatives were huge, and expenditures for new fixed assets and for patronage refunds increased accordingly. The following table tells the story (all figures are in millions).

	1974	1975	1976	Total
Sales	$456.00	$462.00	$530.00	$1,448.00
Earnings	26.15	23.80	18.33	68.28
Patronage Refunds				
Received	12.00	21.20	16.00	49.20
Paid	14.70	11.90	8.40	35.00
Fixed Assets				
Purchased	7.77	15.00	12.40	35.17

Net worth during the three-year period increased from $17 million to $50 million. Total assets increased from $109 million to $182 million, while long-term debt (including bonds and bank borrowings) increased from $50 million to $63 million.

During this period almost half the patronage dividends received ($23.9 million) were from the Cooperative Farm Chemicals Association in Lawrence, Kansas. Additions to fixed assets in the Exchange Division accounted for approximately 50 percent of the total increase in assets during the three years, a portion of the growth coming from the absorption of locally owned exchanges in financial difficulty. Grain, Feed, and Plant Foods Divisions accounted for most of the remaining increase in assets, which was due to the building of new grain terminal storage facilities and enlargement of the soybean processing plant in Mexico.

Farmers and their cooperatives were on an expansion binge in the 1970s, and Missouri Farmers Association was no exception. Lending agencies were encouraging farmers to buy more land and machinery and to erect more buildings. Looking back on these years, an article in the July 1985 issue of *Atlantic Monthly* noted:

> The FmHA [Farmer's Home Administration], production-credit associations, and banks were just as much to blame for plunging as farmers. With acreage values rising at up to 20 percent a year, farmland was an investment that was staying ahead of inflation. Many banks, needing borrowers to generate income on their inflation-pumped deposits, encouraged farmers to leverage themselves to the limit. During the 1970s there were times when lenders quite literally drove up and down the road, knocking on people's doors, and asking them if they could use more credit.

Even the Farm Credit Administration built magnificent home offices during that period. Unfortunately, some of MFA's projects, such as grain storage and bulk fertilizer plants, were built because of pressure from farmers and local boards and not for sound business reasons. In other words, Operating Divisions personnel sometimes initiated requests for expenditures they knew were not feasible, yet later they would be held responsible for the results. This practice was termed "the end run."

At the 1976 convention, attended by seven thousand members, sixty-five resolutions were adopted. Approval was given to building the new solvent-extraction soybean processing plant in Mexico, Missouri, at a cost of $5 million. Kermit Head was manager of the plant and reported that the new facility would process more than sixty thousand bushels per day, or 20 percent of all soybeans grown in Missouri. The employees at the plant totaled 120, and storage capacity was three million bushels.

Also approved in 1976 was the building of a research center in Columbia to do the work of research laboratories at MFA Oil Company, MFA mills, and MFA seed facilities. And to relieve crowded quarters at the home office, a building owned by Missouri Division of Employment Security and located immediately north of the main MFA office building was purchased.

In 1977 MFA closed its meat-packing plant in Springfield. There was no longer enough livestock fed out in that area to supply the plant, and it had become necessary to ship hogs from north and central Missouri and Iowa to keep the plant going. An attempt to process pork for shipment to Japan fizzled after long negotiations. During that time butchers from Japan went to Springfield to teach MFA meatcutters to process meat for the Japanese market.

The two livestock marketing affiliates of MFA did well in 1977. Farmers Livestock Marketing Association (formerly Farmers Livestock Commission Company, renamed on January 31, 1963) of National Stockyards, Illinois, managed by Frank Patton, had a volume of $97 million with savings of $265,000. It handled 590,000 head of livestock and ranked first at National Stockyards in sales of both cattle and hogs. MFA Livestock Association of Marshall, managed by Jim Halsey, marketed 473,000 feeder pigs and 281,000 butcher hogs, which resulted in a savings of $106,000.

During these years, Heinkel, Carpenter, and Maupin continued their legislative activities. On a national level, their efforts were largely funneled through the National Farm Coalition, as described by Heinkel in an article in the April 1977 issue of *The Missouri Farmer.*

> This year the message of farmers was delivered to Congress and to the Administration by a strengthened and maturing National Farm Coalition. Now apparent is the fact that farmers are closer to speaking with one voice than ever before, in the opinion of veteran Washington scene observers. Created seven years ago, this informal alliance of farm leaders has been de-

veloped and strengthened with each legislative challenge. . . .
Coalition membership now includes thirty-six general, commodity, corporative, and farm organizations representing more
than a million agricultural producers.

The sad experience of Progressive Farmers Association (PFA) of
Springfield tightened up Missouri's surveillance of the sale of stocks
and bonds in cooperatives. The PFA, incorporated in 1973, cut a wide
swath in the middle 1970s, with much publicity. To finance the PFA
operation, Estate Builder investments were sold, many to MFA members. MFA officials repeatedly warned of the danger of PFA activities,
but to no avail, apparently because MFA was regarded by some as a
jealous competitor. The end result was a loss of several million dollars
by investors and indictment of some leaders of the PFA organization.

The 1977 fiscal year was less profitable than the previous years had
been, with a gain of $6.5 million on sales of $553 million. Patronage
refunds received were $6 million less than in 1976. Patronage divi-
dends paid out were only $3.75 million, a reduction of $5 million.
Additions to fixed assets were at a record level of $21 million. The
operating divisions where most of these additions occurred were:
Exchange Division, $9.6 million; Grain Division, $5.6 million; and
Plant Foods, $2.5 million.

In 1977 MFA and Land O' Lakes joined together in the formation of
Imperial Packaging Company to own and operate a bag manufacturing plant in Clarksdale, Mississippi. Ralph Hofstad, president of Land
O' Lakes, and Harry Pomeranz, a bag manufacturer in Des Moines,
Iowa, were longtime friends and business associates. Pomeranz owned
a plant in Clarksdale that was not operating at capacity, and he offered
to sell it to MFA and Land O' Lakes. The combined volume of business
of the new owners would bring the plant up to capacity. Pomeranz
was hired to manage Imperial Packaging Company. With no down
payment, the plant was paid for by applying profits to the purchase
price. It turned out to be a very worthwhile investment.

In 1978 the fiscal year was changed to end on May 31; thus there
were only nine months in the business year ending May 31, 1978. Net
earnings were $700,000 on sales of $455 million. The short fiscal year

did not include some patronage refunds ordinarily received in the last three months of the fiscal year. The largest of these was from CF Industries. However, earnings from interregionals dropped considerably, as explained to me by Harvey Strothman, manager of the Plant Foods Division. "The fertilizer industry is sick, particularly nitrogen manufacturing. The industry overbuilt following the high prices of three or four years ago."

In 1978 MFA Milling Company of Springfield entered into a management agreement with Missouri Farmers Association, and in 1981 it became a part of MFA. John F. Johnson, who had long managed MFA Milling Company, had retired in 1974 and been succeeded by Travis Harris. The retirement of Johnson marked an end to the career of one of MFA's most colorful and successful business managers. Johnson was a hard-nosed businessman who had played a major part in the development of animal agriculture in the Ozarks region of southern Missouri and northern Arkansas. He contended that the best measurement of the success of an MFA business unit was not the bottom line but the cost per unit of operation plus market share. He bitterly opposed farmers exchanges getting into grocery store operations because such action took emphasis away from the major objective, that is, the furnishing of farm input items such as feed, fertilizer, and pesticides.

At the MFA Milling Company's annual meetings you could expect to hear Johnson talk about "those good MFA feeds" and "the wonderful hill country down here in the Ozarks." The MFA Milling Company had the lowest operating cost of any feed mill in the country at the height of its volume, and it paid substantial patronage refunds to farmers exchanges, many of which depended on the milling company refund for their net savings. After his retirement, Johnson continued his cattle business, operating three ranches in the Ozarks near Springfield. Although he had several battles with Heinkel and other MFA leaders during his career, after his retirement he became a close friend of both Heinkel's and Rosier's.

In 1978 the prestige of MFA was again demonstrated when President Jimmy Carter agreed to be the principal speaker at the convention held in the Hearnes Auditorium in Columbia. On stage with the president were Secretary of Agriculture Bob Bergland; Senator Herman Talmadge from Georgia; and Senators Tom Eagleton and Jack Danforth, Congressmen Richard Gephardt, Ike Skelton, Tom Coleman, Gene Taylor, Richard Ichord, and Bill Burlison, and Governor Joseph Teasdale—all from Missouri.

Hearnes Auditorium was filled to capacity, and security was tight. Secret-service men were much in evidence, and hospitals and physicians were on alert. President Carter was highly complimentary of Heinkel, the Missouri Farmers Association, and the Missouri congressional delegation. As a peanut farmer in Georgia, the president was familiar with the operations of a farmers cooperative.

Heinkel's remarks at the convention consisted largely of a history of federal farm programs since the 1930s and illustrated his belief that farmers could make or lose more money in a legislative session than their cooperatives could save for them in a year's operations.

> Farmers who survived the ups and downs and the booms and busts of the past 50 years have, with the help of federal programs, made some progress. I am particularly thinking about the improved standard of living on farms made possible by R.E.A. [Rural Electrification Administration] and all that it has done for farm people, especially farm women.
>
> A few years after the turn of the century farmers were portrayed as hicks, rubes, and hayseeds. About the time of World War I it was said that farmers were the salt of the earth—the backbone of the nation and that food would win the war.
>
> Some 18 months after the war ended farm prices collapsed. Farmers were told to diversify—plant and produce some of a lot of things. Supposedly the theory was that maybe something would have a fair price.
>
> But farmers were restless and with good reason. They urged their organizations to have Congress pass some helpful legislation. All farm organizations united and called for passage of the McNary-Haugen farm bill. Congress passed it and the President vetoed it. Congress passed it again, and it was vetoed a second time.
>
> Then a high official stated that if the problems were given time to run their course, nature would correct the problems.

This reminds me of a statement by a great president who said, "The legitimate object of government is to do for the people what needs to be done, but which they cannot, by individual effort, do at all, or do so well, for themselves." It was Abraham Lincoln who made this statement.

This also reminds me that when pneumonia and appendicitis were allowed to run their course (with a little weak treatment) the patient often died.

The only reason very, very few people are now the victims of pneumonia or appendicitis is because of penicillin and the skilled hands of surgeons. We no longer let nature take its course.

Farmers didn't believe or buy this "Let nature take its course" theory. They took their wants and needs to the two political conventions in 1928 and as a result a Farm Board Law was passed in 1929. It proved inadequate and set the stage for the next Farm Act passed in 1933.

The Act of 1933 got farmers out of the woods but was declared unconstitutional in 1936. It was followed by the Soil Conservation and Domestic Allotment Act of 1936. This in turn was followed by the Agricultural Adjustment Act of 1938. The 1938 Act in amended form is still in effect.

The point of all this is that once a Farm Bill was passed and signed by a President, the "farm problem" was officially recognized by the federal government. This set the stage for [the bill's] continued existence to the present day and beyond to 1981. At times it has been weakened and provided too little too late. One such period was in the 1950's, when we wound up with a price crushing surplus of 85 million tons of feed grains and 1 billion 400 million bushels of wheat as we entered the 1960's. This precipitated the Emergency Feed Grain Act of 1961 and succeeding years.

Through the programs of the intervening years from 1933 to 1978 the need for two basic provisions [has] been firmly established. They are non-recourse loans and the machinery for acreage adjustment. In the early 60's "deficiency payments" were added, and in lieu of these the 1973 Act added Target Price payments.

And now the 1977 Farm Act, the best act of all, has added another basic feature, a "farmer held" Security Reserve. It is being effectively administered by Secretary Bergland. This reserve feature together with the other basic features of the 1977 Act as administered by the Secretary has moved farm prices up substantially since August of 1977. Soybeans are up more than a dollar per bushel. Wheat, corn, and milk are up too. Cotton is the only one that is down but is now improving. Livestock is not covered by the Act, however. Cattle and calves are up quite substantially. Hogs are holding their own.

A new Act has also been passed that should aid substantially in further development of our export markets. It provides for several types of help to further sales of farm products.

Another Act recently signed into law greatly increases the lending authority of Farmers Home Administration. This should help farmers who are in a bind with credit problems as well as young farmers.

And still another Act well on its way to passage is a new Food Production Insurance Program. It is designed to consolidate all present crop insurance and disaster programs, and is to be administered by county ASCS [Agricultural Soil Conservation Service] committees, which should be a big improvement. This will be a tremendously important program in these times of inflated production costs if farmers are hit with disaster through no fault of their own.

With all these acts to which I have referred, the secretary of agriculture will be in a position to deal effectively with problems and emergencies as they arise instead of trying to develop a program after an emergency has occurred. In fact, some problems can be averted by preventive action.

The Missouri Legislature is to be commended for having passed the Family Farm Act in 1975 which is designed to keep farming in the hands of family farmers instead of allowing it to be gobbled up by conglomerates and other huge corporations.

It is also to be commended for having passed a law at the recent session to prevent farm land from being bought up by non-resident aliens.

The National Farm Coalition of which MFA is a member, along with some 30 other farm groups, has been very effective in getting the 1977 Act and subsequent Acts passed.

You delegates and other members here in this convention have been very helpful in developing MFA policies that have gone into the programs of the National Farm Coalition. And you have also been very helpful in the passage of the two state laws to which I have referred. For all your help we are deeply grateful.

In conclusion, we are likewise grateful to the United States Congress, including our fine Missouri delegation, for having passed the Food and Agricultural Act of 1977 and to President Carter for having signed it into law.

A. D. Sappington, president of MFA Insurance Companies, died on February 27, 1979, at the age of sixty-six, after a long and distinguished career with MFA. He had been very active in promoting legislation favorable to MFA in both Jefferson City and Washington, D.C. Also he served for nine years as a member of the Missouri State Highway Commission, and he was the first person to serve two terms as chairman of the Board of Governors of the National Association of Independent Insurers. Under his leadership, MFA insurance-premium income grew from $32 million to $244 million. Total assets grew from $48 million to $382 million, and the surplus grew from $12 million to $99 million.

Sappington was not only a business associate but also a close personal friend of mine. He had more influence with Heinkel than anyone else in MFA, and when I reached an impasse, I would call on him for help. He was genuinely interested in people, particularly MFA employees, and both MFA and MFA Insurance Companies owed a great debt of gratitude to A. D. Sappington. Howard Lang, who had been with MFA Insurance Companies since 1949, was elected president to succeed Sappington; Gus Lehr, who had been with the company since 1959, was elected executive vice president.

As the end of the decade approached, interest rates began to rise at an alarming rate. For example, in 1979, interest paid by MFA to the St. Louis Bank for Cooperatives increased $3 million over the previous year. On recommendation of management, all capital expenditures over $200,000 had to be approved by the board of directors, and the St. Louis Bank for Cooperatives also had to approve expenditures in excess of $400,000. The years of quick and easy expansion were over.

Chapter Twelve

Heinkel Defeated
by Thompson, 1979

The year 1979 began with an occurrence that would develop into an uprising on the part of MFA members and end the Fred Heinkel era. Yet the changes that occurred were not so much a result of that one event as a reflection of a growing surge of unrest that had been developing for many years within the organization.

A perception, widely held, was that MFA was spending an undue portion of its resources on legislative and political activities. Fueling this perception were the large number of resolutions at annual conventions devoted to legislative and governmental affairs as well as the preponderance of legislative articles in *The Missouri Farmer.* Legislative committees, organized throughout the state, held frequent, numerous meetings, and political action committees made contributions to candidates. Top officials of MFA, members of the field force, MFA attorneys, and the staff of *The Missouri Farmer* spent what many felt was an excessive amount of time in legislative pursuits. Another perception was that the Democratic Party was favored over the Republican Party.

When I became executive vice president of MFA in late 1968, it was apparent that there also was conflict between activities in Midcontinent and in MFA. The field force in Midcontinent was close to Heinkel and thus tended to influence business decisions based on political considerations rather than financial ones. On the other hand, the majority of MFA retail outlets, membership, and volume of business was in the hands of the Exchange Division of MFA. Division managers for the Exchange Division, all experienced businessmen, included Phil Nickerson, Ranie Thompson, Keith Mitchem, Albert Smith, Don Copenhaver, and Bob Brown. They had a close working relationship with exchange managers and delegates and were in a position to influence election of board members and officers in Missouri Farmers Association, but they had largely steered clear of such activity. Their chief concern was successful operation of MFA retail business. Thus the stage was set for a dramatic change in MFA leadership in 1979.

On January 16, 1979, Norman Baker, manager of the Trenton Farmers Exchange, a unit of the Exchange Division, was fired for failure to comply with policies established by MFA, particularly those relating to grain. This was done following an internal audit by MFA, which revealed numerous violations. Some of the Trenton delegates protested, making trips to Columbia and contacting Heinkel, who was vacationing in Phoenix, Arizona. Heinkel's response to the delegates was that he would check into the situation when he returned to Columbia. In the meantime, there were protests and blockages at the exchange in Trenton. When Heinkel returned, he arranged for an independent audit to be made by Lindburg and Vogel, an accounting firm in Hutchinson, Kansas, to determine if the reasons for firing Baker were valid. This firm served as auditor for Kansas City Terminal Elevator Company, and the elevator company's board members included Heinkel.

I was present when C. E. Lindburg gave his verbal and written reports to Heinkel. Lindburg's reports were even more critical than the internal reports from MFA auditors. Nonetheless, after thinking about the matter over the weekend, Heinkel gave instructions to reinstate Baker.

When I reported this information to Bud Frew, he resigned as head of the Exchange Division, effective April 3, 1979, and Norman Baker was reinstated. Frew was very popular with exchange managers and delegates in territories served by the 112 exchanges in the Exchange Division. They recognized that it was not proper for the board or the board chairman to interfere with the hiring or firing of employees.

In a story in the September 15, 1979, issue of the *Columbia Daily Tribune,* Heinkel stated that he rehired Baker "because that's what MFA's Trenton area farmers wanted. I've always maintained an open door to farmers. In this case, I listened, and they convinced me it was time to intervene in their behalf. Baker was reinstated after it became evident that this was their wish."

A movement to defeat Heinkel at the upcoming convention started rolling shortly thereafter. During the summer of 1979, I received numerous calls from MFA leaders asking me to be a candidate for president. I refused because I did not want to run against Heinkel, with whom I had worked almost forty years. Heinkel had also said that he wanted to serve as president for just one more year and that he planned to turn over more of the management to me during that final year.

Slightly more than one week before the convention, while I was spending the weekend at the Lake of the Ozarks, David Thomas called and told me that Eric G. Thompson, MFA director of Employee Relations, planned to run against Heinkel. As I recall, this was on Sunday, July 29, and on Monday I flew to Chicago to attend a board meeting of CF Industries. While at the meeting, I received a call from MFA headquarters to leave right away—they were sending the company plane to pick me up—so that I could send a letter to delegates in support of Heinkel. I wrote the following letter on the plane as I returned to Columbia:

I'm writing to you in response to the letter you may have received announcing a candidacy for President of the MFA.

The letter indicated I would be [Thompson's] choice for Vice President. The announcement was a complete surprise to me. By no stretch of the imagination are we allied on the same ticket as running mates. For whatever it is worth, my choice for election for MFA President is Fred V. Heinkel. I would hope you will see fit to re-elect me to serve under him as Vice President.

The position of President of an organization of 175,000 members with sales approaching one billion dollars, assets of over $300 million, requires more experience, in my judgment, than four years of personnel work. MFA members, and others in Missouri, have more than $85 million of their savings invested in Missouri Farmers Association and MFA Oil Company. In addition, MFA members have in excess of $79 million invested in patronage equities. Bank borrowings average more than $100 million throughout the year; thus the goodwill and cooperation of the bankers is absolutely essential to MFA—I'm positive they wouldn't look with favor on a relative newcomer, with no experience in cooperative leadership.

First and foremost, MFA must serve its member patrons and remain strong financially. In the last eight years, our net worth has increased from $17 million to $79 million—sales from $240 million to more than $900 million.

In any business organization, improvements can be made, but I think the record for the past several years indicates stability and improvement in our financial position. Our involvement in interregional cooperatives (CF Industries, National Cooperative Refinery, etc.) is an extremely important part of the total MFA and is not to be relegated to some employee in an ambassadorial role—one must be deeply and fully involved in the business activities in those fields to serve as board member and officer of these very large cooperative business operations.

I hope you come to the MFA Convention next Monday, August 6th—we will be looking for you.

At a board meeting called for August 1, 1979, Heinkel recommended that the delegates at the annual convention elect the chairman and vice chairman of the board and that the board elect the president and vice president of Missouri Farmers Association. This was a change advocated by the supporters of Eric Thompson, and it would have required a special membership meeting because it was too late to get it on the agenda for the convention, which was only five days away. The date for that special meeting was set for October 15, but the meeting was never held. At the same board meeting, there was a long discussion on prices charged for supplies and prices paid for grain by farmers exchanges. It was my suggestion that a committee of the board make an investigation and report back to the full board.

During the week before the convention, Thompson asked me to

remain as vice president. I replied that I would not leave or make a decision about anything "until the dust settled." (Later some of Heinkel's supporters tried to interpret this as an act of disloyalty.) I spent most of my time that week contacting exchange managers, fieldmen, and delegates in support of Heinkel. By the night before the convention, however, it had become apparent that Thompson had the election in the bag. Both Clell Carpenter and Hilton Bracey, close friends and advisers to Heinkel, told him that the only chance to salvage the situation was for him to withdraw and throw his support to me. Heinkel thought about it and replied that he would not withdraw.

Thompson, a native of Moniteau County, had been on the staff of MFA for five years as director of Management Development and Training and then as director of Employee Relations. Before joining MFA, he received bachelor's and master's degrees in agricultural economics from the University of Missouri. From 1969 to 1974 he served in the U.S. Air Force and flew more than two hundred missions in Vietnam. In his campaign for president of MFA, Thompson advocated lower prices on farm inputs purchased through farmers exchanges, increased emphasis on the role of directors, elimination of "over-staffing and misguided management of the corporate headquarters," and a new and less costly approach in legislative affairs.

Attorneys for Heinkel and Thompson met and agreed on ground rules for conducting the election for president at the convention. Each nominee was given five minutes to speak, with no other speakers allowed. Howard Lang, president of MFA Insurance Companies, was chairman of the meeting. After Heinkel and Thompson were nominated, I was nominated from the floor for the office of president, but I declined. The vote was 1,088 for Thompson and 615 for Heinkel, and I was reelected vice president without opposition. Besides electing a new president, delegates elected seven new board members: Carlton Spencer, David Hortenstine, Everett Billings, L. E. Manson, Adrian Murray, William Stouffer, and William Umbarger.

Earnings for the 1979 fiscal year were reported as $8.8 million on sales of $836 million. For the decade of the 1970s, under Heinkel's leadership, net earnings had totaled more than $90 million, with more than $40 million paid in cash refunds or retirements of equity. Net worth increased in the ten years from $10.6 million to $58.1 million, total assets went up from $60 million to $278 million, and long-term debt increased from $30 million to $90 million.

The day following the convention, Thompson asked for and received resignations from Clell Carpenter, Jack Hackethorn, and David Thomas. Two months later Stuart Spradling resigned.

In the September 1979 issue of *The Missouri Farmer*, David Bryant wrote the following editorials:

Member Control Is an MFA Reality

Let it be noted that the system works—that farmer ownership and farmer control of MFA remain reality—that the means of exercising member control is yet viable.

Those facts were reaffirmed last month in Columbia, Mo.

Reflecting a deep and growing membership concern relative to direction and responsiveness of their organization, a majority of delegates came to the Annual Convention of MFA determined to effect a change. To that end, they elected a new president and seven new board members.

Whether or not advocated changes are wise is not an issue in this editorial discussion. In a cooperative, as in a democracy, when a majority of the members desires any given action, then that action is necessary and correct.

In order now is a review and re-evaluation of virtually all procedures and policies of this cooperative enterprise and farm organization. Changes can be expected. And the process of review and re-evaluation should, in itself, reassure the membership that MFA is responding to their concerns and their needs.

That, after all is said and done, is what MFA is all about.

A Standing Ovation for F. V. Heinkel

In obvious respect and admiration, 1,703 delegates to the 1979 Annual Convention of MFA accorded a standing ovation to F. V. Heinkel—the man for whom 1,088 of those delegates had refused to vote only minutes earlier.

It was the end of an era—F. V. Heinkel era—in MFA and in agriculture.

For 39 years, the dynamic farmer from Franklin County,

Mo., had headed MFA. In those years, membership increased from about 32,000 farm families to more than 175,000. And the cooperative's business volume climbed from a little more than $100,000 annually to more than $725 million per year. For MFA, the Heinkel era was a period of remarkable growth, development and progress.

The Heinkel influence, however, extended far beyond MFA and the borders of Missouri. Perceptive and forthright, he was widely recognized and acknowledged as a leading spokesman for the interests of farmers. As such, he advised Presidents, Governors and Secretaries of Agriculture, as well as law-makers at the state and national levels.

So even as his bid for a 40th consecutive year as president of MFA was rejected by convention delegates, Heinkel's past dedication to the well being of farmers was never in doubt.

His indelible imprint on MFA and on U.S. agriculture is obvious reality. Through 39 years, he served his fellow farmers capably, effectively and with distinction. The standing ova-tion was fully-earned and well-deserved.

Heinkel's supporters made an attempt to upset Thompson and me in 1980 by running Edwin Sachs, longtime MFA board member and leader from Rolla, for president and Keith McLaughlin for vice president. McLaughlin had been interim manager of the MFA Exchange Division in 1979. The vote was overwhelming for Thompson and me, and there were no further attempts to change MFA leadership.

Heinkel's long and distinguished career was marked by many positions and honors. In addition to his service as president of Missouri Farmers Association for thirty-nine years and as president of MFA Oil Company, MFA Livestock Association, Farmers Livestock Marketing Association, and many other affiliated agencies, he was chairman of the board of MFA Insurance Companies, Farmers Export Company, and the National Advisory Committee on Feed Grains and Wheat. He was vice chairman of the National Council of Farmer Cooperatives and the American Institute of Cooperation. Besides serving on the board of curators of the University of Missouri, he was a member of the Missouri Basin Survey Commission, the Missouri Academy of Squires, the Missouri Advisory Committee on Legislative Reform, and the Public Advisory Committee on Trade Negotiations. Among many recognitions, Heinkel was named Man of the Year in Agriculture of Missouri by *Progressive Farmer* magazine, he received the Distinguished Service to Agriculture Award from the National Farmers Union, and he received honorary doctorates from the University of Missouri and Missouri Valley College.

Among those who worked closely with Heinkel, Roy Reed observed that "he had a very pleasant personality and was especially good one-on-one. He was always natural—never put on an act—had no ulterior motives." Richard Collins recalled that "he had an exceptional memory—names, figures, dates. He had ability to work with diverse groups. He had a genuine concern for farmers as individuals and never refused to talk with a farmer. He was a gentleman in every way." Bob Maupin noted that "one of Mr. Heinkel's greatest attributes was timing and balance. He had a sense of knowing when and when not to do something." And Herman Schulte called him the "greatest 'people' person" he ever knew.

I became acquainted with Heinkel when I went to work for MFA Oil Company in 1938. At that time I was twenty-five years old and he was forty. Hirth and Rosier were the dominant figures in MFA at that time—Heinkel and I were relative newcomers. With only a sixth-grade education, Heinkel's grammar needed polishing, and that was accomplished when he married a schoolteacher. Heinkel acquired stature as a leader very quickly after becoming president of MFA. His innate ability to understand what the opposition was planning to do made him a leader in the legislative field. He was helped by staunch friends such as Congressman Clarence Cannon and Senator Stuart Symington. The fact that he was almost appointed secretary of agriculture by President Kennedy was proof of his national reputation. Heinkel also did a good job of surrounding himself with astute businessmen for most of his career. But his failure to delegate authority and support subordinates, and his attempt to hold on too long, led to his undoing. Such shortcomings, however, should not overshadow his brilliant and rewarding service. Heinkel died on October 31, 1990. His wife had died approximately one year earlier.

Epilogue

U nder Eric Thompson's leadership, several changes occurred quickly, sometimes abruptly. In retrospect, if Heinkel had retired a few years earlier, many of the changes that were made precipitously might have been made in a less divisive manner. Although some of Heinkel's close associates resigned or were terminated, Bud Frew returned as the head of business operations. Management consultants were hired to assist in the planning process, and the management structure was changed. Farmers Livestock Marketing Association of National Stockyards, Illinois, was separated from its status as an MFA affiliate, and MFA Milling Company of Springfield was taken over by MFA. An agreement was reached with MFA Insurance Companies for separation from MFA, with the insurance company changing its name to Shelter Insurance Companies, and for a division of the money in the MFA retirement plan and in MFA Foundation.

In the early 1980s MFA suffered substantial losses, as did other regional cooperatives. The interregional cooperatives that had supplied substantial earnings to MFA in the 1970s suffered greatly reduced profits. To shore up its financial position, MFA sold its ownership in the Cooperative Farm Chemicals Association of Lawrence, Kansas, the Kansas City Terminal Elevator Company, St. Louis Grain Company, Farmers Export Elevator of New Orleans, and the barging operation of Agri-Trans Corporation.

Several MFA-owned operations also were sold, including the soybean processing plant in Mexico, Missouri, and grain terminals on the Mississippi River. Many farmers exchanges were merged or closed where there was a small or negative return on capital.

When Eric Thompson was elected president in 1979, he vowed that he would retire as president after six years, and he did so as of December 31, 1985. Thompson was succeeded by Bud Frew. Under Frew a different style of leadership has emerged—a quiet, no-nonsense manner of conducting business. He has the knack of putting foremost the activities of board members and employees while providing strategy in the background. He is well liked and highly respected by them and by the cooperative community.

In recent years the trend of locally owned cooperatives joining the retail division of MFA has accelerated. In 1992 there were 116 company-operated MFA Agri-Service centers (exchanges) and 46 locally owned affiliates. Significant new ventures have been initiated, including a river terminal at Caruthersville consisting of a grain elevator and warehouses for fertilizer and agricultural chemicals, and a joint venture with Hubbard Pet Foods in which an MFA feed mill was converted to produce pet foods.

In the 1980s an important change was made in the method of selecting the chief executive officer. Since the formal organization of MFA in 1917, the president had been elected by delegates at the annual convention. As far as I know, MFA was the only cooperative that elected its president in this manner. Under new bylaws adopted in 1984, delegates now elect board members, who, in turn, elect a chairman and vice chairman from among their group and select the chief executive officer with the title of president. In 1983, the directors were limited to three 3-year terms, and in the early 1990s the number of directors was reduced from thirty to fifteen.

Rigid belt-tightening, shifting of resources, and employment of the latest technology in all areas are now paying off for MFA. Since 1986, MFA has operated in the black and is now, in 1992, in sound financial position. [Ed. note: In 1994 net worth approaches $87 million.]

It is my sincere belief that Missouri Farmers Association is in good hands and is doing well.

MFA Oil Company
A Brief History

A lthough MFA Oil Company was founded in 1929 in a time of severe national depression, the volume of sales increased each year from the 1930s into the 1970s. Starting with the original twenty-four bulk oil plants of 1929 and 1930, the number of plants had grown to forty-five by 1943.

The first man I hired when I became manager of MFA Oil Company in 1939 was Carl Farmer, to serve as our agent at Marshall. Farmer, a native of Ash Grove, had worked for Sinclair Oil Company. He was a natural-born salesman with little formal education, but he was highly intelligent and had an outstanding personality. Before he went into the navy during World War II, Farmer was largely responsible for the expansion of bulk oil plants and, after the war, for expansion in the mid-South.

Another MFA Oil employee who made an important contribution was C. F. "Charlie" Robertson, a native of Mattoon, Illinois. He was employed in the St. Louis office of MFA Oil Company in June 1930. Robertson, with Irish humor and Irish temper, held several positions, including office manager, sales manager, and assistant general manager. He was closely involved in all important management decisions from the time he joined the oil company until his retirement in 1972.

Ralph Deuser, another veteran employee, transferred from St. Louis when the office was moved to Columbia in 1934. He was purchasing agent and supervisor of the Maintenance Department for most of the forty-plus years he worked for the company.

When MFA Oil Company purchased the refinery in Chanute, Kansas, in 1943, Oscar Cunningham, who had been manager of the refinery under the previous owner, remained in that position. Following World War II, MFA Oil expanded rapidly through the building of bulk oil plants and service stations until supply once again became a problem. In 1948, when MFA Oil purchased Delta Refining Company of Memphis, Tennessee, with a capacity of three thousand barrels per day, it gave Cunningham the additional responsibility of managing Delta. Carl Farmer was sent to the newly acquired refinery to develop sales through cooperatives and to other customers in southeast Missouri and other parts of the mid-South. Farmer remained as head of the company's mid-South division until his retirement in 1981.

By the middle 1950s, refined oil products were plentiful, and it was apparent that ownership of the refineries had served the purpose of supplying products when they were greatly needed, thus enabling MFA Oil Company to engage in an aggressive expansion program. To keep costs competitive, the decision was made to sell both refineries. The Chanute plant was sold in December 1955 and the Delta refinery in June 1956, both at a small profit.

From 1956 to 1965 MFA Oil Company was entirely dependent on major and independent refiners for supply. Other cooperatives had entered the refining business in the 1940s, including the National Cooperative Refinery Association (NCRA), which had its refinery in McPherson, Kansas. After the sale of the Chanute and Memphis refineries, MFA Oil became a part-owner of NCRA. The McPherson refinery now processes seventy-five thousand barrels of crude oil per day and is one of the most modern and efficient refineries in the United States.

Almost from the beginning, MFA Oil Company marketed products classified as agricultural chemicals, the first of these being an oil-based cattle spray. During World War II, DDT was developed as an insecticide. It soon replaced the old cattle spray, marking the real beginning of the agricultural chemical business for MFA Oil Company.

Stuart Spradling, who started work in the MFA Oil Company's testing laboratory while still a student at the University of Missouri, soon developed into an expert in fuels and lubricants and later in the field of agricultural chemicals. Spradling was chairman of the Fuels and Lubricants Committee of the American Petroleum Institute at one time and was highly regarded in the industry. He received his training under Gayle Pipes, the original head of MFA Oil's laboratory in Columbia.

In April 1969 MFA Oil Company and Land O' Lakes purchased an agricultural chemical formulation and packaging plant in Shenandoah, Iowa, from FS Services of Illinois. The plant, Imperial, Inc., under management of Dwight Habermehl, proved to be a highly successful venture, and the company purchased another formulating plant in Albert Lea, Minnesota. In 1980, MFA Oil turned the agricultural chemical business over to MFA, primarily because the great bulk of the sales, amounting to some $25 million annually, was through farmers exchanges. At that time, the company sold its interest in the formulating plants to Cenex of St. Paul.

MFA Oil diversified in the 1960s by getting into the propane business, and in October 1962 Missouri Farmers Association sold its Tire Division to the oil company after having suffered losses for a few years. Tire warehouses and recapping plants were built in Columbia and in Springfield. By 1965 there were 115 bulk oil plants, 3 propane plants, and 250 service stations. The volume of sales was $21.5 million, and the company's net worth was $2.9 million. Sizable patronage refunds were paid annually.

As business grew, supply problems cropped up again. In 1973, just before the Arab oil embargo, MFA Oil entered into a supply agreement with Lion Oil Company of El Dorado, Arkansas, under the management of Bud Bierbaum, who was formerly with Midland Cooperatives and NCRA. In return for a loan of $6.5 million, Lion agreed to make available three thousand barrels per day of finished products. This arrangement was a lifesaver to MFA Oil for the next five years.

Just as the arrangement with Lion Oil was phasing out, MFA Oil Company and other cooperatives were scrambling desperately for sources of supply. CF Industries, the large fertilizer interregional in which Missouri Farmers Association participated, actively promoted the purchase of the Atlantic-Richfield Refinery in East Chicago, Indiana, with a capacity of 125,000 barrels per day. It purchased the refinery in May 1976 at a cost of $80 million for the fixed assets. MFA Oil Company's ownership of the Atlantic-Richfield Refinery, later named Energy Cooperative, Inc. (ECI), was roughly 12.5 percent. The other owners were Midland Cooperatives, Cenex, Land O' Lakes, Farm Bureau Services of Michigan, Landmark, Tennessee Farmers Cooperative, FCX, and CF Industries.

The initial management of ECI operations by CF Industries was marginally successful. However, by May 1981 two main factors had led ECI to file for bankruptcy. The first was that the government was not enforcing federal regulations that guaranteed access to crude oil for all refineries at competitive prices. Then, Ni-Gas, a utility company, unilaterally canceled its contract with ECI to buy a sizable amount of products for use in the making of synthetic natural gas.

The bankruptcy court took more than eleven years to complete its consideration of the case. The owners and unsecured creditors suffered big losses. MFA Oil's share of the loss, after calculating the credit for income tax deductions, was approximately $15 million. However, ECI had furnished a source of supply during a period of rapid expansion. In its few years in business, a 30 percent increase in outlets occurred. Fortunately, MFA Oil was strong enough financially that none of the members' equities were impaired by the loss, and excellent operations since 1981 have continued to strengthen the company.

In 1980, MFA Oil Company and Missouri Farmers Association joined in an effort to build a large ethanol plant near Baton Rouge, Louisiana. The enterprise was headed by Bud Bierbaum and Hein Koolsbergen, former officers in Tosco, an oil refining and marketing company. The proposed plant would have produced 100 million gallons of ethanol per year, with a value of over $200 million. Other participants included Joseph Grain of Minnesota and United Refining Company of Pennsylvania. A loan guarantee of $166 million was secured from the Department of Energy. Unfortunately, the remaining equity capital was not secured, and the project was abandoned in 1983. Total loss for MFA Oil and MFA was approximately $500,000 each. Contributing to the failure of the project was the death of Koolsbergen in 1982.

By mutual agreement, MFA relinquished its ownership of MFA Oil Company in 1985. Between 1946 and 1985, MFA named half the MFA Oil Company board members, and MFA Oil Company member-patrons elected the other half at their annual meeting. Beginning in 1985 MFA Oil entered into a contract with MFA for the use of the emblem for a fee. A close working relationship continues between the two cooperatives.

I retired as president of MFA Oil Company and executive vice president of MFA on May 31, 1981. Dale Creach, who had been with MFA Oil and MFA for fifteen years, became president of MFA Oil Company. Creach, a native of Macks Creek and the son of Ormal Creach, is a graduate of Drury College. He was with Phillips Petroleum Company for four years before becoming an employee of MFA Oil Company in 1967. After working initially as a district man, he spent three years as a regional representative for MFA before returning to MFA Oil Company as sales manager, assistant manager, and then president.

MFA Oil Company has grown and expanded under Creach's management in spite of write-offs on ECI. From 1981 to 1992, net worth increased from $10.8 million to $42 million, and sales from $209 million to $250 million. (The sales figure for 1981 includes $25 million in agricultural chemicals, before that operation was turned over to Missouri Farmers Association.) In 1981 the number of bulk oil plants totaled 116; in succeeding years many of them have been consolidated, so that by 1992 the plants numbered 118. During those years as well, the number of propane plants increased to 65 from 24; 65 new Petro card systems were developed; and the number of employees grew from 468 to 1,045.

MFA Livestock Association
A Brief History

The MFA Livestock Association, like the MFA Oil Company, is no longer an affiliate of Missouri Farmers Association, although it uses the MFA name and emblem by contract, which includes payment of a fee. When MFA Livestock Association was first organized in 1958, with Clell Carpenter as manager, it had two hog-buying stations. Severe losses were suffered in the beginning.

In early 1959, Jim Halsey replaced Carpenter as manager. Halsey had been a vocational agriculture teacher and county agent before going to work for MFA in 1949 as a field representative for the Plant Foods and Seed Divisions. He was later assistant manager of the divisions. Soon after he became manager of the MFA Livestock Association, the organization bought several country buying stations belonging to George Hess and moved its headquarters from Columbia to Marshall.

In 1963, with the aid of experts from the University of Missouri, Halsey started a program of promoting feeder pigs with production and marketing agreements between the association and pig producers. The agreements provided for selection of boars, feeding, and medication, and specified other criteria for the pigs to be marketed through the association.

In 1965, Halsey inaugurated a unique method of marketing feeder pigs called Tel-O-Auction. Buyers in areas that finished pigs would gather in twelve or fourteen locations, and auctioneers, via telephone, would sell pigs by graded lots from MFA buying stations. Buyers had the right to turn down an entire lot of pigs on arrival, but only three lots were turned down in the first twenty-five years of the program. In 1973, the Missouri Pork Producers Association gave an award to Halsey for having "pioneered a unique hog marketing system in Missouri that has resulted in the improvement of swine production, swine quality, and increased income for the Missouri farmers."

In 1978, its twentieth year of operation, MFA Livestock Association marketed 550,000 head of livestock through fourteen auction barns, primarily in central and southern Missouri and in Arkansas. According to Glen Grimes, agricultural economist at the University of Missouri, before the MFA program began, the feeder pig industry in southern Missouri and in northern Arkansas had lacked a dependable year-round market. Farmers were producing everything from choice-quality pigs to razorbacks, and marketing was left to auctions and traders who did not always recognize quality and often paid little or no premium for it. The Tel-O-Auction helped raise feeder pig prices in the entire Ozark region. One feeder pig producer, Floyd Westen of Pettis County, who marketed four thousand pigs through the auction over a three-year period, observed: "I don't know of any pigs in this area that sell for more money than MFA feeder pigs. I figure my pigs bring an average of 5 cents to 8 cents a pound more."

Besides marketing feeder pigs, the association marketed butcher hogs and started a cow-and-calf-marketing program from its Humansville auction barn facility. As the marketing program expanded into new locations, local banks often helped in financing the facilities, since the marketing program increased income for farmers. The association also operated a commission firm at the St. Joseph stockyards, and for a few years it joined with Producers Livestock Commission Company in the operation of 4-Square Marketing Association at Marshall Junction.

Jim Halsey retired in 1985 as president and was replaced by Pete Moles, who had been with the association since its founding in 1958.

The butcher hog operations were sold in September 1988 to Wilson Packing Company. The St. Joseph commission operation was discontinued in 1987; a large auction facility was purchased in Maryville, and the operation moved to that location. In 1991 the volume handled was $129 million with net earnings of $273,000 and 695,000 head of livestock sold.

Appendix Three

Members of the
Board of Directors
Missouri Farmers Association

1917-1994

Abbott, T. E.	El Dorado Springs	1931-1934
Albrecht, William G.	Jerico Springs	1948-1969
Allyn, W. E.	Sheridan	1938-1941
Anderson, G. M.	Galt	1929-1938
Atkins, David	Lebanon	1969-1972, 1976-1979
Atkins, J. Wiley	Lebanon	1921-1933
Bachmann, R. E.	Menfro	1948-1956
Bachtel, Aaron	Brunswick	1923-1944
Bailey, L. E.	Willow Springs	1933-1937
Ball, Ned J.	Montgomery City	1917-1930
Barkley, Kenneth	Canton	1972-1975
Barrett, Walter	Elwood	1917-1920
Becker, Donald	Labadie	1967-
Beckett, William	Columbia	1967-1968
Beezley, H. L.	Springfield	1941-1944
Bess, James	Advance	1963-1978
Billings, Everett	Green Ridge	1979-1982
Bilyeu, Milbern	Ozark	1968-1972
Bishop, C. E.	El Dorado Springs	1922-1928
Block, Eldon	Jacksonville	1963-1969
Bolton, Dean	Fairfax	1963-1981
Botts, John R.	Maysville	1930-1936

219

Bowers, E. A.	Neosho	1935-1941
Brehe, Fred	Marthasville	1969-1981
Breshears, J. C.	Bolivar	1929-1933, 1941-1945
Britt, O. D.	Brunswick	1944-1947
Brown, C. C.	Elsberry	1917-1920
Buford, Welton	Gorin	1917-1923
Bunch, Colonel	Lancaster	1991-
Burch, Jerry	Walker	1983-1985
Burns, Larry Joe	Rector, Ark.	1982-1989
Caldwell, Chester A., Jr.	Blytheville, Ark.	1978-1982
Carrington, F. M.	Safe	1923-1926
Chapman, T. M.	Ozark	1920-1934
Childress, C. F.	Maryville	1920-1923
Clark, Elmer	Dexter	1947-1957
Clemens, Dan	Marshfield	1993-
Clemens, Joe	Marshfield	1972-1983
Clements, C. G.	Grant City	1924-1930
Coats, James A.	Mountain Grove	1978-
Collier, Ora	Albany	1948-1962
Collins, C. C.	Trenton	1938-1945
Collins, George	Chillicothe	1946-1947, 1949-1961
Combs, Tom	Golden City	1981-1986
Conrad, John F.	Clarksville	1955-1967
Cook, Stephen	California	1987-1993
Coolley, Truman	Centralia	1977-1988
Cope, C. M.	Crane	1920-1926
Cope, O. D.	Jenkins	1980-1993
Cott, Kenneth	Slater	1981-1983
Crawford, A. J.	Atlanta	1917-1929
Cross, Robert F.	Stockton	1972-1983
Cunnyngham, B. L.	Morrisville	1944-1950
Darrow, C. W.	Ava	1921-1934
Davison, Barton V.	Gibbs	1948-1966
Degraffenreid, Kenny	Bolivar	1985-1991
DeWitt, T. H.	Green City	1917-1929
Doepel, Edwin	Stuttgart, Ark.	1991-
Dohrman, Forest L.	Sweet Springs	1966-1981
Drennan, Ollin	Kirksville	1944-1948

Edmondson, Ben	Cassville	1932-1935
Ellis, D. E.	Crane	1934-1956
Ellis, Doyle	Lineville, Iowa	1988-
Elson, Charles	Ash Grove	1920-1923
Etter, Priest	Etterville	1944-1948
Farquhar, James	Clearmont	1932-1938
Farrell, Benny	Maryville	1987-1993
Ferguson, W. E.	Rosendale	1923-1929
Fiegenbaum, Martin	Higginsville	1932-1941
Fitzpatrick, Clarence	Higginsville	1917-1919
Foland, Charles	Grant City	1951-1957
Forck, Mike	Jefferson City	1987-
Fulton, F. G.	Daviess County	1918-1919
Gex, John	Graham	1926-1928
Gibson, Norman	Sedalia	1958-1967
Gillespie, Dale	Albany	1947-1948
Goforth, W. H.	Barnard	1929-1932
Goodbrake, T. E.	Clinton	1985-
Gooden, E. C.	Parnell	1920-1926
Gorman, Ed	Wentworth	1935-1950
Graham, J. C.	Pattonsburg	1936-1944
Gratz, Henry J.	Russellville	1940-1944
Griffith, John J.	Dawn	1923-1931
Gruhn, Fred	Lincoln	1982-1992
Gwin, D. C.	Chillicothe	1941-1946
Hall, Raymond	California	1971-1980
Hanan, J. P.	Buffalo	1919-1922
Harshbarger, Don	Centralia	1972-1981
Hartell, A. C.	Plattsburg	1918-1921
Hatcher, Roy D.	Shelbyville	1929-1952
Hays, J. R.	Centralia	1926-1929
Heiman, August H.	Montrose	1919-1920
Heiman, Fred H.	Montrose	1920-1923
Heinkel, Fred V.	Columbia	1935-1979
Hemeyer, Stanley	Montgomery City	1991-1993
Henry, C. D.	Tipton	1940-1950
Hensel, D. F.	Montrose	1928-1936

Hern, Miller	Rocheport	1947-1977
Hetlage, Herman	Wright City	1923-1929, 1936-1971
Higgins, R. P.	Licking	1932-1944
Hillhouse, Clint	Aurora	1941-1944
Hirth, William	Columbia	1917-1940
Holden, Wayne	Birch Tree	1976-1982
Hopper, Bert	Clarence	1920-1926
Hortenstine, David	Brookfield	1979-1992
Howell, Reuben	Dexter	1957-1970
Hudson, J. A.	Columbia	1917-1922
Hume, Harry	Kahoka	1928-1937
Hurst, S. W.	Tipton	1926-1929
Inglish, A. V.	Jamestown	1928-1937
Ingwersen, T. B.	Bowling Green	1917-1918
Isaacs, George Jr.	Faucett	1948-1951
Isaacson, Paul B.	Callao	1990-
James, George	Brunswick	1967-1979
Jasper, Joseph H.	Washington	1947-1962
Jennings, Charles	Dexter	1982-1993
Johnson, W. W.	Shelbyville	1926-1929
Jones, J. M.	Everton	1928-1931, 1934-1937
Jones, Wayne	Cabool	1945-1948
Joyce, H. F.	Lamar	1946-1949, 1950-1959
Karl, William A.	Ste. Genevieve	1944-1949
Kearns, W. A.	Granger	1917-1928
Kelley, George M.	Tipton	1917-1928
Kemp, M. H.	Lockwood	1946-1953
Kertz, Herman	Ste. Genevieve	1953-1971
Kerwin, James	Grant City	1981-
Ketchem, W. H.	Atlanta	1926-1929
Kies, Sam	Bethany	1957-1963
Kircher, P. D.	Harrisonville	1980-1985
Kleinschmidt, Samuel J.	Higginsville	1917-1919
Kline, B. F.	Knobnoster	1917-1919
Kramme, Milford	Owensville	1962-1966
Kreisel, A. C.	Warsaw	1925-1934, 1937-1948
Kullmann, Lawrence	Sedalia	1955-1980

Lancaster, Melvin	Lancaster	1983-1992
Lane, C. E.	Ozark	1927-1941
Lantz, Lester	Sheridan	1941-1944
Lawrence, Charles	Golden City	1929-1932
Leavitt, G. A.	Kirksville	1929-1944
Letsinger, Cecil	Mansfield	1951-1976
Lindner, John	Union	1927-1930
Lischwe, Joseph B.	Dixon	1944-1951, 1952-1955
Littrell, B. B.	Centralia	1935-1938
Littrell, J. S.	Keytesville	1917-1920
Lock, Ervel	La Plata	1978-1990
Loida, Albert	Ste. Genevieve	1938-1944
Long, H. B.	Clinton	1936-1944
Luehrman, Walter	Higginsville	1980-1992
Lynch, O. C.	Catawissa	1930-1936
McClelland, D. V.	Kirksville	1923-1926
McClure, W. E.	Irwin	1917-1919
McNally, A. W.	Kahoka	1937-1941
McNeall, Raymond	Keytesville	1983-1992, 1993-
McShane, Neil	Flemington	1938-1941
Maczuk, Mike	New Haven	1941-1944
Manson, L. E.	Brunswick	1979-1983
Marshall, Joe	Marshall	1966-1972
May, Rex	Milan	1983-1988
May, W. E.	St. Clair	1918-1919
Meals, Chester	Moberly	1945-1964
Meek, Keith	Cameron	1962-1980
Meisner, John	Clarence	1929-1957
Miller, Fred	Holden	1922-1928
Miller, Larry	Long Lane	1987-1993
Miller, Richard	Cassville	1955-1979
Miller, W. S.	St. James	1922-1948
Mooney, L. H.	Rogersville	1933-1969
Morrison, Charles	West Plains	1937-1948
Mortensen, A.	Weatherby	1926-1927
Mueller, John J.	Drake	1929-1935
Mundell, Junius	Browning	1970-1979
Murphy, Wayne	LaGrange	1941-1944

Murray, Adrian	Ash Grove	1979-1983
Murrell, Sam	Lancaster	1948-1978
Myers, Glen	Memphis	1958-1983
Nauman, Frank	Craig	1920-1923
Neuenschwander, A.	Deepwater	1944-1964
Neuenschwander, Arthur	Deepwater	1971-1980
Nicks, Floyd	Owensville	1948-1952
Niebrugge, C. O.	Washington	1917-1920
Niehaus, August	Lamar	1964-1972
Nitsch, Gene	Jackson	1966-1984
Ohlendorf, Chris	Boonville	1922-1940
Orf, A. C.	O'Fallon	1930-1934
Osborne, Everett	Nixa	1956-1968
Patterson, J. S.	Ozark	1949-1951
Pence, R. T.	Marshall	1917-1929
Perry, Larry	Lake Spring	1980-1992
Pierce, Frank	Nashville	1917-1920
Pippins, Bill	Dexter	1970-1983
Pollard, Raymond	Mexico	1929-1935
Potter, Juan	Carthage	1969-1981
Pritchard, J. L.	Knobnoster	1922-1925
Propst, Gerald	Chaffee	1984-1991
Quade, Don	Carthage	1983-1992
Rea, Earl	Marshall	1917-1919
Ream, Dale	Unionville	1961-1964
Rehagen, Otto	Freeburg	1950-1956
Rehagen, Walter	Freeburg	1981-1987
Rickenbrode, F. W.	Avalon	1931-1938
Risser, Otto	Sheridan	1928-1949
Riutcel, F. W.	Martinsburg	1944-1955
Roberts, Frank	Worth	1920-1923
Robertson, Dorsey	Russellville	1962-1965
Robins, Charles D.	Advance	1978-1991
Rosier, A. C.	Butler	1917-1922
Ross, Neal	Sikeston	1978-1983
Rowe, Oakley	Sheridan	1944-1945

Rowles, E. E.	Bolivar	1959-1960
Rybolt, Sherman	Grant City	1917-1918
Sachs, Edwin	Rolla	1956-1981
Samek, Frank	Bolivar	1993-
Schindler, John D.	Shelbina	1930-1936
Schnakenberg, Hugo	Cole Camp	1956-1962
Schnarre, Keith	Centralia	1983-1993
Schowengerdt, E. W.	Mayview	1920-1923
Schunemeyer, Neal	Bernie	1951-1963
Schutte, Don	Mexico	1988-1991
Schwartz, Henry, Sr.	Argyle	1934-1944
Scott, C. A.	Sheridan	1930-1933
Scott, George T.	Versailles	1937-1940
Scroggins, R. L.	Bolivar	1960-1980
Seaman, B. M.	New Boston	1944-1972
Siddens, W. J.	Albany	1919-1920
Simpson, J. E.	Sheridan	1939-1947
Sloan, R. T.	Hamilton	1980-1993
Small, Othor	Cabool	1972-1981
Smutz, B. C.	Brunswick	1917-1923
Sobotka, Frank	Gainesville	1927-1930
Spencer, Carlton	Faucett	1979-
Spicer, James	Stuttgart, Ark.	1991-1992
Sprick, Larry	Warrenton	1981-1987
Steiner, William L.	New Haven	1920-1923, 1924-1927
Steury, Ed	Springfield	1941-1958
Stiles, C. M.	Aldrich	1923-1929
Stouffer, William	Marshall	1979-
Straughan, E. H.	Farmington	1955-1967
Stump, Harlin	Lockwood	1986-1992
Tallon, Tom	Maryville	1924-1930
Thompson, Eric G.	Columbia	1979-1985
Thompson, Tom	Strafford	1929-1932
Tillman, J. W.	Galloway	1934-1937
Umbarger, William	Fairfax	1979-1987
Van Gilder, Earl,	Irwin	1980-1986
Van Houten, James	Clarence	1964-1970

Van Houten, Neal	Clarence	1975-1993
Voris, W. R.	Halfway	1933-1938
Wade, Jeff	Bragg City	1978-1983
Wallach, A. A.	Beaufort	1952-1955
Wallis, L. O.	Springfield	1944-1967
Wangelin, F. G.	Grandin	1936-1944
Watson, W. C.	Sheridan	1933-1939
Watt, G. F.	Mountain View	1929-1932
Weathers, J. S.	Windsor	1921-1927
Weaver, Ed	Birch Tree	1965-1976
Webb, John	Miller	1926-1935
Weber, George	Hermann	1938-1941
Weekley, D. T.	Blackwater	1949-1979
Wheeler, J. P.	Greenfield	1937-1946
White, James L.	Dexter	1989-1992, 1994-
Wiggenstein, C. A.	Fredericktown	1917-1919
Wilkinson, A. K.	Rogersville	1919-1920
Williams, David L.	New Cambria	1967-1979
Williams, O. W.	Bolivar	1950-1955
Wilson, Glennon	Sheridan	1945-1948
Wissbaum, David	Conway	1981-1987
Wood, R. M.	Lamar	1920-1929
Woodard, H. O.	Jasper	1944-1946
Young, John L.	Elsberry	1920-1926
Young, Raymond A.	Columbia	1968-1983
Youtsey, Estes	Gallatin	1917-1927
Youtsey, Turpin	Gallatin	1944-1979
Zahn, Virgil	Marshall	1944-1966

Notes

Preface: What Is MFA?

1. Quoted in "Companies Digging Up Their Past," *Management Review* 71 (January 1982): 32.

2. Frank Stork, "A Passing of the Torch," *Rural Missouri* 40 (April 1987): 3.

3. Joseph G. Knapp, *The Rise of American Cooperative Enterprise, 1620–1920* (Danville, Ill.: Interstate Printers and Publishers, 1969), 193; James V. Rhodes, "Bill Hirth and MFA: The Early Years" (University of Missouri Department of Agricultural Economics working paper 1985-11 [1985]), 20.

Two. The Creation of a Statewide Organization

1. For more information on the Extension Division, see James Olson and Vera Olson, *The University of Missouri: An Illustrated History* (Columbia: University of Missouri Press, 1988), and David Thelen, *Paths of Resistance: Tradition and Democracy in Industrializing Missouri* (Columbia: University of Missouri Press, 1991), 41–42.

2. Vera Busiek Schuttler, *A History of the Missouri Farm Bureau Federation* (n.p.: Missouri Farm Bureau Federation, 1948), 3.

3. Ibid., 19–20.

4. All correspondence quoted from Hirth or to Hirth is in the William Hirth Papers, 1925-1934, Western Historical Manuscript Collection, Ellis Library, University of Missouri, Columbia.

5. William Hirth, "The Fight at the National Capital," *The Missouri Farmer,* April 1, 1918.

Three. Continued Growth: The Early 1920s

1. W. J. Spillman, "'Show-Me' State Shows Us," *Farm Journal* 43 (September 15, 1919): 5.

2. "WPFA Messenger," *The Missouri Farmer,* February 1971.

3. Robert Montgomery, *The Cooperative Pattern in Cotton* (New York: Macmillan, 1929), 46.

4. William Hirth, "'The Old Guard' into the Fray," *The Missouri Farmer,* September 15, 1924.

Four. Politics and Conflict

1. Milo Reno, "An Epoch-Making Occasion," *The Missouri Farmer,* June 1, 1927.

2. Gilbert C. Fite, *Beyond the Fence Rows: A History of Farmland Industries, Inc., 1929–1978* (Columbia: University of Missouri Press, 1978), 29.

3. Ray Derr, *Missouri Farmers in Action: A Public Relations Study* (Columbia: Missouri Farmers Association, 1953), 84.

4. Minutes of the MFA Board Executive Committee, June 30, 1927, MFA Historical Files, Law Department, MFA Corporate Headquarters, Columbia, Missouri.

5. Derr, *Missouri Farmers in Action,* 92.

Five. MFA in the 1930s

1. "Tax Committee Starts in on Huge Job," *The Missouri Farmer,* September 15, 1931.

2. Klinefelter to Hirth, August 20, 1932, Hirth Papers.

3. William Hirth, "The Governorship," *The Missouri Farmer,* January 15, 1936.

4. J. Christopher Schnell, Richard J. Collings, and David W. Dillard, "The Political Impact of the Depression on Missouri," *Missouri Historical Review* 85 (January 1991): 145.

5. Quoted in H. E. Klinefelter, "A Great Managers' Meeting," *The Missouri Farmer,* January 15, 1936.

Six. The End of an Era

1. Theodore Saloutos, "William A. Hirth, Middle Western Agrarian," *Mississippi Valley Historical Review* 38 (September 1951): 215–32.

2. H. E. Klinefelter, "William Hirth, the Man," *The Missouri Farmer,* December 15, 1943, and December 15, 1946. *The Missouri Farmer* changed from a biweekly publication to a monthly one in March 1948.

Seven. Expanding Business Ventures: The 1940s

1. Fite, *Beyond the Fence Rows,* 112.

Eight. MFA in the 1950s

1. Derr, *Missouri Farmers in Action,* 187.

Nine. Reorganization: The 1960s

1. Richard Collins, "Everybody's Talking about MFA!" *The Missouri Farmer,* January 1961.

2. Clarence Cannon, "We Need Fair Farm Legislation," ibid., October 1960.

3. Jim Reeves, *First Twenty Years: The Story of Mid-America Dairymen* (Republic, Mo.: Western Printing, 1989), 204–5.

Index

Abbott, T. E., 219
Adams, B. R., 102
Adrian: elevator, 82, 188; exchange, 75
Agency for International Development (AID), 182
Agricultural Adjustment Act (1938), 10, 197
Agricultural Adjustment Administration (U.S.), 5
Agricultural Cooperative Development International (ACDI), 182
Agricultural Extension Service (U.S.), 40, 41
Agricultural Marketing Act (1929), 3
Agricultural Money (AGMO), 174-75
Agricultural Soil Conservation Service, 198
Agricultural Wheel, the, 14, 28, 35, 37
Agri-Service centers (exchanges). *See* specific locations
Agri-Trans Corporation, 191, 208
Albany: exchange, 48, 174
Albrecht, William G., 219
Aldrich: farm club, 51-52
Alford, G. M., 74
Allen, Mrs. S. D., 57
Allersmeyer, Albert, 40
Allister, J. W., 67

Allyn, W. E., 219
American Cotton Growers Exchange, 65
American Press, 177-78
Anderson, G. M., 219
Anthony Salt Company, 88
Argyle: exchange, 74
Armstrong, State Representative James W., 91, 136
Armstrong, W. L., 25; pictured, 113
Arthur Andersen and Company, 170, 179
Artificial Breeding Association, Springfield, 146-47, 155. *See also* Dairy Breeders Division
Ash Grove: exchange, 50, 75
Atkins, David, 219
Atkins, J. Wiley, 76, 81, 85, 219
Auditing Department, 87, 163-64
Audrain County: farm clubs, 34
Aurora: exchange, 97

Bachmann, R. E., 219
Bachtel, Aaron, 3, 24-26, 67, 219; pictured, 113
Bachtel, Virgil, 26
Bagnell: exchange, 73
Bailey, L. E., 219

Baker, Harold, 175
Baker, Norman, 201-2
Baldi, Jim, 172
Bales, State Senator D. L., 91
Ball, Ned J., 36, 44, 49, 54, 76, 82, 219; elected president of MFA, 52
Ballew, Bill, 176, 177
Ballew, R. W., 149
Bank for Cooperatives, 5, 6, 138-39; Louisville, 139; St. Louis, 134, 139, 152, 186, 199
Barker, George, 174
Barkley, Kenneth, 219
Barnard: exchange, 190
Barnett: exchange, 103
Barney, Baxter, 191
Barrett, Walter, 36, 219
Barton County: farm clubs, 27, 52
Baruch, Bernard, 64
Beacon, The, 158
Beal, W. A., 75
Beaufort: exchange, 186
Becker, Donald, 188, 219
Beckett, William, 158, 163, 173, 176, 177, 219; biographical information, 153; pictured, 123
Bedison: exchange, 74
Beezley, H. L., 149, 219
Benton, Dale, 100, 101
Bergland, Secretary of Agriculture Bob, 195, 198
Bernie: exchange, 174
Berry, Charles, 100
Bess, James, 188, 219
Bierbaum, Bud, 213, 214
Billings, Everett, 204, 219
Billings: exchange, 50, 75
Bilyeu, Milbern, 219
Bingham, Judge Robert, 64
Bishop, C. E., 219
Black, Albert G., 140
Black, Jim, 177-78
Blackwater: exchange, 27
Blanton, H. J., 88
Block, Eldon, 219
Bockhorst, Garrett, 30

Bois d'Arc: exchange, 74
Bolckow: exchange, 74
Bolivar: exchange, 51, 137-38, 149, 174
Bolton, Dean, 188, 219
Bolzenius, Ralph, 190
Booker, Ralph, 83
Boone County: exchange, 145, 147; farm clubs, 29, 31, 34. *See also* Columbia
Boonville: bulk oil plant, 84
Boss, E. L., 75
Botts, John R., 219
Bowers, E. A., 220
Bowles, Claud, 174
Boynton: exchange, 74
Bracey, Hilton, 165, 175, 182, 204
Bradley, Carlos, 134
Brandt, John, 149
Branscomb, J. C., 75
Branson: exchange, 75; farm clubs, 29
Brehe, Fred, 220
Breshears, J. C., 220
Britt, O. D., 220
Broach, Leonard F., 85, 102
Bronaugh: exchange, 84, 186
Brookfield: exchange, 74
Brookline: exchange, 74
Brooks, Harold, 161, 162, 174
Brooks, Stratton D., 67
Brown, Bob, 201
Brown, C. C., 36, 220
Brown, Dorothy, 97
Brown, John, 139
Browning, O. J., 75
Browning: exchange, 48, 174; farm club, 50
Brucks, Charles, 75, 134
Bruning, Walter, 85
Bryant, David, 171
Bucklin: bulk oil plant, 84
Buffalo: exchange, 48, 174
Buford, Welton, 36, 220
Bullock, E. H., 33, 41
Bunch, Colonel, 220
Burch, Jerry, 220
Burch, Jim, 134

Burley Tobacco Growers Association, 64

Burlison, Congressman Bill, 196

Burns, Larry Joe, 220

Burt, Earl, 75, 109

Butts, Hadley, 134

Cabool: creamery, 74, 138, 142, 172; farm clubs, 51

Caldwell, Chester A., Jr., 220

California: bulk oil plant, 84; exchange, 74, 97, 161

California Fruit Growers Exchange, 140

Callao: exchange, 48

Camdenton: grocery, 101

Camp Clover Leaf Point, 57

Cannon, Congressman Clarence, 72, 94, 140, 149, 153, 156, 166, 207

Capper, Senator Arthur, 153

Capper-Volstead Act (1922), 3, 11

Carpenter, L. C. "Clell," 159-60, 173, 174, 189, 190, 193, 204, 205, 216; pictured, 125

Carrington, F. M., 220

Carson, John, 157

Carter, President Jimmy, 195-96, 199

Carthage: exchange, 53

Caruthersville: elevator, 172, 188, 209; exchange, 190

Cass County: farm clubs, 34

Catawissa: exchange, 133, 189

Cavermo, Judge Xemophom, 95

Cellar, Dick, 190

Cenex, 214

Central Cooperative, 103-4, 137, 138, 144, 145, 147, 163, 176, 184, 186

Central Farmers Fertilizer Company, 148, 155, 170

Centralia: exchange, 48, 174; farm clubs, 29, 30

CF Industries, 8, 177, 191, 195, 203, 213, 214. *See also* Central Farmers Fertilizer Company

Chapman, T. M., 220

Chariton County: farm clubs, 33, 34

Charity: exchange, 74

Childress, C. F., 220

Chillicothe: creamery, 138, 142; produce plant, 62; seed processing plant, 147

Chlebowski, Harry, 186

Clarence: farm club, 52

Clark, State Senator A. M., 91

Clark, Congressman Champ, 45

Clark, Elmer, 220

Clark: exchange, 74

Claxton, Jim, 184

Clayton Antitrust Act (1914), 2, 11

Clemens, Dan, 220

Clemens, Joe, 220

Clements, C. G., 220

Clinton: bulk oil plant, 84; creamery, 74, 143; elevator, 149; produce plant, 62, 143

Clyde, Frank, 74

Coast-to-Coast, 186

Coats, James A., 220

Coleman, Congressman Tom, 196

Collier, Ora, 134, 220

Collins, C. C., 143, 220

Collins, George, 220

Collins, Richard, 171, 204

Columbia: home offices, 104, 120-21, 135-36, 152, 155, 193; MFA Oil Company headquarters, 85, 97; research center, 193; site of conventions, 151; tire plant, 213. *See also* Boone County

Combs, Tom, 220

Committee on Taxation and Government Reform, 91-92. *See also* Legislation

Commodity Division, 161

Conboy, Bill, 134

Conrad, John F., 220

Consumers Cooperative Association (CCA), 149, 155, 170

Conway: exchange, 75

Cook, John, 103, 109, 142

Cook, Stephen, 220

Coolidge, President Calvin, 69, 71, 72

Coolley, Truman, 220
Cooperative Association No. 1, 48
Cooperative Farm Chemicals Association (CFCA), Lawrence, Kans., 83, 171, 177, 191, 192, 208
Cooperative Fertilizers International (CFI), 182
Cooperative League, 149
Cooperative Marketing Act (1926), 3
Cooperative Stock Act (1919), 84
Cooper County: farm clubs, 27
Cope, C. M., 220
Cope, O. D., 220
Copenhaver, Don, 164, 201
Corn Belt Committee, 71-72, 75, 76
Cornell Seed Company, 88
Cott, Kenneth, 220
Cowden, Howard A., 48, 73, 143, 149, 150; biographical information, 51; first full-time paid secretary of MFA, 58; pictured, 115; relationship with Hirth, 59-60, 68, 75-83, 107. *See also* Cowden Oil Company; Farmland Industries, Inc.
Cowden Oil Company, 77
Cowgill: exchange, 190
Craig, Anderson, 33
Crane: exchange, 138
Cravens, Al, 172
Crawford, A. J., 36, 46, 61, 69, 76, 77, 220; elected president of MFA, 70
Creach, Dale: biographical information, 215; pictured, 129
Creach, Ormal, 176, 181, 184; biographical information, 163; pictured, 125
Creameries. *See* Producers Creamery Company; specific locations
Creighton: exchange, 74
Crighton, William T., 99, 103, 109, 142, 164, 172; pictured, 119
Crocker: bulk oil plant, 84
Cross, Robert F., 220
Cunningham, Oscar, 212
Cunningham, Shelton, 174, 176
Cunnyngham, B. L., 220

Cuno, F. L., 39, 84
Curry, State Senator J. E., 150

Dairy Breeders Division, 164, 170
Dallas County: farmers association, 49
Dalton, Governor John M., 169
Danball, J. R., 95
Danforth, Senator Jack, 196
Darby, Homer, 163, 170
Darling and Company, 88, 148
Darrow, C. W., 220
Davison, Barton V., 220
Davison, John, 74
Day, Sammy, 174
Deering, Katheryn, 142
Degraffenreid, Kenny, 220
Delta Refining Company, 152, 156. *See also* MFA Oil Company
DeMott, F. H., 75
Dempsey, Leon, 174
Denham, Glen, 136
Dennis, Bob, 74
Derr, Ray: *Missouri Farmers in Action*, xii, 22, 76, 77, 82, 158
Deuser, Ralph, 211-12
DeWitt, T. H. (Tom), 36, 37, 70, 73, 77, 78, 80, 82, 220; elected president of MFA, 76
Dierking, H. H., 142
Distinguished Service to Agriculture Awards, 153
Doepel, Edwin, 220
Dohrman, Forest L., 188, 220
Dolbeare, Kenneth, 174
Dole, Senator Robert, 126, 175
Donnelly, Governor Phil, 159
Dowell, Lois, 97
Dowling, Melvin, 172
Drennan, Ollin, 220
Drescher, A. B., 62, 85, 87
Drier, Alex, 160
Dunlap, Fred, 49
Dunlap: exchange, 74
Dutzow: exchange, 74

Eagleton, Senator Thomas, xiii, 184, 196

Eales, Mrs. H. V., 57
Edmondson, Ben, 221
Edwards, Fred, 142
Ekstrom, John, 176, 179, 184, 186
Eldon: exchange, 103
El Dorado Springs: creamery, 142; exchange, 174
Elevators. *See* specific locations
Ellis, D. E., 143, 221
Ellis, Doyle, 221
Ellis, Elmer, 175
Ellis, George B., 23, 32
Elsberry: farm clubs, 48
Elson, Charles, 221
Emma: creamery, 101, 138, 142; elevator, 151; exchange, 75
Emmons, Vernie, 181
Employee Relations, 179, 202, 204
Employee Training, 163. *See also* Personnel and Management Training
Energy Cooperative, Inc. (ECI), 214, 215
Ethel: exchange, 73
Etter, Priest, 221
Eugene: exchange, 144–45
Evans, Jim, 174
Evans, Thurman, 141
Exchange Division, 161, 164, 184, 186, 188, 190, 192, 194, 201, 206. *See also* specific locations; State Exchanges
Exeter: bulk oil plant, 84

Fair Play: exchange, 186
Family Farm Act (1975), 198
Farm Bureau Services of Michigan, 214
Farm Club Mill and Feed Company: Kansas City, 63; Springfield, 62. *See also* MFA Milling Company
Farm Credit Administration (FCA, U.S.), 5, 134, 139, 145, 192
Farmer, Carl, 211, 212
Farmers Alliance, 2, 14, 21, 22, 28, 35, 37
Farmers and Laborers' Union, 15

Farmers Chemical Company, Joplin, 83, 155, 184
Farmers Export Company, 1, 144, 171–72, 177, 208
Farmers Home Administration (U.S.), 192, 198
Farmers Livestock Commission Company (National Stockyards, Ill.), xiv, 47–48, 61, 73, 100, 161
Farmers Livestock Marketing Association (National Stockyards, Ill.), xiv, 193, 208
Farmers Union, 15, 23, 78, 96, 155, 171; Grain Terminal Association, 191
Farmland Industries, Inc., 8, 83, 184. *See also* Cowden, Howard
Far-Mar-Co, 171
Farm Supply Division, 104, 141, 153, 161, 163, 164, 170, 176, 177, 190
Farnen, Frank, 63, 103, 149
Farnham, Lee, 87, 93, 99, 103, 109, 168; pictured, 118
Farquhar, James, 221
Farrell, Benny, 221
Faurot, Don, 40
Faurot, F. W., 40
Fawcett, John, 146
FCX, 214
FEDECOOP, 182
Federal Farm Board, 3, 10
Federal Intermediate Credit Banks, 3
Federal Land Bank System, 3
Federal Trade Commission, 156, 157
Feed Division, 141, 170, 190, 192. *See also* Grain Division
Ferguson, Claud, 75
Ferguson, W. A., 33
Ferguson, W. E., 221
Fertilizer Division, 176, 177
Feyen, Robert, 161
Fick, Larry, 164
Fiegenbaum, Martin, 221
Fillmore: exchange, 74
First Missouri Corporation, 170–71
Fite, Gilbert: *Beyond the Fence Rows,* 76, 149

Fitzpatrick, Clarence, 36, 44–45, 221
Fitzpatrick, Thomas, 74
Fleming, John, 74
Foland, Charles, 221
Food Administration (U.S.), 45–46
Food and Agricultural Act (1977), 199
Forck, Mike, 221
Fordland: exchange, 50, 97
4-Square Marketing Association, 217
Franklin, Mrs. Ben, 57
Franklin County: farm clubs, 30–31,
    35; farmers association, 133–34
Freeburg: exchange, 84
Freeland, State Representative W. E., 91
Freeman, Secretary of Agriculture
    Orville, 127, 166
Frew, B. L. "Bud," 1, 201, 208; biograph-
    ical information, 186; elected presi-
    dent of MFA, 209; pictured, 130
FS Services, 213
Fuller, Charles, 136
Fulton, F. G., 221

Galt: exchange, 74
Gargus, Jim, 101
Gates, Carl, 73
Gause, Dan, 49, 52, 54, 58; elected
    president of MFA, 56
Gephardt, Congressman Richard, 196
Gex, John, 221
Gibson, Norman, 221
Gifford: exchange, 75
Gilbert, John, 190
Gillespie, Dale, 174, 221
Gilpin, C. S., 46
Glasgow: exchange, 75
Glendale: farm clubs, 27
Goeke, Joseph, 38, 59, 87, 108, 163
Goforth, W. H., 221
Golden City: exchange, 75
Gonnerman, Clarence, 164, 177; bio-
    graphical information, 142
Goodbrake, T. E., 221
Gooden, E. C., 221
Gorman, Ed, 221
Graham, J. C., 221

Grain Division, 141, 145, 147, 155, 164,
    170, 179, 192, 194. *See also* Feed
    Division
Grandin: exchange, 94
Grange, the, 2, 14, 23, 35, 37, 42
Grange League Federation (GLF), 140
Grantham, Ben, 75
Gratz, Henry J., 221
Gray, Chester, 52–53
Graznak, Mike, 171
Green City: exchange, 145
Greene County: exchange, 174; farm
    club, 50; sales association, 50. *See
    also* Springfield
Greenfield: exchange, 186
Griffith, John J., 81, 221
Grimes, Glen, 217
Groves, Fred, 139
Growmark. *See* FS Services; Illinois
    Farm Supply
Gruhn, Fred, 221
Grundy County: farm club, 54
Gumm, Hubert, 174
Gwin, D. C., 221

Haag, Herman, 134, 148, 150, 151, 159,
    163; biographical information, 141–
    42
Habermehl, Dwight, 213
Hackethorn, Jack, 171, 205; biographi-
    cal information, 160
Halfway: exchange, 74
Hall, Raymond, 221
Halsey, Jim, 163, 174, 193, 216–17; pic-
    tured, 128
Hamilton: exchange, 186
Hampton, Ralph, 186
Hanan, J. P., 221
Hanman, Gary, 172
Harding, President Warren G., 56
Hardy, D. M., 139
Harris, Travis, 134, 195
Harshbarger, Don, 221
Hartell, A. C., 221
Hatcher, Roy D., 86, 137, 142, 143, 149,
    153, 154, 221

Haugen, Congressman Gilbert, 69, 73
Hawkins, Harley, 174
Haynes, Kit, 162
Hays, J. R., 221
Hayter, Howard, 174
Hayti: elevator, 172; fertilizer plant, 175
Head, Kermit, 163, 167, 192–93
Heether, Jim, 163, 176
Heidbreder, A. F., 75
Heiman, August H., 221
Heiman, Fred H., 221
Heinkel, Cora Bell McDaniel (mother), 133
Heinkel, Dorothy Riley (wife), 150, 207
Heinkel, Fred V., xiii, 96, 99, 102, 103, 221: considered for secretary of agriculture, 165–66; death of, 207; pictured, 120, 122, 123, 127; as president of MFA, 133–208 *passim*
Heinkel, William G. (father), 133
Heinmann, Burdett, 172
Heisel, George, 25; pictured, 113
Heisel, W. J., 25; pictured, 113
Helvig, J. A., 62
Hemeyer, Stanley, 221
Henley: exchange, 144, 147
Henry, C. D., 221
Hensel, D. F., 221
Hensley, Glenn, 162
Herman, Harry, 146
Hermann: bulk oil plant, 84
Hern, Miller, 187, 222
Herr, F. X., 67
Herring, W. S., 149
Hess, George, 216
Hetlage, Herman, 222
Higgins, R. P., 222
Higginsville: bulk oil plant, 84; exchange, 190
Hill, Albert Ross, 23
Hillhouse, Clint, 222
Hirth, Henry (father), 19, 21
Hirth, Lilliam Vincent (wife), 22
Hirth, Mildred Orr (daughter-in-law), 135
Hirth, Susan Orr (granddaughter), 135

Hirth, William, xiii, 19–109 *passim,* 161, 169, 180, 207, 222; battle over producers contract, 64–66; conflicts with Extension Division, 40–45, 107; considered for secretary of agriculture, 69–70, 95; death of, 105; early influences on, 19–22; elected president of MFA, 81; as farmer, 89, 107; founds farm clubs, 23–31; founds *The Missouri Farmer,* 22–24; pictured, 111; relationship with Howard Cowden, 59–60, 68, 75–83, 107; *Romance of the Missouri Farmers Association,* 27; runs for governor, 97–99
Hirth, William V. (son), 135
Hoelscher, Fred, 100
Hoffman, Alfred, 177, 179, 182
Hofstad, Ralph, 83, 194
Holden, Wayne, 222
Hoover, Herbert: as head of Food Administration, 45, 46
Hoover and Allison Company, 88
Hopper, Bert, 222
Horn, Walter, 155
Hortenstine, David, 204, 222
Houston: farm clubs, 51; grocery, 101
Howell, Reuben, 222
Hubbard Pet Foods, 209
Hudson, J. A., 36, 42, 44, 45, 46, 222; biographical information, 37; death of, 106
Huettemann, Roy, 61
Hulbert, L. S., 66
Hulen, Rubey, 66, 77, 94, 138
Hull, Ill.: elevator, 188
Humansville: auction barn, 217
Hume, Harry, 222
Humphrey, A. S., 56
Humphrey, Hubert: as senator, 126; as vice president, 175
Hurst, S. W., 222
Hyde, Governor Arthur M., 56

Ichord, Congressman Richard, 196
Iconium: exchange, 74

Illinois Farm Supply, 83
Illinois Grain Company, 171, 191
Imperial, Inc., 213
Imperial Packaging Company, 194
Inglish, A. V., 222
Ingwersen, T. B., 33, 222; elected first president of MFA, 36
Iowa Farmers Cooperative Elevator Association, 35
Iowa Farmers Grain Dealers Association, 171, 191
Iowa Farmers Union, 58, 69
Isaacs, George Jr., 222
Isaacson, Paul B., 222

James, George, 222
Janssen, Dale, 151
Jasper, Joseph H., 222
Jasper: exchange, 75
Jennings, Charles, 222
Jobe, David, 1, 164
Joffee, State Representative Jerome M., 91
John M. Shawhan Agency, 87
Johnson, Chet, 190
Johnson, Jack, 174
Johnson, John F., 62, 74, 99-100, 103, 109, 163; pictured, 115; retirement of, 195
Johnson, O. R., 134
Johnson, W. W., 222
Johnson, Wes, 172
Johnston, Earl, 100
Jones, Ida Mae, 142
Jones, J. M., 222
Jones, State Representative Langdon R., 91
Jones, Wayne, 222
Joplin: fertilizer plant, 155
Jordan, Sam, 30, 35, 40, 41
Joseph Grain, 214
Joyce, H. F., 222
Joyce, J. C., 74
Junior Farmers Association (JFA), 57

Kansas City: flour and feed mill, 38; Terminal Elevator Company, 83, 145, 155, 201, 208. *See also* Farm Club Mill and Feed Company; MFA Grain and Feed Company
Karl, William A., 222
Kearns, W. A., 36, 222
Keithley, Paul, 164
Kelley, George M. ("Cotton Top"), 36, 39, 61, 63, 70, 77, 136, 222; elected president of MFA, 69
Kemp, M. H., 222
Kendrick, Senator John Benjamin, 71
Kennedy, President John F., 127, 165-66, 207
Kennedy, Robert, 166
Kent, George, 164
Kephart, Dave, 174
Kertz, Herman, 222
Kerwin, James, 222
Ketchem, W. H., 222
Kidd, Harold, 100
Kies, Sam, 222
Kircher, P. D., 222
Kirksville: creamery, 138, 142; exchange, 74; produce plant, 62
Kitt, Randall, 158
Kleinschmidt, Samuel J., 36, 43, 222; elected president of MFA, 39
Kline, B. F., 36, 222
Klinefelter, H. E. ("Kline"), 30, 89, 94, 98, 103, 107, 109, 133, 158, 159, 184; biographical information, 93; death of, 162
Knapp, Joseph G.: *Rise of American Cooperative Enterprise,* xii
Knowles, S. P., 146
Kohl, John, 25; pictured, 113
Koolsbergen, Hein, 214
Kramme, Milford, 222
Kreisel, A. C., 222
Kreutzer, John, 75
Kullmann, Lawrence, 187, 222

LaBelle: exchange, 174
Laclede County: farm clubs, 34
Ladue: exchange, 74

Lafayette County: farmers association, 33–34
LaForce, Mrs. Charles, 57
Lamar: elevator, 188
Lancaster, Melvin, 223
Landmark, 214
Land O'Lakes, 83, 194, 213, 214
Lane, C. E. ("Chart"), 74, 94, 96, 99, 100, 223; biographical information, 81; death of, 105
Lang, Howard, 199, 204
Lantz, Lester, 223
Larson, Sid, 169
Law Department, 163
Lawrence, Charles H., 75, 223
Lay, Steve, 176
Leavitt, G. A., 223
Lebanon: bulk oil plant, 84; creamery, 142; exchange, 174
Legislation: national, 45–46, 140, 156–58, 160, 168, 193–94, 197–99; state, 46, 58, 69, 90–92, 136, 150–51, 158–59, 168, 198, 200
Lehman, D. W., 74
Lehmkuhl, Al, 178
Lehr, Gus, 199
Leonard: exchange, 75
Letsinger, Cecil, 187, 223
Lexington: exchange, 174
Liege: exchange, 74
Limbaugh, State Representative Rush H., 91
Lincoln: bulk oil plant, 84; exchange, 75
Lindburg and Vogel, 201
Lindner, John, 81, 223
Lion Oil Company, 213
Lischwe, Joseph B., 223
Litton, Congressman Jerry, 145
Littrell, B. B., 223
Littrell, J. S., 36, 46, 223
Livonia: exchange, 74
Lloyd, Vern, 164
Lock, Ervel, 223
Lockwood: exchange, 75
Lohman, Ralph, 141

Lohman: exchange, 75
Loida, Albert, 223
Long, H. B., 223
Longlane: exchange, 74
Loso, Don, 179
Louisiana: elevator, 188
Loutch, Art, 148, 164
Love, John, 75
Lubin, David, 32
Luehrman, Walter, 223
Lynch, O. C., 223

McCarthy, George E. ("Mac"), 58, 82; biographical information, 39–40, 138; death of, 105
McClelland, D. V., 223
McClure, W. E., 36, 223
McCormack, A. L., 99
McDermott, Mrs. C. B., 56, 57
McDonald, T. D., 74
McDonough, Bob, 147, 176
McKelvie, Governor Sam R., 56
McKittrick: exchange, 48
McLaughlin, Keith, 190, 206
McNally, A. W., 223
McNary-Haugen farm-relief bill, 10, 70–73, 196
McNeall, Raymond, 223
McNeill, J. R., 75
Macon: bulk oil plant, 84; packing plant, 161
McQuerter, Loryn, 164
McShane, Neil, 223
McWilliams, C. M., 40, 41
Maczuk, Mike, 223
Magruder, Leroy, 174
Management Services, 164, 177. *See also* Personnel and Management Training
Manson, L. E., 204, 223
Maples, Irene, 97
Marionville: exchange, 97
Marshall, Joe, 223
Marshall: bulk oil plant, 84, 211; exchange, 103, 174, 176; research farm, 184–85; seed plant, 147, 152.

See also MFA Livestock
Association
Marshfield: exchange, 74
Marthasville: bulk oil plant, 84
Martin, Ovid, 175
Martin, Perry, 100, 174
Martinsburg: exchange, 48
Maryland Heights: farm supply ware-
house, 141; fertilizer plant, 151, 152,
176
Maryville: auction barn, 218;
exchange, 174
Maupin, Bob, 189–90, 193, 204
May, Rex, 223
May, W. E., 39, 223
Mayes, Jewell, 32
Maysville: bulk oil plant, 84, 167
Maze, Maurice, 100, 147, 163
Meals, Chester, 223
Medill: produce plant, 62
Meek, J. R., 76
Meek, Keith, 188, 223
Meisner, John, 143, 223
Memphis: exchange, 48, 174
Mennonites: as MFA members, 68
Meta: exchange, 73
Mexico: elevator, 188; soybean plant,
143, 147, 163, 167, 192–93, 208
Meyer, A. J., 42–43, 44
MFA, Inc.: company emblem, 48; con-
stitution, 37; corporate offices,
104, 120–21, 135–36, 152, 155, 193;
creation of divisions, 141; delegate
representation, 156, 187, 209; dues,
39, 60, 95, 103, 152–53; first board
of directors, 34, 36; first conven-
tion, 35; Old Guard emblem, 67–
68; producers contract, 63–68, 96;
role of field secretaries, 173–74.
See also specific divisions and
locations
MFA Cooperator, The, 145
MFA Dairy Products Company, 142,
143, 164
MFA Delta Dealers, 175
MFA Foundation, 180–82, 208

MFA Grain and Feed Company, 103,
134, 137, 148; Kansas City, 101, 149;
St. Joseph, 155; St. Louis, 145. *See
also* Feed Division; Grain Division
MFA Insurance Companies, xiv, 190,
204; creation of, 104, 143–44, 163;
separation from MFA, 208
MFA Livestock Association, xiv, 163,
193; history of, 216–18; Tel-O-
Auction, 185, 217
MFA Milling Company, Springfield, 57,
62, 74, 81, 99, 100, 103, 104, 116,
134, 137–38, 139, 141, 146, 159, 160,
163, 166, 175, 195, 208
MFA Oil Company, xiv, 57, 74, 89, 97,
103, 109, 141, 166, 174, 185, 203;
becomes a nonstock cooperative,
148; founding of, 83–85; history of,
211–15; refineries, 138, 152, 156,
212, 214; separation from MFA,
Inc., 215
MFA Oilogram, The, 145
MFA Packing Company, 146
Mid-America Dairymen (Mid-Am), xiv,
172–73
Midcontinent Farmers Association,
173, 174, 190, 200
Midland Cooperatives, 214
Milk Producers Federation. *See*
National Cooperative Milk Pro-
ducers Federation
Miller, A. D., 84, 85, 89
Miller, Fred, 223
Miller, Larry, 223
Miller, M. F., 134, 153
Miller, Richard, 187, 223
Miller, W. S., 50, 74, 81, 100, 223; bio-
graphical information, 51; death of,
160–61
Mississippi Chemical Corporation
(MCC), 155, 170, 175, 191
Mississippi Federated, 171
Missouri Association of County Farm
Bureau Boards, 33
Missouri Basin Survey Commission:
Heinkel serves on, 158

Missouri Cattle Feeders Association, 24

Missouri Corn Growers Association, 24

Missouri Dairy Association, 24

Missouri Farm Bureau Federation (MFBF), 41, 44-45, 73, 75, 78, 87, 107, 139

Missouri Farmer, The: "After Thoughts," 23; becomes official organ of MFA, 34, 37; bought by FMA, 135; changes to weekly format, 154; founding of, 22-24; Jim Riley (humorous character), 54; linotype shop, 89, 112; "Our Women's Department," 56; "You Ask About," 185

Missouri Farm Management Association, 24

Missouri Pork Producers Association, 217

Missouri State Board of Agriculture, 30, 32

Mitchell, Wayne, 174

Mitchem, Keith, 201

Moberly: exchange, 103

Moles, Pete, 217; pictured, 128

Monett: creamery, 142; exchange, 138; grocery, 101

Montgomery, Robert: *The Cooperative Pattern in Cotton,* 63-64

Montgomery City: exchange, 48

Moody, C. L., 56; elected president of MFA, 58

Mooney, L. H., 223

Moore, A. C., 54

Morgan, State Senator J. G., 91

Morrison, Charles, 223

Morrison: exchange, 75, 84

Morrow, Bob, 144

Morse, Lowell, 152

Mortenson, A., 134, 137, 149, 223

Morwood, Clyde, 138, 163

Mountain View: exchange, 100; farm clubs, 51

Mueller, John J., 223

Mundell, Junius, 223

Murphy, Wayne, 223

Murray, Adrian, 204, 224

Murrell, Sam, 187, 224

Mustain, Wendell, 174

Myers, Frank, 35

Myers, Glen, 188, 224

National Cooperative Milk Producers Federation, 6, 139

National Cooperative Refinery Association (NCRA), 83, 203, 212

National Council of Farmer Cooperatives, 6, 140, 162, 168

National Farm Coalition, 193, 198-99

National Federation of Grain Cooperatives, 6

Nauman, Frank, 224

Neill, Lloyd, 141, 164

Neosho: exchange, 97, 174

Neuenschwander, A., 224

Neuenschwander, Arthur, 143, 224

New Cambria: exchange, 75

Newcomer Corporation, 166

Newcomer School House ("birthplace of MFA"), 24, 25, 101, 112, 169

Nickerson, Phil, 201

Nicks, Floyd, 224

Niebrugge, C. O., 36, 224

Niehaus, August, 224

Nitsch, Gene, 188, 224

Non-Stock Cooperative Act, 62

Norborne: exchange, 190

Nordyke, S. A., 74

Nourse, Edwin, 4-5, 10

O'Bryant, Jack, 161

O'Fallon: bulk oil plant, 84

Ohlendorf, Chris, 61, 81, 224

O'Malley, R. Emmett, 98-99

Operating Divisions, 144, 152, 162, 163, 170, 176, 192

Orf, A. C., 224

Organization Department, 163

Osborne, Everett, 224

Owensville: bulk oil plant, 84; exchange, 75, 114

Ozark: exchange, 75

Packing Division, 145, 153, 161, 170, 177

Packwood, Gene, 164

Palmyra: fertilizer plant, 176

Park, Governor Guy, 98–99

Parker, State Representative Jones H., 91

Parker, Paul, 176

Passaic: elevator, 40; farm club, 39

Patrons of Husbandry. *See* Grange, the

Patterson, H. B., 53, 56

Patterson, J. S., 224

Patton, Frank, 193

Patton, Guy, 174

Patton, Jim, 162

Payne, A. W., 74

Peers: exchange, 74

Pence, R. T., 36, 37, 42, 61, 76–77, 224

Pence, William Hirth, 77

Pendergast, Tom, 98, 140

Penick, Thomas E., 25; pictured, 113

Peppard Seed Company, 88

Perry, Larry, 224

Perryville: exchange, 174

Personnel and Management Training, 190. *See also* Employee Training; Management Services

Peters, F. G., 87

Pfahl, Karl, 89, 107

Pierce, Frank, 36, 224

Pike, Francis, 21

Pike, John F., 21

Pilot Grove: exchange, 161

Pinchot, Governor Gifford, 93

Pipes, Gayle, 213

Pippins, Bill, 224

Pitts, Lonnie, 174

Planters Fertilizer Company, 175

Plant Foods Division, 141, 153, 155, 164, 170, 174, 177, 188, 190, 192, 195, 216

Polk County: farm clubs, 51; farmers association, 48, 51

Pollard, Raymond, 224

Pollock: exchange, 74

Polly, George, 178, 184

Polsten, Gust C., 30

Pomeranz, Harry, 194

Porter, Gerald, 174

Potter, Juan, 224

Poultry and Egg Division, 164, 170, 174

Powell, Bill, 172

Preston, D. C., 74

Pritchard, J. L., 224

Producers Creamery Company, Springfield, 74, 81, 99, 103, 138, 139, 142, 146, 155, 165–66. *See also* Cabool; Chillicothe; Clinton; Emma; Kirksville

Producers Grain Commission Company, St. Louis, 61, 155

Producers Grocery Company, 100, 101

Producers Livestock Commission Company, 217

Producers Produce Company, 57, 73, 74, 117, 137; Chillicothe, 77, 87, 96; Sedalia, 141–42; Shelbina, 62, 103, 104, 109, 137, 155; Springfield, 81, 87, 93, 99, 100, 101, 103, 138, 139, 168–69

Production Credit Association, 6, 175

Progressive Farmers Association (PFA), 194

Propst, Gerald, 224

Purchasing Department, 62, 63, 74, 86, 101, 103

Purdy, Allan, 181

Quade, Don, 224

Rally Day, 57–58

Rapps, Henry, 74

Rauch, G. L., 75

Ray County: farm clubs, 29, 34

Rea, Earl, 36, 46, 224

Ream, Dale, 224

Reed, Roy, 134, 141, 174, 207

Reeds Spring: exchange, 74

Reeves, Jim: *First Twenty Years: The Story of Mid-America Dairymen,* 172

Rehagen, Otto, 224
Rehagen, Walter, 224
Reid, G. O., 57
Reid, Mrs. G. O., 57
Reno, Milo, 58, 69, 71, 78, 85
Renshaw, George, 29, 75
Rhodes, James, xii
Rickenbrode, F. W., 224
Risser, Otto, 224
Riutcel, F. W., 224
Roach, Cornelius, 35
Roberts, Frank, 224
Robertson, C. F. ("Charlie"), 211
Robertson, Dorsey, 224
Robins, Charles D., 224
Rochdale Society (England), 2, 11
Roderick, A. M., 74
Rogers, W. B., 74
Rogersville: exchange, 50
Rolla: bulk oil plant, 84; exchange, 74
Roosevelt, President Franklin D., 94–95
Rose, Guy, 75
Rosier, A. C., 36, 46, 49, 82, 97, 103, 141, 224
Rosier, Russell J., 93, 105, 108, 109, 136, 142, 143, 150, 159, 163, 170, 173, 176, 207; described, 82–83; pictured, 118, 120, 123; retirement of, 188–89
Ross, George, 151–52
Ross, Neal, 224
Rosson, Lloyd, 149
Rowe, Oakley, 224
Rowles, E. E., 225
Rubey, Congressman Thomas, 69
Rural Electrification Administration, 196
Russellville: bulk oil plant, 84; exchange, 74
Rybolt, Sherman, 36, 225

Sachs, Edwin, 187, 206, 225
St. Clair: elevator, 181
Ste. Genevieve County: farm clubs, 34
Ste. Genevieve: bulk oil plant, 84
St. James: exchange, 51, 74, 100, 160;

farm club, 50–51; produce plant, 62
St. Joseph: farm supply warehouse, 141; feed mill, 148, 152; produce plant, 59, 62; site of conventions, 58; stockyards, 217, 218. *See also* MFA Grain and Feed Company
St. Louis: Grain Company, 171, 191, 208; poultry plant, 164. *See also* MFA Grain and Feed Company
Saline County: farmers association, 35, 50
Salisbury: exchange, 174
Saloutos, Theodore, 106
Samek, Frank, 225
Sanders, Wayne, 190
Sanitary Milk Products, 172
Santa Rosa: exchange, 74
Sapiro, Aaron, 4–5, 10, 63–64
Sappington, A. D., 144, 153, 156–57, 158, 159, 160, 163, 173, 176; biographical information, 138; death of, 199; pictured, 122
Satterwhite, Lloyd, 190
Schelp, Ed, 75, 134, 151
Schindler, John D., 89, 92, 225
Schmutz, S. R., 34
Schnakenberg, Hugo, 225
Schnarre, Keith, 225
Schowengerdt, E. W., 36, 225
Schuermann, Julius, 61
Schulte, Herman, 164, 176, 207; biographical information, 147
Schulte, Otto, 144, 147, 179
Schunemeyer, Neal, 225
Schutte, Don, 225
Schuttler, Vera: *A History of the Missouri Farm Bureau Federation*, 41–42, 44
Schventer, Fred, 40
Schwartz, Henry, Sr., 225
Scotland County: farm clubs, 34
Scott, C. A., 225
Scott, Frank, 76
Scott, George T., 225
Scott, John, 100–101

Scroggins, Del, 101
Scroggins, R. L., 188, 225
Seaman, B. M., 187, 225
Sedalia: exchange, 161; farm supply
   warehouse, 141; poultry plant, 164,
   170; produce plant, 59, 143; site of
   conventions, 35, 39, 49, 52, 63, 70,
   73, 79, 85, 102, 104, 114, 137, 140,
   149. *See also* Producers Produce
   Company
Seed Division, 141, 147, 161, 164, 170,
   176, 177, 190, 216
Seits, Mr., 49
Seymour: exchange, 50
Shelbina: bulk oil plant, 84; exchange,
   174; poultry plant, 164, 170. *See
   also* Producers Produce Company
Shelby County: farm clubs, 52
Shelter Insurance Companies. *See*
   MFA Insurance Companies
Sherman Antitrust Act (1890), 2, 11
Shirkey, Howard, 139
Shorter, Lyle, 174
Siddens, W. J., 225
Silvey, Jack, 108, 109, 136, 141, 143,
   149, 159, 162, 163; biographical
   information, 104; leaves MFA, 144;
   pictured, 129
Simon, B. D., 48; Simon Construction
   Company, 104
Simpson, J. E., 225
Simpson, John, 96
Skelton, Congressman Ike, 196
Slater: elevator, 48
Sloan, R. T., 225
Small, Othor, 225
Smith, Albert, 161-62, 201
Smith-Lever Act (1914), 40
Smoot, B. P., 34
Smutz, B. C., 36, 225
Smutz, Earl, 25; pictured, 113
Sobotka, Frank, 225
Soil Conservation and Domestic Allot-
   ment Act (1936), 197
Spears, Sam, 54
Spencer, Carlton, 204, 225

Spicer, James, 225
Spillman, W. J., 49
Spradling, Stuart L., 184, 205, 213
Sprick, Larry, 225
Springfield: bulk oil plant, 85, 139;
   farm supply warehouse, 141; hatch-
   ery, 139; packing plant, 161, 189,
   193; produce plant, 59, 62; Seed
   Company, 88; site of conventions,
   54-56; stockyards, 73, 139, 152; tire
   plant, 213. *See also* Artificial Breed-
   ing Association; Farm Club Mill and
   Feed Company; Greene County;
   MFA Milling Company; Producers
   Creamery Company; Producers Pro-
   duce Company
Square Deal Milk Producers, 172
Square Deal Stock Tonic, 135
Squires: exchange, 74
Stahl: exchange, 74
Standard Oil Company, 77, 84, 185
Stanley, Mr., 53
Stanton, Frank, 178
Stark, Lloyd, 99, 104
State Exchanges, 170, 174, 184. *See
   also* Exchange Division
Stauffacher, Casper, 97
Steiner, William L., 58, 225; elected
   president of MFA, 63
Stephens, E. Sidney, 90
Stephens College, Columbia, 88-89;
   site of conventions, 124, 151
Steury, Ed, 225
Stevenson, F. G., 146, 164
Stice, Leslie, 171
Stiles, C. M., 52, 70, 225; elected
   president of MFA, 73
Stockton, Delmar, 172
Stockton: exchange, 48; oil plant, 167
Stone, Wilbert, 149
Stone County: WPFA, 57
Stork, Frank, xii
Stouffer, William, 204, 225
Stoutland: exchange, 74
Strafford: exchange, 50
Straughan, E. H., 225

Streeter, Billy, 190
Strid, Henry, 164
Strothman, Harvey, 182, 190, 195
Stump, Harlin, 225
Success Mills, 88
Sullivan: exchange, 100, 147
Supply and Marketing Divisions, 178, 184, 190
Sweet Springs: elevator, 151; oil plant, 167
Swinger, Harold, 147
Symington, Senator Stuart, 165-66, 207

Talley, A. C., 22
Tallon, Tom, 225
Talmadge, Senator Herman, 196
Taylor, Congressman Gene, 196
Taylor, Jack [Timothy Hays], 145-46
Teasdale, Governor Joseph, 196
Tel-O-Auction. *See* MFA Livestock Association
Tennessee Farmers Cooperative, 171, 214
Thomas, David, 174, 190, 202, 205
Thomas, Don, 182
Thompson, Eric G., 225; biographical information, 204; elected president of MFA, 200-209 *passim;* pictured, 130
Thompson, Ranie, 174, 201
Thompson, Tom, 225
Thompson, W. H., 33
Thurston, M. F., 89
Tillman, J. W., 225
Tipton: exchange, 75
Tire Division, 161, 164, 170
Toler, William, 181
Transportation Division, 151-52, 171
Trenton: exchange, 201
Trigsle, Floyd, 33
Triplett, N. H., 74
Truman: Harry S.: as senator, 140; as president, 158

Umbarger, William, 204, 225
Union: bulk oil plant, 85; exchange, 74; farm club, 35; poultry plant, 164

Unionville: exchange, 174
United Refining Company, 214
U.S. Department of Agriculture, 94; Heinkel appointed to Feed and Grain Committee of, 166
U.S. Department of Energy, 214
U.S. House: Interstate and Foreign Commerce Committee, 156
U.S. Senate: Agriculture Committee, 46
U.S. Feed Grain Council, 145
University of Missouri: College of Agriculture, 22, 23, 40-45; Extension Division, creation of, 40-41; Heinkel serves on board of curators, 158; medical school, 159; site of conventions, 151, 187

Vandalia: exchange, 174
Van Gilder, Earl, 225
Van Houten, James, 225
Van Houten, Neal, 226
Van Houten, R. H., 52
Vernon County: farm clubs, 29, 34
Versailles: exchange, 103, 149
Violet: exchange, 74
Vista: exchange, 74
Volunteer Overseas Cooperative Assistance (VOCA), 182
Voorhis, Jerry, 162
Voris, W. R., 226

Wade, Brick, 74
Wade, Jeff, 226
Walker, Naomi, 97
Walker, W. W., 36
Wallace, Secretary of Agriculture Henry, 92
Wallach, A. A., 226
Wallis, L. O., 143, 146, 154-55, 176, 226
Walnut Grove: exchange, 50, 75; farm club, 54
Walser, Ron, 161
Wangelin, F. G., 94, 226
Warren, Glen, 141
Warren County: farmers association, 30

Warsaw: exchange, 186; grocery, 101
Washburn Crosby, 88
Washington: elevator, 48; exchange, 147
Waters, Henry J., 23, 49, 58
Watson, W. C., 226
Watt, G. F., 226
Wayland, Carolyn, 142
Weathers, J. S., 226
Weaver, Ed, 226
Weaver, H. H., 33
Webb, John, 226
Weber, George, 226
Weekley, D. T., 187, 226
Welty, Elmer, 149
Westen, Floyd, 217
West Plains: exchange, 137-38, 186
Wheeler, J. P., 226
Wheeler, Lawrence, 174
Whitaker, State Representative O. B., 91
White, Edward J., 106
White, James L., 226
Whittington, Clarence, 75
Widel, Albert, 27
Wiggenstein, C. A., 36, 226
Wilcox: exchange, 74
Wilkinson, A. K., 226
Willard: exchange, 50
Williams, Carl, 65
Williams, David L., 226
Williams, O. W., 226
Willow Grove: farm club, 27
Willow Springs: farm clubs, 51; oil plant, 167

Wilson, Glennon, 226
Windsor: bulk oil plant, 85
Winter, E. H., 30
Wisbrock, William, 85
Wisdom: exchange, 74
Wissbaum, David, 226
Women's Progressive Farmers Association (WPFA), 56-57
Wood, Art, 174
Wood, R. M., 226
Woodard, H. O., 75, 226
Woodson, Idalee L., 106
World War I: effect of on farmers, 3
World War II: effect of on farmers, 6-7
Worthington: exchange, 74
Wright, J. Kelly, 33
Wright City: bulk oil plant, 85
Wurmb, Robert O., 180-81
Wyaconda: exchange, 48
Wyatt, Judd, 145
Wyss, George, 74

Young, Frank B., 47-48, 100, 109, 146; death of, 161; pictured, 115
Young, John L., 226
Young, Marvin, 100, 176, 181
Young, Raymond A., 226; becomes head of MFA Oil, 102; as executive vice president, 176-79; pictured, 119, 123, 126; retirement of, 215
Youtsey, Estes, 36, 226
Youtsey, Turpin, 187, 226
Yowell, R. O., 74, 142

Zahn, Virgil, 22